GRAY HAT

VULNERABILITY SCANNING & PENETRATION TESTING

4 BOOKS IN 1

BOOK 1
GRAY HAT ESSENTIALS: A BEGINNER'S GUIDE TO VULNERABILITY SCANNING

BOOK 2
INTERMEDIATE GRAY HAT TACTICS: PENETRATION TESTING DEMYSTIFIED

BOOK 3
ADVANCED GRAY HAT EXPLOITS: BEYOND THE BASICS

BOOK 4
MASTERING GRAY HAT ETHICAL HACKING: EXPERT-LEVEL PENETRATION TESTING

ROB BOTWRIGHT

Published by Rob Botwright
Library of Congress Cataloging-in-Publication Data
ISBN 978-1-83938-537-7
Cover design by Rizzo

Disclaimer

The contents of this book are based on extensive research and the best available historical sources. However, the author and publisher make no claims, promises, or guarantees about the accuracy, completeness, or adequacy of the information contained herein. The information in this book is provided on an "as is" basis, and the author and publisher disclaim any and all liability for any errors, omissions, or inaccuracies in the information or for any actions taken in reliance on such information.

The opinions and views expressed in this book are those of the author and do not necessarily reflect the official policy or position of any organization or individual mentioned in this book. Any reference to specific people, places, or events is intended only to provide historical context and is not intended to defame or malign any group, individual, or entity.

The information in this book is intended for educational and entertainment purposes only. It is not intended to be a substitute for professional advice or judgment. Readers are encouraged to conduct their own research and to seek professional advice where appropriate.

Every effort has been made to obtain necessary permissions and acknowledgments for all images and other copyrighted material used in this book. Any errors or omissions in this regard are unintentional, and the author and publisher will correct them in future editions.

TABLE OF CONTENTS – BOOK 1 - GRAY HAT ESSENTIALS: A BEGINNER'S GUIDE TO VULNERABILITY SCANNING

TABLE OF CONTENTS – BOOK 2 - INTERMEDIATE GRAY HAT TACTICS: PENETRATION TESTING DEMYSTIFIED

TABLE OF CONTENTS – BOOK 3 - ADVANCED GRAY HAT EXPLOITS: BEYOND THE BASICS

TABLE OF CONTENTS – BOOK 4 - MASTERING GRAY HAT ETHICAL HACKING: EXPERT-LEVEL PENETRATION TESTING

Introduction

Welcome to the "Gray Hat Vulnerability Scanning & Penetration Testing" book bundle, a comprehensive collection designed to take you on an exciting and educational journey into the realm of ethical hacking, vulnerability scanning, and penetration testing. In an increasingly interconnected and digital world, cybersecurity has become a paramount concern for individuals and organizations alike. Understanding how to identify vulnerabilities, assess risks, and defend against cyber threats has never been more critical.

This bundle is a roadmap that spans from beginner to expert, offering a structured and progressive approach to mastering the techniques and strategies employed by cybersecurity professionals and ethical hackers. Across four meticulously crafted volumes, you will traverse the landscape of cybersecurity, learning to think like a hacker while maintaining an unwavering commitment to ethical conduct and legal practices.

Book 1: Gray Hat Essentials: A Beginner's Guide to Vulnerability Scanning Our journey begins with the essentials. In this foundational volume, you will gain a clear understanding of what vulnerability scanning entails and how it forms the bedrock of penetration testing. From defining vulnerabilities to initiating scans and interpreting results, this book equips beginners with the knowledge needed to embark on their cybersecurity odyssey.

Book 2: Intermediate Gray Hat Tactics: Penetration Testing Demystified Building upon the fundamentals, this intermediate guide demystifies the art of penetration testing. It delves deeper into the tactics and techniques used by cybersecurity experts to identify weaknesses, exploit vulnerabilities, and fortify digital defenses. Whether you're an aspiring ethical hacker or a professional seeking to expand your skill set, this volume offers insights that will sharpen your abilities.

Book 3: Advanced Gray Hat Exploits: Beyond the Basics As we progress, we delve into advanced territory. This book explores the world of sophisticated exploits, intricate vulnerabilities, and the strategies employed by real-world hackers. It challenges readers to think critically, adopt a hacker's mindset, and confront complex scenarios. With a focus on offensive security, you will learn how to outsmart adversaries and secure systems against advanced threats.

Book 4: Mastering Gray Hat Ethical Hacking: Expert-Level Penetration Testing Our journey culminates in the pursuit of mastery. In this expert-level volume, you will acquire the skills and knowledge necessary to navigate the intricate landscape of ethical hacking and penetration testing. From advanced exploitation techniques to post-exploitation strategies, you will be prepared to tackle the most challenging cybersecurity scenarios.

Throughout this bundle, we emphasize the importance of ethical conduct and lawful hacking practices. Our goal is not only to equip you with technical expertise but also to instill a sense of responsibility and integrity in your approach to cybersecurity. Ethical hacking is not about subverting the law but rather about using your knowledge and skills to protect digital assets and safeguard the integrity of digital spaces.

As you embark on this journey through the "Gray Hat Vulnerability Scanning & Penetration Testing" book bundle, we encourage you to embrace the challenges and opportunities that lie ahead. The world of cybersecurity is ever-evolving, and your commitment to continuous learning and ethical practice will play a vital role in defending against cyber threats.

So, let's embark on this exciting adventure together, where knowledge is power, and ethical hacking is the key to securing our digital future. Whether you're a novice or an experienced professional, there's something here for everyone. Let's get started

BOOK 1
GRAY HAT ESSENTIALS
A BEGINNER'S GUIDE TO VULNERABILITY SCANNING

ROB BOTWRIGHT

Chapter 1: Introduction to Vulnerability Scanning

Vulnerability scanning is a crucial aspect of cybersecurity that plays a pivotal role in identifying and addressing weaknesses in computer systems and networks. It serves as the initial step in the process of fortifying an organization's digital infrastructure against potential threats and attacks. By conducting vulnerability scans, organizations can proactively assess their IT environments, pinpoint vulnerabilities, and take appropriate measures to remediate them.

These scans are essentially automated assessments that involve the use of specialized software tools to scan and analyze various components of a network or system, such as software applications, operating systems, and network devices. Vulnerability scanners examine these elements for known security vulnerabilities, misconfigurations, and weaknesses that could potentially be exploited by malicious actors.

Understanding Cybersecurity Fundamentals

To effectively navigate the world of vulnerability scanning, it's essential to have a foundational understanding of cybersecurity principles. Cybersecurity encompasses a wide range of practices, technologies, and strategies designed to protect digital assets from unauthorized access, data breaches, and cyberattacks. It involves safeguarding not only the confidentiality and integrity of data but also the availability of critical systems and services.

One of the fundamental concepts in cybersecurity is the CIA triad, which stands for Confidentiality, Integrity, and Availability. Confidentiality ensures that sensitive information remains protected from unauthorized access.

Integrity ensures that data remains unaltered and trustworthy. Availability ensures that systems and data are accessible when needed.

Setting Up Your Scanning Environment

Before diving into vulnerability scanning, it's essential to establish a proper scanning environment. This includes selecting the appropriate hardware and software tools necessary to conduct scans effectively. Hardware requirements may vary depending on the size and complexity of the network or system being scanned. Additionally, organizations must ensure that scanning tools are up to date with the latest security vulnerabilities and patches.

Network configuration plays a crucial role in scanning success. It's essential to have a clear understanding of the network topology, including the placement of firewalls, routers, switches, and other network security devices. Properly configuring the scanning environment helps ensure that scans are accurate and do not disrupt normal business operations.

Scanning Tools and Techniques

Once the scanning environment is set up, it's time to explore the various scanning tools and techniques available. Vulnerability scanners come in different flavors, with some focusing on specific types of vulnerabilities or target platforms. Open-source and commercial tools are widely used, each offering its unique features and capabilities.

Commonly used vulnerability scanning tools include Nessus, Qualys, OpenVAS, and Rapid7's Nexpose. These tools employ a range of scanning techniques, such as port scanning, service identification, banner grabbing, and vulnerability signature checks. Some scanners also support authenticated scanning, which allows them to log in to target systems to perform a more in-depth assessment.

Identifying Common Vulnerabilities

As the scanning process unfolds, the focus shifts toward identifying common vulnerabilities and weaknesses within the target environment. Vulnerability databases and repositories, such as the Common Vulnerabilities and Exposures (CVE) database, National Vulnerability Database (NVD), and vendor-specific sources, serve as valuable references during this phase.

Common vulnerabilities often include issues like outdated software versions, missing security patches, weak passwords, misconfigured settings, and unsecured network services. By cross-referencing scan results with known vulnerabilities from these databases, organizations can prioritize remediation efforts and address the most critical issues first.

Vulnerability Assessment Best Practices

To make the most of vulnerability scanning, organizations should adopt best practices that enhance the effectiveness of their assessment efforts. These practices encompass a range of activities, including regular and consistent scanning schedules, proper documentation of scan results, and adherence to industry standards and regulations.

Regular scanning is essential to maintaining an up-to-date view of the organization's security posture. This helps detect new vulnerabilities as they emerge and ensures that previously identified vulnerabilities have been addressed. Additionally, organizations should establish a clear process for tracking and managing vulnerabilities, from discovery to remediation.

Reporting and Documentation

The insights gained from vulnerability scans are of little value if they are not properly documented and communicated to the relevant stakeholders. Reporting and documentation play a critical role in the vulnerability management process.

Effective reports provide actionable information to support decision-making and remediation efforts.

Vulnerability scan reports typically include details on the vulnerabilities discovered, their severity levels, potential impact, and recommended remediation steps. These reports should be concise, easy to understand, and tailored to the audience, whether it's IT teams, executives, or compliance auditors. Clear and timely communication is essential for driving the remediation process forward.

Basic Penetration Testing Concepts

Vulnerability scanning lays the foundation for a deeper level of security assessment known as penetration testing. While vulnerability scanning identifies weaknesses, penetration testing goes a step further by simulating real-world attacks to determine if vulnerabilities can be exploited. Understanding basic penetration testing concepts is essential for organizations looking to bolster their security measures.

Penetration testing involves a systematic approach to evaluating security controls, identifying vulnerabilities, and exploiting them to gain unauthorized access or privileges. Unlike vulnerability scanning, penetration testing often requires skilled ethical hackers or penetration testers who possess the knowledge and expertise to mimic the tactics of malicious actors.

Securing Your Scanning Activities

As organizations engage in vulnerability scanning and penetration testing, it's crucial to ensure that these activities are conducted securely. Without proper safeguards in place, scanning and testing can inadvertently introduce risks or disrupt normal business operations. Therefore, securing scanning activities is paramount.

Security measures may include isolating scanning activities from the production environment, implementing access controls, and obtaining proper authorization to conduct scanning and testing. Additionally, organizations should coordinate with internal teams to avoid false positives and false negatives that could impact system availability or trigger unnecessary alarms.

Building a Career in Cybersecurity

For individuals interested in pursuing a career in cybersecurity, mastering vulnerability scanning, penetration testing, and related skills can open the door to a variety of exciting and challenging opportunities. The demand for cybersecurity professionals continues to grow as organizations recognize the critical importance of protecting their digital assets.

Building a successful career in cybersecurity often begins with a solid educational foundation and hands-on experience. Many professionals start by earning certifications like Certified Ethical Hacker (CEH), Certified Information Systems Security Professional (CISSP), or CompTIA Security+ to validate their knowledge and skills.

In addition to formal education and certifications, networking and staying current with industry trends are essential. Engaging with cybersecurity communities, attending conferences, and participating in Capture The Flag (CTF) competitions can provide valuable insights and help individuals stay at the forefront of the field.

Conclusion

In summary, vulnerability scanning serves as a fundamental component of cybersecurity, allowing organizations to proactively identify and address vulnerabilities in their IT environments. By understanding cybersecurity fundamentals, setting up the right scanning environment, and employing the appropriate tools and techniques, organizations can enhance their security posture and protect critical assets.

Effective vulnerability management encompasses best practices, including regular scanning, thorough reporting, and clear documentation. Building on this foundation, penetration testing takes security assessment to the next level by simulating real-world attacks. Securing scanning activities and pursuing a career in cybersecurity are vital aspects of ensuring that organizations remain resilient in the face of evolving threats in the digital landscape.

Vulnerability scanning is a powerful tool in the realm of cybersecurity, and understanding its benefits is crucial for safeguarding digital assets and data. When it comes to securing your digital infrastructure, knowledge is indeed power. First and foremost, vulnerability scanning provides you with a proactive approach to identifying and addressing potential weaknesses within your network or system. It's like having a trusted security guard constantly patrolling your premises, looking for any signs of vulnerability or suspicious activity. By regularly scanning your network and systems, you gain a real-time view of your organization's security posture. This means that you are not caught off guard by unknown vulnerabilities that could be exploited by cybercriminals. It's akin to having a radar that can detect incoming threats, even before they become a problem.

One of the most significant benefits of vulnerability scanning is that it helps you prioritize your security efforts. In the vast world of cybersecurity, it's easy to get overwhelmed by the sheer volume of potential vulnerabilities and threats. Vulnerability scanning helps you focus on the most critical issues that require immediate attention, allowing you to allocate your resources effectively.

Moreover, vulnerability scanning contributes to the overall efficiency of your cybersecurity efforts. Instead of spending countless hours manually searching for vulnerabilities, the scanning process automates this task, saving you time and resources. It's like having a dedicated assistant who can handle the tedious work while you focus on strategic security measures. The financial aspect of vulnerability scanning is also worth considering. In the long run, investing in a robust scanning program can actually save you money. How, you might ask? Well, by identifying vulnerabilities early and preventing potential breaches, you avoid the costly aftermath of security incidents, including data breaches, legal fees, and reputational damage.

Think of vulnerability scanning as an insurance policy for your digital assets. It's a proactive step that helps you mitigate risks and prevent potential disasters. After all, it's much easier and cost-effective to fix a vulnerability before it's exploited than to deal with the fallout of a successful cyberattack. Another significant advantage of vulnerability scanning is its role in compliance and regulatory requirements. Many industries and jurisdictions have specific regulations that mandate regular vulnerability assessments and security checks. By conducting vulnerability scans, you not only meet these requirements but also demonstrate your commitment to security to regulators, partners, and customers. Furthermore, vulnerability scanning contributes to a culture of security within your organization. When employees know that regular scans are part of the security protocol, they become more vigilant about their own actions. It's akin to having everyone on board as active participants in safeguarding the digital environment.

Now, let's talk about the peace of mind that vulnerability scanning brings. Knowing that you have a proactive defense mechanism in place can reduce anxiety and stress related to cybersecurity. It's like having a security blanket for your digital assets, providing a sense of comfort and confidence.

Moreover, vulnerability scanning helps you make informed decisions regarding your IT infrastructure. It provides valuable data and insights that guide your choices when it comes to system upgrades, patch management, and the implementation of additional security measures. It's akin to having a compass that points you in the right direction.

Another critical aspect is the ability to adapt to evolving threats. Cybersecurity is a dynamic field, and new vulnerabilities and attack techniques emerge regularly. Vulnerability scanning keeps you up-to-date with the latest threats, allowing you to adjust your security measures accordingly. It's like having a weather forecast that helps you prepare for changing conditions.

Additionally, vulnerability scanning promotes transparency and accountability within your organization. When you have a clear record of scans and their results, it becomes easier to track progress over time and hold responsible parties accountable for security lapses. It's like having a digital trail that helps you trace your steps and identify areas for improvement.

Moreover, vulnerability scanning can be a valuable tool for vendor and third-party risk management. It allows you to assess the security posture of suppliers, partners, and service providers, ensuring that they meet the necessary security standards and don't introduce vulnerabilities into your ecosystem. In summary, the benefits of vulnerability scanning are numerous and far-reaching. It's a proactive and cost-effective approach to cybersecurity that helps you identify vulnerabilities, prioritize actions, and safeguard your digital assets. It offers peace of mind, fosters a culture of security, and keeps you informed about evolving threats. Ultimately, it's a vital tool for staying ahead in the ever-changing landscape of cybersecurity.

Chapter 2: Understanding Cybersecurity Fundamentals

Understanding key concepts in cybersecurity is like learning the language of digital security, enabling you to navigate the complex landscape of protecting digital assets and data. Cybersecurity, at its core, revolves around safeguarding information systems, networks, and digital resources from unauthorized access, breaches, and cyberattacks.

One fundamental concept in cybersecurity is confidentiality, which ensures that sensitive data remains confidential and protected from unauthorized disclosure. Imagine it as a vault, keeping your most valuable secrets safe from prying eyes.

Another critical concept is integrity, which guarantees the accuracy and trustworthiness of data. Think of it as a digital seal ensuring that your data remains intact and unaltered.

Availability, the third pillar of the cybersecurity triad, ensures that systems and data are accessible when needed, akin to a reliable utility service that is always there when you require it.

Authentication, a key concept in cybersecurity, involves verifying the identity of users or systems. It's like checking someone's identification before granting access to a secure area.

Authorization, closely related to authentication, determines what actions and resources users or systems are allowed to access once their identity is confirmed. Think of it as the permissions and privileges granted to individuals within an organization.

Encryption is a fundamental technique that converts data into a secure code to prevent unauthorized access. It's like encoding a message so that only the intended recipient can decode and read it.

Firewalls are like digital barriers that protect your network from unauthorized access and cyber threats, similar to security guards stationed at the entrance to a secure facility.

Intrusion Detection Systems (IDS) and Intrusion Prevention Systems (IPS) act as vigilant sentinels, detecting and mitigating potential threats within your network, much like security cameras and alarms in a physical setting.

Patch Management involves regularly updating software and systems to address known vulnerabilities and weaknesses. It's akin to regularly servicing your car to ensure it runs smoothly and efficiently.

Antivirus software is like a digital immune system, scanning for and removing malicious software that could compromise your system's health.

Phishing, a prevalent cyber threat, involves fraudulent attempts to deceive individuals into revealing sensitive information. Think of it as a digital con artist trying to trick you into divulging personal details.

Social engineering attacks leverage human psychology to manipulate individuals into divulging confidential information or performing actions that benefit attackers. It's like a skilled actor convincing you to trust them with your secrets.

Malware, short for malicious software, includes viruses, worms, Trojans, and other harmful programs designed to disrupt, damage, or gain unauthorized access to systems. Think of them as digital pests that can infest your system.

Zero-day vulnerabilities are like hidden traps that cybercriminals discover before security experts can patch them, leaving systems vulnerable until a fix is available.

Distributed Denial of Service (DDoS) attacks involve overwhelming a target system or network with a flood of traffic, rendering it unavailable to users. It's akin to a massive crowd blocking the entrance to a building, preventing anyone from entering.

Incident Response is like having a well-prepared emergency plan that guides your actions when a cybersecurity incident occurs, helping you contain and recover from the breach effectively.

Security Policies and Procedures are the rules and guidelines that govern how organizations should protect their digital assets, much like a set of laws that ensure order and safety within a society.

The Principle of Least Privilege (PoLP) advocates granting individuals or systems the minimum level of access necessary to perform their tasks, reducing the risk of unauthorized actions. It's like giving employees access to only the rooms they need to do their jobs.

Multi-factor Authentication (MFA) adds an extra layer of security by requiring users to provide multiple forms of verification before granting access, making it more challenging for unauthorized individuals to gain entry.

Security Awareness Training is akin to teaching people how to stay safe in a city by educating them about potential risks and how to avoid them.

Access Control involves managing who can access what within a digital environment, much like key cards or locks that restrict entry to specific areas.

Cybersecurity Frameworks, such as NIST Cybersecurity Framework and ISO/IEC 27001, provide comprehensive guidelines and best practices for organizations to establish robust cybersecurity programs, acting as roadmaps to navigate the complex cybersecurity landscape.

Risk Assessment is like conducting a safety inspection of a building to identify potential hazards and assess their impact, helping organizations make informed decisions about their cybersecurity investments.

The Cyber Kill Chain is a concept used to understand and prevent cyberattacks, breaking down the stages of an attack into a series of steps, akin to identifying the stages of a heist and implementing security measures to stop the criminals in their tracks.

Red Team vs. Blue Team exercises involve simulated cyberattacks (Red Team) and defense measures (Blue Team), helping organizations test their security measures and identify weaknesses, similar to mock battles or drills in other fields.

Incident Response Plans are like fire escape plans; they provide a structured approach to dealing with cybersecurity incidents, ensuring that organizations respond swiftly and effectively to minimize damage.

By grasping these key concepts in cybersecurity, individuals and organizations can navigate the digital landscape more effectively, making informed decisions to protect their digital assets and maintain a robust security posture.

Understanding the importance of cybersecurity is like recognizing the significance of locking your doors and windows to keep your home safe from intruders, only in the digital realm. In today's interconnected world, where virtually every aspect of our lives depends on technology, cybersecurity has become a paramount concern.

Imagine your personal and financial information as precious treasures that need safeguarding. Just as you wouldn't leave your valuable possessions unattended in an open area, you shouldn't neglect the protection of your digital assets. Cybersecurity serves as the digital locks and alarm systems that keep your virtual treasures secure.

At its core, cybersecurity is about protecting information, systems, and networks from unauthorized access, attacks, and damage. Think of it as a shield that guards the digital realm against a multitude of threats, ranging from hackers and cybercriminals to viruses and malware.

Nowadays, the digital world is an integral part of our daily lives. We rely on the internet for communication, banking, shopping, entertainment, and work. As we embrace the convenience and efficiency of this interconnected world, we also become more vulnerable to cybersecurity threats. It's like living in a city with countless opportunities and amenities but being aware of the risks that come with urban living.

One of the key aspects of cybersecurity is confidentiality. It ensures that sensitive information remains private and accessible only to authorized individuals or entities. Imagine your personal diary, filled with your innermost thoughts and secrets. Just as you would want to keep it locked away from prying eyes, you want your digital data to be confidential.

Confidentiality is particularly crucial when it comes to personal data, financial records, and intellectual property. Protecting this information is not only a matter of personal privacy but also a legal and ethical obligation. Cybersecurity measures, such as encryption and access controls, play a vital role in preserving confidentiality.

Integrity is another fundamental pillar of cybersecurity. It guarantees the accuracy and trustworthiness of data. Imagine a contract or legal document that must remain unaltered to maintain its validity. Just as you want to ensure the integrity of such documents, you need to ensure the integrity of your digital data.

Integrity becomes essential when dealing with critical systems, financial transactions, and communication. Any unauthorized modification or tampering with data can lead to severe consequences, both in personal and business contexts. Cybersecurity measures, such as checksums and digital signatures, help maintain data integrity.

Availability is the third cornerstone of cybersecurity. It ensures that systems and data are accessible when needed. Think of it as the electricity that powers your home or the water that flows from your tap. Just as you rely on these utilities for daily life, you depend on the availability of digital resources.

Downtime due to cyberattacks or technical failures can disrupt businesses, affect productivity, and even impact essential services like healthcare and emergency response. Cybersecurity measures, such as redundancy and disaster recovery plans, help ensure the availability of critical systems and data.

Authentication is a crucial concept in cybersecurity, akin to checking someone's identification before granting access to a secure area. It involves verifying the identity of users or systems. In the digital realm, this means confirming that individuals or entities are who they claim to be before granting them access to sensitive information or resources.

Authorization goes hand in hand with authentication. It determines what actions and resources users or systems are allowed to access once their identity is confirmed. Think of it as granting permissions and privileges within an organization or digital environment. Proper authorization ensures that individuals only have access to what is necessary for their roles or tasks.

Encryption is a powerful tool in the cybersecurity arsenal. It involves converting data into a secure code to prevent unauthorized access. Imagine it as encoding a message so that only the intended recipient can decode and read it. Encryption is used to protect sensitive data during transmission and storage, ensuring that even if intercepted, it remains unreadable to unauthorized parties.

Firewalls act as digital barriers, much like security guards stationed at the entrance to a secure facility. They monitor incoming and outgoing network traffic, blocking or allowing data packets based on predefined security rules. Firewalls are essential for protecting networks from unauthorized access, malware, and cyber threats.

Intrusion Detection Systems (IDS) and Intrusion Prevention Systems (IPS) function as vigilant sentinels, detecting and mitigating potential threats within your network, much like security cameras and alarms in a physical setting. They monitor network traffic for suspicious activity, alerting administrators or taking automated actions to prevent security breaches.

Patch Management involves regularly updating software and systems to address known vulnerabilities and weaknesses. It's akin to regularly servicing your car to ensure it runs smoothly and efficiently. Failing to apply patches can leave systems exposed to cyberattacks that target known vulnerabilities.

Antivirus software is like a digital immune system, scanning for and removing malicious software that could compromise your system's health. It detects and eliminates viruses, worms, Trojans, and other types of malware, ensuring the overall security and performance of your devices.

Phishing is a prevalent cyber threat that involves fraudulent attempts to deceive individuals into revealing sensitive information. Think of it as a digital con artist trying to trick you into divulging personal details. Phishing attacks often use email or messages that appear legitimate to lure victims into providing passwords, financial information, or access credentials.

Social engineering attacks leverage human psychology to manipulate individuals into divulging confidential information or performing actions that benefit attackers. It's like a skilled actor convincing you to trust them with your secrets. Social engineers exploit trust, fear, or curiosity to deceive targets, making this form of attack highly effective and dangerous.

Malware, short for malicious software, includes viruses, worms, Trojans, and other harmful programs designed to disrupt, damage, or gain unauthorized access to systems. Think of them as digital pests that can infest your system, causing harm and chaos. Malware can spread through email attachments, infected websites, or compromised software.

Zero-day vulnerabilities are like hidden traps that cybercriminals discover before security experts can patch them, leaving systems vulnerable until a fix is available. These vulnerabilities are called "zero-day" because there are zero days of protection; once exploited, they can cause significant damage. Organizations must remain vigilant and have mitigation strategies in place.

Distributed Denial of Service (DDoS) attacks involve overwhelming a target system or network with a flood of traffic, rendering it unavailable to users. It's akin to a massive crowd blocking the entrance to a building, preventing anyone from entering. DDoS attacks can disrupt online services, websites, and even critical infrastructure, highlighting the importance of robust cybersecurity measures.

Incident Response is like having a well-prepared emergency plan that guides your actions when a cybersecurity incident occurs. It helps you contain and recover from the breach effectively, minimizing damage and downtime. Incident response plans involve identifying the incident, containing the threat, eradicating it, recovering affected systems, and learning from the incident to prevent future occurrences.

Security Policies and Procedures are the rules and guidelines that govern how organizations should protect their digital assets. Think of them as a set of laws that ensure order and safety within a society. Security policies outline the organization's stance on security, while procedures provide step-by-step instructions for implementing security measures.

The Principle of Least Privilege (PoLP) advocates granting individuals or systems the minimum level of access necessary to perform their tasks. It's like giving employees access to only the rooms they need to do their jobs, preventing unauthorized actions and reducing the attack surface.

Multi-factor Authentication (MFA) adds an extra layer of security by requiring users to provide multiple forms of verification before granting access. It's like having multiple locks on your front door, making it more challenging for unauthorized individuals to gain entry. MFA often involves something you know (password), something you have (smartphone or token), or something you are (fingerprint or facial recognition).

Security Awareness Training is akin to teaching people how to stay safe in a city by educating them about potential risks and how to avoid them. Cybersecurity awareness programs teach individuals about common threats, safe practices, and the importance of security measures. Informed and vigilant users are an organization's first line of defense against cyber threats.

Access Control involves managing who can access what within a digital environment, much like key cards or locks that restrict entry to specific areas. Access control ensures that users have appropriate permissions and only access resources necessary for their roles. It helps prevent unauthorized access and data breaches.

Cybersecurity Frameworks, such as NIST Cybersecurity Framework and ISO/IEC 27001, provide comprehensive guidelines and best practices for organizations to establish robust cybersecurity programs. Think of them as roadmaps that help organizations navigate the complex cybersecurity landscape, ensuring that they address all essential aspects of security.

Risk Assessment is like conducting a safety inspection of a building to identify potential hazards and assess their impact. It helps organizations make informed decisions about their cybersecurity investments, focusing on areas of highest risk. By understanding their vulnerabilities and threats, organizations can prioritize security measures effectively.

The Cyber Kill Chain is a concept used to understand and prevent cyberattacks. It breaks down the stages of an attack into a series of steps, helping organizations identify and interrupt the attack chain before it succeeds. Think of it as identifying the stages of a heist and implementing security measures to stop the criminals in their tracks.

Red Team vs. Blue Team exercises involve simulated cyberattacks (Red Team) and defense measures (Blue Team). These exercises help organizations test their security measures and identify weaknesses. Think of it as mock battles or drills in other fields, where teams compete to improve their skills and strategies.

Incident Response Plans are like fire escape plans; they provide a structured approach to dealing with cybersecurity incidents. They ensure that organizations respond swiftly and effectively to minimize damage and recovery time. Incident response plans involve defining roles, establishing communication channels, and outlining actions to take during and after an incident.

By grasping these key concepts in cybersecurity, individuals and organizations can navigate the digital landscape more effectively. They can make informed decisions to protect their digital assets and maintain a robust security posture in an increasingly connected and digital world.

Chapter 3: Setting Up Your Scanning Environment

Setting up your scanning environment is a critical step in the world of vulnerability scanning and penetration testing, much like preparing a canvas before painting a masterpiece. The scanning environment provides the foundation upon which you'll conduct your assessments, and getting it right is essential for accurate results and efficient operations.

First and foremost, you need to select the appropriate hardware for your scanning activities, akin to choosing the right tools for a specific task. The hardware requirements may vary depending on the size and complexity of the network or system you intend to scan. It's essential to have hardware that can handle the demands of your scanning tools and the network being assessed.

Consider the processing power, memory, and storage capacity of the hardware. Faster processors and ample memory can significantly improve scanning performance. Additionally, having sufficient storage space is crucial for storing scan results and logs, which can be valuable for analysis and reporting.

Furthermore, staying up-to-date with the latest hardware technology can ensure that your scanning activities are not hindered by hardware limitations. Technology evolves rapidly, and having modern hardware can help you keep pace with the ever-increasing demands of cybersecurity assessments.

Once you've selected the appropriate hardware, you'll need to install and configure the necessary software tools for vulnerability scanning. Think of this as setting up your artist's palette with the right colors and brushes before starting your painting. The software tools you choose should align with your scanning objectives and the target environment.

Open-source and commercial vulnerability scanning tools are widely available, each offering its unique features and capabilities. Popular options include Nessus, Qualys, OpenVAS, and Rapid7's Nexpose. Take the time to evaluate these tools and select the one that best suits your needs. Consider factors like the types of vulnerabilities you need to scan for, the scalability of the tool, and the level of automation it offers.

Software updates are crucial in the world of vulnerability scanning. Just as you ensure your painting supplies are in good condition, keeping your scanning tools up to date is essential. Vulnerability scanners regularly receive updates that include new vulnerability checks, bug fixes, and improvements. By keeping your tools current, you ensure that you can scan for the latest vulnerabilities and benefit from enhanced features and reliability.

Now, let's talk about network configuration, which plays a pivotal role in the success of your scanning activities. Think of it as preparing the canvas upon which your painting will take shape. You need a clear understanding of the network topology, including the placement of firewalls, routers, switches, and other network security devices.

Mapping out your network architecture helps you identify potential scanning bottlenecks and areas where scans may be blocked or disrupted. You must know the locations of critical assets, such as servers and databases, as well as the paths that scanning traffic will traverse.

Properly configuring your scanning environment also involves considering the placement of scanning devices and sensors. Similar to choosing the right angle and lighting for a photograph, the location of your scanning devices can impact the accuracy of your assessments. Ideally, scanners should be strategically placed to cover all areas of your network, ensuring comprehensive coverage.

Firewalls and network security devices can sometimes interfere with scanning activities, much like obstacles in your artistic workspace. It's essential to coordinate with your network and security teams to ensure that scans are not blocked or flagged as suspicious activities. This collaboration helps prevent false positives and false negatives in your scan results.

Additionally, consider the timing of your scans. Just as lighting conditions can affect the outcome of a painting, the timing of your scans can impact their effectiveness. Avoid conducting scans during peak usage times when network traffic is high, as this can lead to performance issues and inaccurate results. Instead, schedule scans during periods of lower activity to minimize disruptions.

Another critical aspect of setting up your scanning environment is ensuring that you have the necessary permissions and authorizations to conduct scanning activities. Think of this as obtaining the proper permits and clearances before starting a construction project. Scanning can be seen as a form of active probing, and unauthorized scanning can trigger security alarms or even legal consequences.

Obtain explicit authorization from relevant stakeholders, including senior management, network administrators, and data owners, before initiating scans. Document the scope, objectives, and expected outcomes of your scanning activities to ensure that everyone is aligned on the goals and potential impact.

Moreover, it's crucial to establish a clear process for tracking and managing vulnerabilities identified during scanning. Think of this as maintaining a ledger of expenses and income for a financial project. Vulnerabilities should be documented, categorized, and prioritized based on their severity and potential impact on the organization.

Implement a system for assigning responsibility for vulnerability remediation and tracking progress. Just as a project manager keeps tabs on the progress of a construction project, someone should oversee the vulnerability management process to ensure that identified issues are addressed promptly and effectively.

Lastly, consider the regulatory and compliance requirements that may affect your scanning environment. Just as building codes dictate the construction standards for physical structures, regulations and industry standards may impose specific requirements on vulnerability scanning and penetration testing activities.

Different industries and jurisdictions may have specific rules governing cybersecurity assessments. Ensure that your scanning activities align with these requirements to avoid compliance issues and potential legal ramifications.

In summary, establishing your scanning environment is a crucial step in the journey of vulnerability scanning and penetration testing. It's the canvas upon which you'll create your security assessments, and getting it right is essential for accurate results and effective cybersecurity. By carefully selecting hardware, configuring software tools, understanding network architecture, obtaining authorizations, and considering compliance requirements, you set the stage for successful and impactful scanning activities.

Configuring your network for scanning is a crucial element of the vulnerability assessment and penetration testing process, much like setting up the stage for a performance. Your network's layout, security measures, and accessibility all play vital roles in the success of your scanning activities, and understanding how to configure them effectively is essential.

First and foremost, consider the network topology you're dealing with, much like understanding the layout of a theater where a play will be performed. Mapping out your network's structure, including the placement of routers, switches, firewalls, and other network devices, is essential for a successful scanning operation.

Identify critical assets within your network, such as servers, databases, and network segments, as these are the focal points of your scanning activities. Understanding their locations and configurations will help you target your scans effectively.

Just as a well-lit stage is essential for a theatrical performance, proper lighting in your network environment is crucial for scanning. Ensure that all network segments and devices are appropriately powered and operational, as scanning relies on the availability of the target systems.

Network security measures, much like security personnel in a theater, are essential for maintaining order and safety. Firewalls, intrusion detection systems (IDS), and intrusion prevention systems (IPS) are your first line of defense. Ensure that these security devices are properly configured to allow scanning traffic while still protecting your network from potential threats.

Additionally, coordinate with your network and security teams to ensure that scans are authorized and do not trigger security alerts or alarms. Collaboration is key to preventing disruptions and false positives during scanning activities.

Now, let's delve into the placement of scanning devices and sensors. Just as stage props and equipment need to be strategically arranged, the location of your scanning devices can impact the accuracy and coverage of your assessments.

Strategically position scanning devices to cover all critical areas of your network, ensuring that no segment or asset is overlooked. Think of these devices as the cameras capturing every angle of a performance, providing you with a comprehensive view of your network's vulnerabilities.

Consider the bandwidth and capacity of your scanning devices, as they must handle the volume of scanning traffic generated during assessments. Adequate resources are essential to ensure that scans run efficiently without overloading the scanning infrastructure.

Furthermore, the timing of your scans can significantly impact their effectiveness. Just as scheduling a performance at the right time ensures maximum attendance, scheduling scans during periods of lower network activity minimizes disruptions and resource contention.

Avoid conducting scans during peak usage times when network traffic is at its highest, as this can lead to performance issues and inaccurate results. Instead, schedule scans during off-peak hours to ensure that your scanning activities do not adversely affect network operations.

Additionally, you should implement mechanisms to limit the impact of scanning on your network's performance. Bandwidth throttling and rate limiting can help control the amount of scanning traffic generated, ensuring that it does not overwhelm your network resources.

Now, let's discuss the importance of permissions and authorizations. Just as actors need permission to perform on a stage, scanning activities require explicit authorization to prevent potential disruptions and legal issues.

Obtain authorization from relevant stakeholders, including senior management, network administrators, and data owners, before initiating scans. Clearly communicate the scope, objectives, and expected outcomes of your scanning activities to ensure that everyone is aligned on the goals and potential impact.

Moreover, it's crucial to maintain transparency throughout the scanning process. Just as audience members have the right to know the details of a performance, stakeholders should be kept informed about the progress of scanning activities, any issues encountered, and the results obtained.

Establish a clear process for tracking and managing vulnerabilities identified during scanning, much like maintaining a log of performances and their outcomes. Document vulnerabilities, categorize them based on their severity, and prioritize them for remediation.

Assign responsibility for vulnerability remediation and track progress to ensure that identified issues are addressed promptly and effectively. Similar to coordinating cast and crew for a theater production, having a well-organized team responsible for vulnerability management is essential.

Lastly, consider the regulatory and compliance requirements that may affect your scanning activities. Just as theaters must adhere to safety regulations and licensing requirements, organizations conducting vulnerability assessments and penetration tests must comply with relevant laws and industry standards.

Different industries and jurisdictions may impose specific rules governing cybersecurity assessments. Ensure that your scanning activities align with these requirements to avoid compliance issues and potential legal consequences.

In summary, configuring your network for scanning is a critical aspect of vulnerability assessment and penetration testing. It's the stage upon which your security assessments will unfold, and careful configuration is essential for accurate results and the success of your cybersecurity efforts. By understanding your network's topology, ensuring proper security measures, strategically placing scanning devices, scheduling scans thoughtfully, obtaining authorizations, maintaining transparency, and considering compliance requirements, you set the stage for effective and impactful scanning activities.

Chapter 4: Scanning Tools and Techniques

Exploring the world of vulnerability scanning and penetration testing tools is like opening a toolbox filled with instruments of cybersecurity. These essential tools are your companions on the journey to identify weaknesses and secure your digital assets effectively.

One of the foundational tools in your arsenal is the vulnerability scanner. Think of it as a detective's magnifying glass, used to inspect your digital landscape for potential vulnerabilities. Vulnerability scanners, such as Nessus, OpenVAS, and Qualys, systematically scan your network and systems, identifying known vulnerabilities and misconfigurations.

These tools use a database of known vulnerabilities to compare your system's configuration and software versions, much like detectives referencing a database of known criminals. When a match is found, it means there's a potential security gap that needs attention.

Intriguingly, some vulnerability scanners are like expert detectives who can not only identify vulnerabilities but also provide recommendations for remediation. They offer insights into how to patch or mitigate the identified vulnerabilities, helping you bolster your defenses.

Another indispensable tool in your kit is the port scanner, similar to a locksmith's kit used to check which doors are open and which are locked. Port scanners, like Nmap, scan your network to identify open ports on target systems. An open port can be seen as a potential entry point for attackers, and knowing which ports are open is crucial for assessing the security posture of your network.

Beyond identifying open ports, port scanners can also determine the services running on those ports, providing valuable information about the target systems. This information helps you understand the attack surface and potential vulnerabilities.

Furthermore, just as a locksmith may carry specialized tools for different locks, there are specialized port scanners designed for specific tasks. Some focus on service detection, while others excel at version detection or operating system fingerprinting. These specialized scanners offer more detailed insights into the target systems.

Network mapping tools are akin to creating a blueprint of a building before planning a renovation. These tools, such as Wireshark and Zenmap, help you visualize your network's layout, discover connected devices, and map out network topologies. Understanding your network's structure is essential for effective scanning and assessment.

Packet analyzers, like Wireshark, are your digital magnifying glasses for inspecting network traffic. These tools capture and analyze network packets, allowing you to dissect communication between devices. Just as forensic experts examine evidence, packet analyzers help you investigate network activity, detect anomalies, and identify potential security threats.

Similarly, wireless network scanning tools are like metal detectors used to find hidden treasures. They help you identify and assess wireless networks in your vicinity. Tools like Aircrack-ng and Kismet can detect nearby Wi-Fi networks, identify their security protocols, and even assess their vulnerabilities. This is crucial for securing your wireless infrastructure and preventing unauthorized access.

Web application scanners are essential when it comes to securing web-based assets, much like having a locksmith who specializes in securing doors and locks. Web applications are a common target for cyberattacks, making it crucial to scan them for vulnerabilities.

Web vulnerability scanners, such as OWASP ZAP and Burp Suite, crawl web applications, identify potential flaws like SQL injection, cross-site scripting (XSS), and insecure authentication mechanisms. They help you patch vulnerabilities that could be exploited by attackers aiming to compromise your web applications.

Database scanners are your investigators focused on securing your data vaults. Databases often store sensitive information, and securing them is paramount. Database scanners, like SQLMap, assess database systems for potential vulnerabilities and weaknesses. They identify vulnerabilities that could lead to data breaches and provide guidance on how to mitigate them.

Password cracking tools are like safecrackers, attempting to uncover the secret combinations guarding your digital treasures. Passwords remain a weak point in many security systems, and it's essential to assess the strength of user credentials. Password cracking tools, such as John the Ripper and Hashcat, attempt to crack passwords through various techniques like brute-force attacks and dictionary attacks. They help organizations identify weak passwords and enforce stronger password policies.

Similarly, social engineering tools, like SET (Social Engineering Toolkit), simulate real-world attacks that manipulate human behavior. Just as a skilled con artist might use psychological tricks to gain access to a secure area, social engineering tools help you assess the susceptibility of your organization's employees to social engineering attacks. They test your employees' awareness and help you educate them on potential threats.

While scanning and probing are essential, data analysis tools are your means of making sense of the information gathered. Log analysis tools, like Splunk and ELK Stack, help you centralize and analyze logs from various sources, enabling you to detect anomalies, security incidents, and potential threats. It's like having a team of analysts dissecting clues from a crime scene to uncover the truth.

Moreover, reporting and documentation tools are your storytellers, conveying the findings of your scanning and testing activities. Effective reporting is crucial for communicating vulnerabilities and risks to stakeholders, similar to a detective providing a detailed report of their investigation.

Tools like Dradis and Nessus provide capabilities for generating comprehensive reports that include vulnerability details, risk assessments, and recommended remediation steps. These reports are essential for decision-makers and IT teams to prioritize and address security issues.

Collaboration tools, such as Slack and Microsoft Teams, are like your communication hub, facilitating effective teamwork during scanning and testing activities. They enable your security team to collaborate in real-time, share findings, and coordinate response efforts. Just as detectives rely on teamwork to solve complex cases, collaboration tools foster cooperation among cybersecurity professionals.

Lastly, consider the importance of automation in your scanning toolkit. Automation tools, like Ansible and Puppet, help streamline vulnerability remediation and security configuration management. They enable you to automate the deployment of security patches and configuration changes across your network, reducing the attack surface and minimizing vulnerabilities.

In summary, essential scanning tools are the instruments that enable you to identify, assess, and mitigate vulnerabilities and security risks in your digital environment. These tools, ranging from vulnerability scanners and port scanners to packet analyzers and password cracking utilities, are essential for maintaining a robust cybersecurity posture. By mastering the use of these tools, you can effectively secure your digital assets and stay one step ahead of potential threats.

Navigating the realm of effective scanning techniques is akin to mastering various strokes and techniques in the world of art, where each technique brings its unique approach to capturing the essence of your subject—the vulnerabilities within your digital landscape.

One of the fundamental techniques in your scanning repertoire is the "Full Port Scan," similar to sketching the initial outline of your artwork. This technique involves scanning all possible ports on a target system. It provides a comprehensive view of the target's open ports and services, helping you identify potential entry points for attackers.

Another valuable technique is the "Service Version Detection," akin to adding intricate details to your artwork. This technique goes beyond identifying open ports; it determines the specific versions of services running on those ports. Knowing the exact service versions is essential for assessing their vulnerabilities accurately.

Similarly, the "Operating System Fingerprinting" technique is like recognizing the artist's signature on a painting. It helps you identify the underlying operating system of a target system based on its network responses. This information is valuable for tailoring your scanning and testing activities to the target's environment.

The "Incremental Scanning" technique is comparable to adding layers of colors and textures to your artwork. Rather than scanning the entire target network in one pass, incremental scanning divides the scanning process into smaller, more manageable segments. This approach helps distribute scanning traffic and resources, reducing the risk of disruptions.

Focused scanning is a technique similar to zooming in on a specific detail of your artwork. It involves targeting a particular range of IP addresses, ports, or services within your network. Focused scanning is useful when you want to assess specific areas or assets in your network without scanning the entire environment.

Conversely, "Comprehensive Network Scanning" is like creating a panoramic masterpiece, scanning your entire network landscape. This technique scans all IP addresses and ports within your network, providing a complete overview of your digital terrain. Comprehensive scanning is essential for identifying hidden vulnerabilities and ensuring thorough coverage.

The "Timing-Based Scanning" technique is akin to adjusting the brush strokes in your artwork to achieve different effects. Timing-based scanning involves varying the timing and intervals between scan requests to avoid triggering security alerts or rate limiting mechanisms. This technique helps ensure that your scans go undetected and provide accurate results.

Customized scanning scripts are like personalized brushes in an artist's collection, tailored to your specific needs. These scripts allow you to create scanning routines that align with your organization's requirements and objectives. Custom scripts offer flexibility and control over your scanning activities.

Vulnerability-specific scanning techniques are like using specialized brushes for different painting styles. These techniques focus on scanning for specific vulnerabilities or weaknesses, such as SQL injection or cross-site scripting (XSS). They help you target known threats and assess the security of critical areas in your network.

Scanning with authentication credentials is akin to having privileged access to your artwork's creation process. This technique involves scanning target systems with valid credentials, allowing you to assess the security configuration and vulnerabilities from an insider's perspective. It's essential for evaluating the effectiveness of access controls and privilege management.

When it comes to web application scanning, "Crawling and Scanning" is like exploring every nook and cranny of a complex painting. This technique involves crawling web applications to discover their structure and content before scanning for vulnerabilities. It helps ensure comprehensive coverage and accurate assessments of web applications.

"Session-Based Scanning" for web applications is like capturing dynamic elements in your artwork. This technique simulates user sessions, interacting with web applications like a real user would. It's crucial for identifying vulnerabilities that may only manifest during specific user interactions.

Authenticated web application scanning is like examining the hidden layers of a painting. This technique involves scanning web applications with user credentials to access restricted areas and assess their security. It helps uncover vulnerabilities that may be accessible only to authenticated users.

External scanning is like painting the exterior of a building, focusing on what's visible to the outside world. This technique involves scanning systems and assets accessible from the internet, helping you identify vulnerabilities that may be exploited by external attackers.

Internal scanning, on the other hand, is like inspecting the building's interior, looking for hidden flaws. This technique assesses systems and assets within your internal network, focusing on vulnerabilities that may pose a threat from within your organization.

"Non-Intrusive Scanning" is like using a gentle touch in your artwork, avoiding any potential disruption. This technique involves scanning without actively probing or interacting with target systems. It's ideal for assessing vulnerabilities without risking any impact on the target's stability.

"Interactive Scanning" is akin to an artist engaging with their subject to capture its essence. This technique involves interactive sessions with target systems, actively probing and testing for vulnerabilities. It provides a more comprehensive assessment but may require additional precautions to avoid disruptions.

Furthermore, "Incremental Testing" is like refining your artwork in multiple iterations. This technique involves conducting successive rounds of scanning and testing, each building upon the findings and insights from the previous iteration. It allows you to track the progress of vulnerability remediation efforts and measure the effectiveness of security improvements.

"Continuous Scanning" is like maintaining an ongoing dialogue with your artwork, ensuring it stays relevant and up to date. This technique involves regularly scheduled scanning and testing activities to continuously monitor your network's security posture. It helps you stay vigilant against emerging threats and vulnerabilities.

Lastly, "External Validation" is like seeking feedback from fellow artists to improve your artwork. This technique involves engaging third-party security experts or penetration testers to validate your scanning results and provide an independent assessment of your network's security. It ensures objectivity and thorough scrutiny of your security measures.

In summary, effective scanning techniques are the brushes and strokes that allow you to create a comprehensive and accurate picture of your network's vulnerabilities and security posture. By mastering these techniques, you can assess your digital landscape with precision, identify weaknesses, and take proactive measures to enhance your cybersecurity defenses.

Chapter 5: Identifying Common Vulnerabilities

Recognizing common vulnerabilities is like becoming a detective who can spot subtle clues in a crime scene. In the world of cybersecurity, understanding these vulnerabilities is crucial for safeguarding your digital assets and maintaining a robust security posture.

One of the most prevalent vulnerabilities is "Unpatched Software," much like an unlocked door in a secure building. Unpatched software refers to the presence of known security vulnerabilities in the software applications and operating systems running on your systems. These vulnerabilities can be exploited by attackers to gain unauthorized access or compromise your systems. Regularly applying security patches and updates is essential to mitigate this risk.

Similarly, "Weak or Default Passwords" are like using a simple combination lock to secure a valuable item. Weak passwords, easily guessable or commonly used credentials, pose a significant security risk. Attackers can use brute force or dictionary attacks to gain access to accounts and systems protected by weak passwords. Implementing strong password policies, enforcing password complexity, and using multi-factor authentication (MFA) can enhance password security.

The "Lack of User Training" vulnerability is similar to a lack of awareness about potential dangers. Users who are not adequately trained in cybersecurity practices can inadvertently fall victim to phishing attacks, social engineering tactics, or unknowingly engage in risky behaviors. Providing regular cybersecurity training and awareness programs helps users recognize and respond to security threats effectively.

"Outdated or Unsupported Software" is like using old, worn-out tools that are no longer effective. Operating systems and software that are no longer supported by vendors are susceptible to unpatched vulnerabilities. Attackers can target these systems, knowing that security updates and patches will not be available. It's crucial to retire or upgrade unsupported software to mitigate this risk.

The "Missing Security Updates" vulnerability is akin to forgetting to lock your car when parked in a busy area. Failure to apply security updates and patches promptly leaves systems exposed to known vulnerabilities. Attackers actively scan for unpatched systems to exploit weaknesses. Regularly monitoring and applying security updates is essential for reducing this risk.

"Open Ports and Services" vulnerabilities are like leaving multiple entrances open in a building. Open ports and services on networked systems can serve as potential entry points for attackers. Identifying and closing unnecessary open ports and services helps reduce the attack surface and minimize exposure to threats.

The "Insufficient Data Encryption" vulnerability is similar to sending sensitive information through an unsecured postal service. Insufficient data encryption exposes data in transit to interception and eavesdropping. Implementing strong encryption protocols for data in transit, such as HTTPS for web traffic and VPNs for remote access, helps protect sensitive information.

"SQL Injection" vulnerabilities are like allowing unauthorized individuals to alter records in a filing system. SQL injection occurs when attackers manipulate input fields to execute arbitrary SQL queries against a database. This can lead to unauthorized access, data manipulation, or even data theft. Implementing input validation and using prepared statements can help prevent SQL injection attacks.

"Cross-Site Scripting (XSS)" vulnerabilities are similar to someone leaving hidden messages in a book that others might read. XSS attacks involve injecting malicious scripts into web applications, which can then be executed by unsuspecting users. This can lead to theft of user data, session hijacking, or defacement of websites. Implementing input validation and output encoding in web applications helps mitigate this risk.

The "Inadequate Access Controls" vulnerability is like failing to lock certain doors in a high-security facility. Inadequate access controls can allow unauthorized individuals to gain access to sensitive resources or systems. Implementing proper access controls, role-based permissions, and least privilege principles helps restrict access to authorized users only.

"Security Misconfigurations" are similar to leaving the blueprint of a secure building in plain sight. Misconfigured settings in software, servers, or devices can create security weaknesses that attackers can exploit. Regularly auditing and reviewing configurations, removing unnecessary services, and following security best practices can help prevent misconfigurations.

The "Insecure File Uploads" vulnerability is akin to allowing strangers to deposit packages without inspection. Allowing users to upload files to a web application without proper validation can lead to the execution of malicious code or the spread of malware. Implementing strict file upload controls and scanning uploaded files for malware helps mitigate this risk.

"Missing or Weak Authentication" vulnerabilities are like using a simple combination lock to secure a vault. Weak authentication mechanisms, such as single-factor authentication or default credentials, can be exploited by attackers to gain unauthorized access. Implementing strong authentication methods, including multi-factor authentication (MFA), enhances security.

"Cross-Site Request Forgery (CSRF)" vulnerabilities are similar to someone tricking you into signing documents without your knowledge. CSRF attacks involve manipulating a user's web browser to perform actions without their consent, leading to unauthorized actions being taken on their behalf. Implementing anti-CSRF tokens and secure session management helps prevent these attacks.

"Sensitive Data Exposure" vulnerabilities are like leaving confidential documents in an unlocked cabinet. Storing sensitive data without proper encryption or protection can lead to data breaches. Encrypting sensitive data at rest and in transit, implementing access controls, and following data protection regulations are crucial for safeguarding sensitive information.

"Broken Authentication" vulnerabilities are similar to someone easily picking locks to access restricted areas. Broken authentication mechanisms, such as session fixation or session hijacking, can allow attackers to gain unauthorized access to user accounts. Implementing secure authentication processes and regularly monitoring for suspicious activities help mitigate this risk.

The "Misuse of Security Tokens" vulnerability is akin to someone using a master key improperly. Security tokens, such as API keys or OAuth tokens, can be misused or leaked, leading to unauthorized access or data breaches. Implementing token management best practices and monitoring token usage helps prevent misuse.

In summary, recognizing common vulnerabilities is an essential skill in the realm of cybersecurity. Just as a detective identifies clues at a crime scene, cybersecurity professionals identify vulnerabilities that can be exploited by attackers. By understanding and addressing these vulnerabilities, organizations can strengthen their defenses and protect their digital assets effectively.

Navigating the vast landscape of cybersecurity is a bit like exploring a library filled with books containing valuable information on vulnerabilities and threats. These books, metaphorically speaking, are the vulnerability databases, and they play a pivotal role in helping cybersecurity professionals stay informed and proactive in the battle against security risks.

Imagine these databases as well-organized collections, each containing a wealth of knowledge about vulnerabilities, security patches, and potential threats. These resources serve as essential references for anyone involved in cybersecurity, from network administrators to penetration testers and security analysts.

One of the most well-known vulnerability databases is the National Vulnerability Database (NVD), often considered the grand library of vulnerabilities. The NVD is a comprehensive repository of known vulnerabilities, categorized and cataloged for easy reference. It's like an expansive encyclopedia of vulnerabilities, where each entry provides critical information about the security issue, its severity, and available patches or mitigations.

Similarly, the Common Vulnerabilities and Exposures (CVE) database is a valuable resource, akin to an index in a reference book. CVE assigns unique identifiers to vulnerabilities, making it easier for professionals to search and cross-reference vulnerabilities across different databases and resources. This standardization helps streamline communication about vulnerabilities and ensures a common understanding of the issues at hand.

In addition to these widely recognized databases, there are specialized resources tailored to specific technologies and industries. For instance, the Common Weakness Enumeration (CWE) database focuses on identifying and categorizing software weaknesses and design flaws. It's like a specialized library for software developers, offering guidance on addressing common coding issues that can lead to vulnerabilities.

Furthermore, organizations like the Open Web Application Security Project (OWASP) maintain their databases, such as the OWASP Top Ten. These resources concentrate on web application security, providing insights into the most prevalent vulnerabilities in web applications, such as SQL injection and cross-site scripting (XSS). They're like dedicated sections in a library, where experts focus on specific topics to provide in-depth knowledge.

Accessing vulnerability databases is akin to browsing through a library's catalog system. Users can search for vulnerabilities based on keywords, software names, or unique identifiers like CVE numbers. This allows cybersecurity professionals to quickly locate information about vulnerabilities relevant to their systems and applications.

Each entry in a vulnerability database is like a book, containing essential details about a specific security issue. These entries typically include a description of the vulnerability, its severity, affected software versions, and references to related resources, such as security advisories and patches. It's as if each book offers a comprehensive summary of a particular topic.

Severity ratings assigned to vulnerabilities, often expressed using Common Vulnerability Scoring System (CVSS) scores, help users prioritize their response efforts. Just like a library's rating system for books, CVSS scores indicate the potential impact and exploitability of a vulnerability. This information guides cybersecurity professionals in determining which vulnerabilities require immediate attention and which can be addressed later.

Moreover, vulnerability databases provide historical data, much like a library's archives. This historical context helps users understand the evolution of vulnerabilities, including when they were first discovered, how they've been exploited, and the remediation efforts undertaken over time. It's like reading through the pages of history to gain insights into the past.

One of the significant advantages of utilizing vulnerability databases is their role in proactive security management. Just as reading books on various subjects enhances your knowledge, regularly checking vulnerability databases allows organizations to stay ahead of potential threats. By staying informed about the latest vulnerabilities and patches, security teams can take proactive measures to protect their systems.

For example, when a new vulnerability is discovered and added to a database, security professionals can access the relevant information immediately. They can assess the vulnerability's impact on their systems, determine if any of their assets are affected, and plan the appropriate response. It's like receiving an alert about a new book release and being one of the first to read it.

Furthermore, vulnerability databases offer guidance on mitigation strategies and patches, similar to books that provide solutions to common problems. When security teams identify vulnerabilities in their systems, they can refer to the database entries for recommended actions. These recommendations may include applying vendor-provided patches, implementing workarounds, or configuring security controls to mitigate the risk.

Collaboration and knowledge sharing are vital aspects of utilizing vulnerability databases, just as discussions among readers enhance understanding. Cybersecurity professionals often rely on these databases to share insights, exchange information about emerging threats, and collaborate on strategies for addressing vulnerabilities. It's like joining a community of experts who discuss and share their expertise.

Security researchers and organizations contribute to the wealth of knowledge in vulnerability databases. They discover and report vulnerabilities, share details about their findings, and collaborate to develop solutions. This collective effort is essential for the continuous improvement of security measures and the timely response to emerging threats. It's like authors contributing chapters to a collaborative book, each adding their expertise to the collective knowledge.

In addition to staying informed about vulnerabilities, organizations can use vulnerability databases as references for compliance and risk management. Just as legal libraries help lawyers navigate the complexities of the law, vulnerability databases assist organizations in complying with security regulations and standards. They provide information about vulnerabilities that may impact compliance efforts and help organizations prioritize remediation activities.

Moreover, cybersecurity professionals often use vulnerability databases to support their penetration testing and vulnerability assessment activities. These databases serve as a valuable source of information when conducting security tests on systems and applications. By referencing the databases, testers can identify potential weaknesses, assess their severity, and provide recommendations for remediation. It's like having a comprehensive guidebook for conducting security assessments.

In summary, vulnerability databases are like well-maintained libraries for cybersecurity professionals, offering a wealth of information about vulnerabilities, patches, and threats. These resources play a crucial role in proactive security management, enabling organizations to stay informed, prioritize their response efforts, and collaborate with the broader cybersecurity community. Just as books empower readers with knowledge, vulnerability databases empower security professionals with the information they need to protect their digital assets effectively.

Chapter 6: Vulnerability Assessment Best Practices

Navigating the vulnerability scanning process is akin to following a well-orchestrated dance, where each step leads to a harmonious and secure outcome. This vulnerability scanning workflow is the choreography that helps organizations identify and address potential security weaknesses in their digital environments.

It all begins with the "Preparation" phase, much like warming up before a dance performance. In this phase, you define the scope of your vulnerability scanning, identifying the assets and systems to be scanned. You also consider the goals of the scan—are you looking for specific vulnerabilities, conducting a routine check, or preparing for a compliance audit?

Next comes the "Configuration" step, which is like choosing the right music for your dance. Here, you configure your scanning tools, selecting the appropriate settings and parameters for the scan. You determine which types of scans to perform, whether it's a full port scan, a web application scan, or a database vulnerability assessment.

Once your tools are finely tuned, it's time to "Initiate" the scan, much like stepping onto the dance floor as the music begins. You launch the scans against the selected targets, allowing the scanning tools to do their work. It's essential to monitor the progress of the scan to ensure it's proceeding as expected.

As the scan progresses, vulnerabilities start to emerge, much like dancers gracefully executing their moves. These vulnerabilities are identified by the scanning tools, and each one is categorized based on severity and potential impact.

Just as a choreographer watches dancers closely, you watch the scanning results closely.

The "Assessment" phase is where you dive deep into the vulnerabilities found during the scan. It's like analyzing the performance of each dancer to identify areas for improvement. In this phase, you assess the vulnerabilities to understand their significance, exploitability, and potential impact on your organization.

Some vulnerabilities may turn out to be false positives, similar to a dancer executing a move incorrectly during practice. It's essential to verify and validate vulnerabilities to ensure they are genuine threats. You also prioritize vulnerabilities based on their severity, addressing the most critical ones first.

With a clear understanding of the vulnerabilities, it's time to "Remediate" them, much like refining dance routines to perfection. Remediation involves applying patches, implementing security controls, or making configuration changes to mitigate the identified vulnerabilities. Just as a choreographer guides dancers to improve their moves, you guide the organization to enhance its security posture.

Communication is a vital aspect of the vulnerability scanning workflow, similar to providing feedback to dancers. During the "Communication" phase, you report the scan results to relevant stakeholders. This includes sharing information about the vulnerabilities, their potential impact, and the actions taken to remediate them. Effective communication helps ensure everyone is on the same page regarding security risks and actions taken.

As with any dance performance, practice makes perfect. In the "Continuous Improvement" phase, you assess the effectiveness of your vulnerability scanning process and look for ways to enhance it. You may refine scanning configurations, update tools, or adjust scanning schedules based on lessons learned from previous scans. Continuous improvement ensures that your vulnerability scanning process remains effective over time.

Now, let's delve into the specifics of each phase in more detail.

In the "Preparation" phase, you begin by defining the scope of your vulnerability scan. You identify the assets and systems that will be scanned, taking into account factors such as network segments, IP ranges, and critical infrastructure. This step is essential to ensure that the scan focuses on the areas of greatest concern.

Next, you establish clear objectives for the scan. Are you conducting a routine scan to identify common vulnerabilities, or are you preparing for a compliance audit that requires specific checks? Understanding the goals of the scan helps you tailor the scanning process to meet your organization's needs.

Moving on to the "Configuration" phase, you select the appropriate scanning tools and configure them for your specific requirements. You decide on the scanning frequency—are you conducting periodic scans, continuous monitoring, or one-time assessments? Your choice depends on your organization's risk tolerance and security policies.

Within the scanning tools, you set parameters and options, such as scan intensity and coverage. You choose the scanning profiles that match your objectives, whether it's a comprehensive network scan or a focused web application assessment. This phase is like choosing the dance style and music tempo that align with your performance goals.

With the tools finely tuned, you "Initiate" the scan. This involves launching the scans against the selected targets, whether they are internal systems, external assets, or web applications. Monitoring the scan's progress is crucial at this stage to ensure it proceeds as expected and does not disrupt normal operations. It's like watching the dancers closely to ensure they follow the choreography.

As vulnerabilities begin to surface, you enter the "Assessment" phase. Here, you dive deep into each vulnerability to understand its nature and potential impact. You assess vulnerabilities based on their severity, exploitability, and relevance to your organization. Just as a choreographer evaluates each dancer's performance, you evaluate each vulnerability's significance.

During the assessment, you may discover false positives—vulnerabilities that initially appeared to be threats but are not. It's essential to verify and validate vulnerabilities to separate genuine risks from false alarms. Prioritization is key, as you determine which vulnerabilities require immediate attention and which can be addressed in later stages.

After assessing the vulnerabilities, you enter the "Remediation" phase. This is where you take action to address and mitigate the identified vulnerabilities. Remediation may involve applying security patches, configuring security controls, or implementing compensating measures. It's like refining the dance routines to eliminate errors and improve overall performance.

Communication is vital throughout the vulnerability scanning workflow. In the "Communication" phase, you report the scan results to relevant stakeholders, including IT teams, management, and compliance officers. Your reports provide clear information about the vulnerabilities, their potential impact, and the actions taken to remediate them. Effective communication ensures that everyone is aware of security risks and the progress of vulnerability management efforts.

Lastly, the "Continuous Improvement" phase is about refining and enhancing your vulnerability scanning process over time. You review the effectiveness of your scans, assess the accuracy of vulnerability assessments, and identify areas for improvement. This phase ensures that your scanning process remains robust and aligned with your organization's evolving security needs.

In summary, the vulnerability scanning workflow is a well-structured process that helps organizations identify, assess, and remediate security vulnerabilities effectively. Just as a dance performance requires careful planning, practice, and refinement, the vulnerability scanning process relies on thorough preparation, configuration, assessment, and remediation. By following this workflow, organizations can proactively manage security risks and maintain a strong security posture.

Navigating the sea of vulnerabilities can feel a bit like sorting through a treasure chest filled with valuable gems. Each vulnerability represents a potential security risk, but not all are equally significant, and that's where vulnerability prioritization techniques come into play—helping organizations focus their efforts on addressing the most critical threats.

Think of vulnerability prioritization as having a map that guides you to the most valuable treasures within that chest. It helps you determine which vulnerabilities to address first, ensuring that your limited resources are allocated where they matter most.

One of the primary techniques in vulnerability prioritization is the Common Vulnerability Scoring System (CVSS), which is like a rating system for the gems in your treasure chest. CVSS assigns scores to vulnerabilities based on their severity, impact, and exploitability. These scores help organizations quickly identify the most critical vulnerabilities and prioritize them for remediation.

However, CVSS scores are just the beginning. The "Asset and Business Impact" technique goes beyond the technical aspects of vulnerabilities and considers their potential impact on your organization's assets and operations. It's like assessing the value of each gem in your treasure chest. By understanding which vulnerabilities could harm your critical assets or disrupt your business processes, you can prioritize them accordingly.

The "Threat Intelligence" technique is akin to having a trusted guide who provides insights into the behavior of potential adversaries. This technique involves gathering threat intelligence to identify whether specific vulnerabilities are actively being exploited in the wild. Just as a guide warns you about dangerous paths, threat intelligence helps you focus on vulnerabilities that are currently posing a real threat to your organization.

"Exploitability Analysis" is like evaluating the tools and techniques needed to unlock the potential of a gem. This technique assesses the likelihood that a vulnerability will be exploited successfully. By understanding the ease with which an attacker can exploit a vulnerability, you can prioritize those that are more likely to be weaponized against your organization.

Moreover, the "Vulnerability Age" technique is similar to assessing the historical significance of a gem. Older vulnerabilities may have been known and addressed by vendors or the security community, reducing their immediate risk. Prioritizing newer vulnerabilities ensures that you're focusing on those that may not yet have widely available patches or mitigations.

The "Business Context" technique involves understanding the specific impact of a vulnerability on your organization's operations. It's like considering whether a gem fits perfectly into a particular piece of jewelry. By examining how a vulnerability aligns with your business objectives, you can prioritize those that have the potential to disrupt critical processes or services.

"Remediation Difficulty" is similar to evaluating the effort required to polish a gem and make it shine. Some vulnerabilities are easier to remediate than others due to factors like the availability of patches or the complexity of mitigations. Prioritizing vulnerabilities based on remediation difficulty ensures that you address the low-hanging fruit first.

"Cumulative Risk" takes into account the potential impact of multiple vulnerabilities when exploited together. It's like recognizing that a collection of gems may be more valuable than each gem individually. By assessing the combined risk of vulnerabilities when used in tandem, you can prioritize those that, when chained together, pose a significant threat to your organization.

The "Compliance and Regulatory Requirements" technique is akin to following a set of rules and guidelines for handling precious gems. Some industries have specific compliance requirements that dictate how vulnerabilities should be prioritized and remediated. Adhering to these regulations ensures that you remain in compliance while addressing security risks.

"Asset Criticality" is like determining the value of certain gems in your collection. By assessing the criticality of assets impacted by a vulnerability, you can prioritize those vulnerabilities that pose the greatest risk to your most important assets. This approach aligns vulnerability management with your organization's strategic objectives.

The "External Exposure" technique involves evaluating which vulnerabilities are accessible from the internet. It's like considering which gems in your collection are on display for potential thieves to see. Prioritizing externally exposed vulnerabilities is essential for protecting your organization from threats originating outside your network perimeter.

"Attack Vector Analysis" is akin to understanding the paths attackers may take to exploit vulnerabilities. Some vulnerabilities may require attackers to follow complex routes, while others have straightforward attack vectors. By analyzing attack vectors, you can prioritize vulnerabilities that are more likely to be targeted by various adversaries.

"Predictive Analysis" is like having a crystal ball that forecasts the future value of gems. This technique involves using historical data and threat trends to predict which vulnerabilities are likely to become high-priority targets in the near future. It helps you proactively address emerging threats.

Additionally, the "Scanning and Monitoring" technique involves continuously scanning and monitoring your environment for vulnerabilities. It's like regularly inspecting your gem collection to ensure none have been stolen or damaged. By maintaining ongoing visibility into your vulnerabilities, you can identify new risks as they emerge and address them promptly.

Collaboration is key in vulnerability prioritization. Just as a group of experts may assess the value of different gems collectively, involving various stakeholders in the process can lead to more informed decisions. Collaboration ensures that different perspectives and expertise are considered when prioritizing vulnerabilities.

In summary, vulnerability prioritization techniques are the compass that guides organizations through the complex landscape of security risks. Like an experienced gemologist who identifies the most valuable gems in a collection, these techniques help organizations focus on addressing the most critical vulnerabilities first. By carefully considering factors such as severity, impact, threat intelligence, exploitability, and business context, organizations can prioritize their efforts effectively and enhance their cybersecurity defenses.

Chapter 7: Reporting and Documentation

Creating effective reports in the realm of cybersecurity is akin to crafting a compelling story that conveys essential information and guides decision-making. Just as a well-written story captivates its audience, a well-structured and informative cybersecurity report ensures that stakeholders understand the security landscape and can take appropriate actions.

Imagine yourself as a storyteller, narrating the cybersecurity journey through your report. To start, you need to define your audience, much like identifying who will be listening to your story. Understanding your audience's level of technical expertise, interests, and objectives is essential for tailoring the report's content and tone to their needs.

The introduction of your report serves as the opening chapter of your story. Here, you set the stage by providing context and background information. Explain the purpose of the report, the scope of your analysis, and the timeframe it covers. Just as the first chapter of a book draws readers in, the introduction should capture the reader's attention and convey the report's significance.

Moving on to the "Executive Summary," think of this section as the book's blurb—a concise overview that highlights the main points and key findings. In cybersecurity reports, the executive summary is a crucial element for busy stakeholders who need a quick grasp of the report's content without diving into the details.

The "Methodology" section is like revealing the research methods used to gather information for your story. Here, you explain how data was collected, the tools and techniques employed, and any specific methodologies or frameworks followed. Transparency in your methodology builds trust and credibility in your report.

Now, let's delve into the heart of your report—the "Findings" chapter. This is where you present the core of your story, much like the unfolding plot in a book. Organize your findings logically, grouping related information together. For example, if you're reporting on vulnerabilities, categorize them by severity or affected systems. Provide detailed descriptions of each finding, including its impact and potential risks.

Accompany your findings with evidence and supporting data, much like a novelist using quotes and references to substantiate the story. In cybersecurity reports, evidence can include logs, screenshots, and vulnerability scan results. Visual aids like charts and graphs can help convey complex information in a digestible format.

In the "Analysis" section, you offer insights and interpretations of your findings, similar to a book's analysis of characters' motivations and actions. Explain the implications of the vulnerabilities or security incidents you've identified. Discuss the potential consequences if these issues are left unaddressed and provide recommendations for mitigation.

When writing your report, consider the narrative flow. Just as a book follows a logical sequence of events, your report should lead the reader from one section to the next in a cohesive manner. Ensure that each section flows naturally into the next, allowing the reader to follow the story of your cybersecurity assessment effortlessly.

While conveying your findings and analysis, maintain a balance between technical details and accessibility. Think of it as ensuring that your story is engaging for both experts and non-experts. Use plain language to explain technical concepts and provide definitions or context for terms that may be unfamiliar to some readers.

In the "Recommendations" section, you play the role of the guide who suggests the best course of action to address the challenges presented in your report. Provide clear and actionable recommendations for mitigating vulnerabilities, improving security controls, or addressing any identified gaps. Prioritize recommendations based on their potential impact and urgency.

Just as a book's characters may face dilemmas and choices, the decision-makers who read your report may need to make critical decisions. Your recommendations should empower them to make informed choices that enhance the organization's cybersecurity posture.

Consider including a "Risk Assessment" section, similar to a book's assessment of the risks and consequences characters face. In cybersecurity reports, a risk assessment provides a quantitative or qualitative evaluation of the potential risks associated with the findings. It helps stakeholders understand the magnitude of the security risks and aids in decision-making.

In the "Conclusion" section, you bring your report to a close, summarizing the key takeaways and emphasizing the importance of the findings and recommendations. Just as a book's conclusion ties up loose ends and leaves a lasting impression, your report's conclusion should leave stakeholders with a clear understanding of the security situation and the steps needed to address it.

As you progress through your report, maintain a reader-centric approach. Think about what your audience needs to know and how the information can be presented most effectively. Use headings, subheadings, and clear formatting to make the report easily scannable and digestible.

Consider providing an "Appendix" or "Glossary" section, similar to a book's reference section. This is where you can include additional technical details, documentation, or definitions that may be relevant to some readers but not essential for the main narrative. An appendix allows you to provide supplementary information without cluttering the main report.

Lastly, the "Distribution" phase is like publishing your story for the world to read. Determine who needs to receive the report and in what format. Some stakeholders may prefer printed copies, while others may prefer digital formats. Ensure that the report reaches the right hands promptly.

Remember that effective report generation is not just about conveying information but also about influencing decision-making and actions. Just as a well-told story can inspire and resonate with readers, a well-crafted cybersecurity report can drive positive changes in an organization's security practices.

In summary, creating effective reports in cybersecurity is an art of storytelling. By understanding your audience, structuring your report logically, providing clear findings and recommendations, and maintaining a reader-centric approach, you can convey the cybersecurity story effectively. Just as a compelling story captivates its audience, an effective cybersecurity report informs and empowers stakeholders to take action in improving security.

Navigating the complex world of compliance in the realm of cybersecurity is akin to following a well-structured guidebook—one that ensures your organization adheres to the regulations, standards, and best practices governing information security.

Imagine this guidebook as a comprehensive manual, carefully outlining the steps your organization must take to achieve and maintain compliance. To start your journey, it's crucial to understand the landscape of compliance and the significance it holds.

First and foremost, you need to identify the specific compliance requirements that apply to your organization. Think of this step as recognizing the map that guides you on your journey. Regulations such as GDPR, HIPAA, PCI DSS, or ISO 27001 are like distinct routes, each with its own set of requirements and objectives. Understanding which regulations are applicable to your industry and geography is the initial key to compliance.

Once you've identified the relevant regulations, it's time to assess your current compliance posture. Think of this as evaluating your starting point on the map. This assessment involves a thorough examination of your organization's existing security controls, policies, and practices to determine where you stand concerning compliance requirements. You may need to conduct security audits, risk assessments, or gap analyses to gain a clear picture of your current state.

With your starting point established, you can begin the journey toward compliance. Think of this as the route you'll take to reach your destination. To navigate this route effectively, you'll need a well-structured plan—a compliance roadmap, if you will. This plan outlines the specific actions, milestones, and timelines required to achieve and maintain compliance.

Documentation plays a pivotal role in this journey, much like keeping a detailed journal during a trip. It helps you record your progress, track your actions, and provide evidence of compliance efforts. Your documentation should encompass a wide range of aspects, including policies, procedures, risk assessments, incident response plans, and security controls.

Let's explore some key elements of documentation for compliance in more detail:

Policies and Procedures: Think of these as the road signs and traffic rules on your compliance journey. Policies define your organization's stance on security matters, while procedures detail the steps to follow in various scenarios. Properly documented policies and procedures ensure that everyone in your organization understands their responsibilities and how to meet compliance requirements.

Risk Assessments: These are like weather forecasts on your journey—predicting potential challenges and hazards. Conducting regular risk assessments helps you identify vulnerabilities, threats, and risks to your organization's information assets. Documenting these assessments provides evidence of your proactive approach to risk management.

Security Controls: Consider these as the tools and equipment you need for your journey. Documenting the security controls you have in place, such as firewalls, encryption protocols, and access controls, demonstrates your commitment to safeguarding sensitive data and complying with security standards.

Incident Response Plans: Just as you'd have a plan for handling unexpected detours or emergencies during a trip, an incident response plan outlines how your organization will respond to security incidents. Documenting these plans ensures that your team knows how to react when faced with security breaches, helping to minimize their impact.

Training and Awareness Programs: Think of these as educational resources that equip your team with the knowledge and skills needed for a successful journey. Documenting your training programs and employee awareness initiatives demonstrates your commitment to maintaining a security-aware workforce.

Compliance Reports and Audits: These are like checkpoints along your route, where you assess your progress.

Documenting compliance reports and audit results provides a record of your ongoing efforts to meet regulatory requirements. It also helps you identify areas for improvement and corrective actions.

Data Retention Policies: Consider these as guidelines for what to pack and what to leave behind on your journey. Documenting data retention policies helps ensure that your organization retains and disposes of data in compliance with legal and regulatory requirements.

Change Management Procedures: These are like guidelines for adapting to unexpected roadblocks or detours. Documenting change management procedures ensures that modifications to your IT environment are carried out in a controlled and compliant manner.

Vendor Management and Third-Party Assessments: Just as you'd need to vet and collaborate with service providers during your journey, documenting vendor management processes and third-party assessments ensures that your partners meet your security and compliance standards.

Evidence of Compliance: Think of this as your travel diary, containing all the documentation and records that serve as proof of your compliance efforts. This includes records of security assessments, training completion, incident response actions, and any other activities related to compliance.

Documentation isn't just about creating files and records; it's about maintaining a living and evolving repository of information that supports your compliance journey. It provides transparency, accountability, and traceability, allowing you to demonstrate your commitment to meeting regulatory requirements.

Moreover, documentation aids in communication with auditors, regulators, and stakeholders. It's like having a clear and detailed map to show others the path you've taken and the milestones you've achieved in your compliance journey.

This transparency builds trust and credibility, making it easier to navigate the compliance landscape.

Documentation also helps your organization adapt to changes in compliance requirements. Regulations and standards can evolve over time, much like the terrain on a long journey. By maintaining well-documented processes and controls, you can more effectively align your security practices with the latest compliance requirements.

To ensure effective documentation for compliance, consider implementing a robust document management system. This system should provide version control, access controls, and retention policies to keep your documentation organized, secure, and up to date.

In summary, documentation for compliance is the roadmap, journal, and communication tool that guides your organization on the journey to meeting regulatory requirements. Just as a well-kept travel journal captures the memories and experiences of a trip, effective documentation captures your compliance efforts and ensures that you reach your destination successfully.

Chapter 8: Basic Penetration Testing Concepts

Imagine yourself as a digital detective, tasked with unraveling the mysteries of computer systems, networks, and applications—a modern-day Sherlock Holmes in the realm of cybersecurity. This exciting adventure is known as penetration testing, a practice that simulates real-world attacks to uncover vulnerabilities and weaknesses in an organization's security defenses.

In this chapter, we embark on a journey into the world of penetration testing, a field that combines technical expertise, creativity, and an ethical mindset to protect digital assets and information. Picture it as an engaging detective story where you play the role of the investigator, seeking hidden clues that could compromise security.

But before we dive into the intricacies of penetration testing, let's set the stage by understanding its essence and significance in the ever-evolving landscape of cybersecurity.

At its core, penetration testing is akin to stress-testing the locks and alarms of a fortified castle. Instead of wielding swords and shields, penetration testers harness their knowledge of cybersecurity, hacking techniques, and the digital terrain to challenge an organization's defenses. They do this with the explicit permission of the organization, making it a lawful and ethical endeavor.

Why is penetration testing essential, you might wonder? Well, think of it as a proactive security measure—a preventative measure rather than a reactive one. In a world where cyber threats are continually evolving, organizations can't rely solely on firewalls and antivirus software to protect their digital assets. Penetration testing offers a proactive approach to identifying and addressing vulnerabilities before malicious actors can exploit them.

Just as a castle's guards must anticipate the strategies of potential intruders, organizations must be vigilant in their approach to cybersecurity. Penetration testing is a valuable tool for assessing an organization's security posture. It mimics the tactics and techniques of real attackers, allowing organizations to uncover weaknesses that might otherwise remain hidden.

Penetration testing isn't about hacking for malicious purposes—it's a practice conducted by ethical hackers, often referred to as "white hat" hackers. These individuals use their skills to strengthen security rather than exploit it. They act as allies, not adversaries, in the quest to protect digital assets.

Now, let's explore the key components and methodologies that make up the fascinating world of penetration testing.

At the heart of penetration testing is the concept of "authorized access." Think of it as the key to the castle gates—an agreement between the organization and the penetration tester, granting permission to test the organization's security defenses. This authorization distinguishes penetration testing from malicious hacking and ensures that the tester operates within legal and ethical boundaries.

The scope of penetration testing can be likened to a treasure map—it defines the boundaries of the testing engagement. It outlines which systems, networks, and applications are within the scope of the test and specifies any limitations or constraints. A well-defined scope helps focus the testing efforts on areas of greatest concern.

Now, let's talk about the various methodologies that penetration testers employ to uncover vulnerabilities. One of the most widely used methodologies is the "Open Web

Application Security Project (OWASP) Top Ten." This framework identifies the ten most critical web application security risks, providing a structured approach for testing web applications. It's like a checklist for a detective, ensuring that no critical vulnerabilities are overlooked.

Another popular methodology is the "Penetration Testing Execution Standard (PTES)," which offers a comprehensive and standardized approach to penetration testing. It breaks down the testing process into seven phases, from pre-engagement interactions to reporting. PTES is like a roadmap that guides penetration testers through the entire testing process.

Additionally, the "Common Vulnerability Scoring System (CVSS)" is used to assess the severity of vulnerabilities discovered during penetration testing. CVSS assigns scores based on factors like impact, exploitability, and ease of remediation. It helps organizations prioritize the vulnerabilities that require immediate attention, much like a detective categorizes clues by importance.

Penetration testers use a wide array of tools and techniques to simulate attacks. These tools range from network scanners and vulnerability scanners to password cracking tools and exploit frameworks. Just as a detective uses specialized equipment to gather evidence, penetration testers leverage these tools to uncover vulnerabilities and weaknesses.

Communication is a crucial aspect of penetration testing, akin to the detective's ability to gather and share information. Penetration testers maintain open lines of communication with the organization throughout the engagement. They provide regular updates on their progress, share findings, and collaborate with the organization's security team.

Now, you might be wondering about the types of penetration testing engagements. Well, there are several, each serving a unique purpose. "Black box testing" is like solving a mystery with no prior knowledge—the tester has no information about the target environment. "White box testing," on the other hand, is akin to having all the information—a tester has full knowledge of the target system. "Gray box testing" falls in between, with partial information about the target.

"External testing" focuses on assessing the security of external-facing systems, such as websites and remote access portals. It's like investigating the castle's exterior defenses. "Internal testing" delves into the security of systems within the organization's network, much like inspecting the inner workings of the castle. "Social engineering testing" involves manipulating human behavior through tactics like phishing to test the organization's susceptibility to such attacks.

As the field of cybersecurity continues to evolve, penetration testing plays a critical role in safeguarding digital assets and information. It's not merely a technical exercise but a strategic approach to proactively identify and address security vulnerabilities. Ethical hackers who conduct penetration testing serve as guardians of digital fortresses, working diligently to strengthen defenses and protect against ever-present threats.

In the chapters ahead, we'll delve deeper into the various phases of penetration testing, the tools and techniques used by ethical hackers, and real-world examples of successful testing engagements. Our journey through the world of penetration testing will equip you with the knowledge and insights needed to understand this dynamic field and its crucial role in modern cybersecurity. So, fasten your seatbelt, dear reader, as we embark on this exciting adventure together.

Welcome to the world of penetration testing methodologies, where ethical hackers adopt a structured and systematic approach to uncover vulnerabilities and weaknesses in information systems. Think of these methodologies as roadmaps that guide penetration testers through the complex terrain of security assessments, ensuring a comprehensive and effective evaluation of an organization's defenses.

To start our journey, let's explore the core principles that underpin penetration testing methodologies. At its heart, penetration testing is about replicating the actions of malicious attackers in a controlled and ethical manner. It's like a game of chess, where the tester strategically plans and executes moves to expose vulnerabilities and assess an organization's security posture.

One fundamental principle is "authorized access," akin to a chess match that only begins when both players agree to the rules. Penetration testers must obtain explicit permission from the organization to conduct their assessments. This ensures that the testing is conducted within legal and ethical boundaries.

The "scope" of a penetration test is like defining the boundaries of the chessboard. It specifies which systems, networks, and applications are within the scope of the assessment and outlines any limitations or constraints. A well-defined scope ensures that the testing efforts are focused on areas of concern and relevance.

Now, let's delve into some of the prominent penetration testing methodologies that guide ethical hackers in their assessments.

One of the most recognized methodologies is the "Open Web Application Security Project (OWASP) Testing Guide." Think of this as a comprehensive guidebook for testing web applications. It provides a structured approach to identifying and mitigating vulnerabilities specific to web applications, such as injection flaws, cross-site scripting (XSS), and broken authentication.

Another widely adopted methodology is the "Penetration Testing Execution Standard (PTES)," which offers a holistic and standardized approach to penetration testing. PTES divides the testing process into seven distinct phases, from pre-engagement interactions to reporting. It's like a well-organized itinerary that ensures that no critical step is overlooked.

Furthermore, the "Common Vulnerability Scoring System (CVSS)" plays a crucial role in assessing the severity of vulnerabilities discovered during penetration testing. CVSS assigns scores based on factors like impact, exploitability, and ease of remediation. It's like a scoring system that helps prioritize vulnerabilities, ensuring that the most critical ones are addressed first.

The "Information Systems Security Assessment Framework (ISSAF)" is another valuable resource for penetration testers. It provides a structured methodology for assessing the security of information systems. Think of it as a toolkit that includes various techniques and processes for conducting comprehensive assessments.

Now, let's explore the phases that commonly make up penetration testing methodologies.

The first phase, "Pre-engagement Interactions," is like sending a friendly letter to your chess opponent before the match. It involves establishing clear communication with the organization, defining the scope, and obtaining the necessary permissions and agreements.

Next comes "Intelligence Gathering," where the tester collects information about the target, much like studying your opponent's previous chess games. This phase involves reconnaissance, data gathering, and information analysis to better understand the organization's infrastructure and potential vulnerabilities.

The "Threat Modeling" phase is akin to strategizing your chess moves based on your opponent's strengths and weaknesses. In penetration testing, this phase involves identifying potential threats and attack vectors that could be leveraged against the target.

Now, it's time for "Vulnerability Analysis," which is like analyzing your opponent's previous games to spot their weaknesses. Penetration testers assess the target for known vulnerabilities, using tools and techniques to identify potential security flaws.

Once vulnerabilities are identified, it's time for "Exploitation," which is like executing a well-planned chess move to capture your opponent's pieces. In this phase, testers attempt to exploit the identified vulnerabilities to gain unauthorized access or control over the target.

The "Post-Exploitation" phase is reminiscent of consolidating your advantage after a successful chess move. Here, penetration testers aim to maintain access to the target, escalate privileges, and gather additional information for further exploitation or reporting.

Finally, we arrive at the "Reporting" phase, which is like summarizing the outcomes of a chess match. In this phase, testers document their findings, including vulnerabilities, exploitation results, and recommendations for remediation. A well-documented report is a valuable resource for the organization to improve its security posture.

Throughout these phases, penetration testers leverage a wide array of tools and techniques. Think of these tools as your chess pieces, each serving a specific purpose in the game. Network scanners, vulnerability scanners, password cracking tools, and exploit frameworks are like the knights, bishops, rooks, and pawns in your cybersecurity chess match.

Effective communication is also a cornerstone of penetration testing methodologies. Just as chess players must communicate moves clearly, testers maintain open lines of communication with the organization. They provide regular updates on progress, share findings, and collaborate with the organization's security team.

Moreover, penetration testers often encounter different types of penetration testing engagements. "Black box testing" is like approaching a chess match with no prior knowledge of your opponent's strategies—it's a blind assessment. "White box testing," on the other hand, is akin to having access to your opponent's playbook—you have full knowledge of the target's systems. "Gray box testing" falls in between, with partial information about the target.

"External testing" focuses on assessing the security of external-facing systems, such as websites and remote access portals. It's like examining the defenses on the outer walls of a castle. "Internal testing" delves into the security of systems within the organization's network, much like exploring the inner chambers of the castle. "Social engineering testing" involves manipulating human behavior through tactics like phishing to assess an organization's susceptibility to such attacks.

In summary, penetration testing methodologies serve as invaluable guides for ethical hackers, helping them navigate the complex landscape of security assessments. These methodologies provide structure, principles, and best practices for conducting effective penetration tests. Just as chess players follow a set of rules and strategies, penetration testers use these methodologies to identify vulnerabilities, assess security postures, and contribute to the ongoing improvement of information security. In the chapters ahead, we'll explore each phase and aspect of penetration testing in greater detail, equipping you with the knowledge and skills needed to understand this dynamic field and its crucial role in cybersecurity. So, get ready to dive deeper into the fascinating world of penetration testing!

Chapter 9: Securing Your Scanning Activities

In the realm of cybersecurity, securing scanning tools and processes is like safeguarding your trusted toolkit to ensure it doesn't fall into the wrong hands. These tools and processes are essential for vulnerability scanning and penetration testing, but they can also pose risks if not properly managed.

Let's begin our exploration by understanding the importance of securing scanning tools and processes. Think of it as locking the doors and windows of your cybersecurity fortress. In a world where malicious actors are constantly seeking vulnerabilities to exploit, it's essential to ensure that the tools and processes used for security assessments don't become weapons in the wrong hands.

One key principle in securing scanning tools and processes is "access control." Consider it as setting up security checkpoints in your fortress. Access control involves limiting who can use scanning tools and access sensitive information related to security assessments. Only authorized individuals with a legitimate need should have access to these resources.

Now, let's delve into some practical steps and best practices for securing scanning tools and processes:

Authentication and Authorization: Think of this as issuing access badges to your trusted team members. Implement strong authentication mechanisms, such as two-factor authentication (2FA), to ensure that only authorized users can access scanning tools and initiate security assessments. Additionally, use role-based access control (RBAC) to assign specific permissions based on job roles and responsibilities.

Inventory Management: Consider it like keeping track of all the tools in your toolkit. Maintain an inventory of scanning tools and their versions to ensure that they are up to date and properly licensed. This prevents the use of outdated or unauthorized tools that may have security vulnerabilities.

Secure Storage: Just as you'd secure your valuable assets in a vault, protect scanning tools and related data in a secure storage environment. Use encryption to safeguard sensitive information, such as scan results and configuration files. Store tools and data in access-controlled repositories.

Regular Updates and Patch Management: Think of this as maintaining and sharpening your tools. Stay vigilant about updates and patches for scanning tools to address known vulnerabilities. Ensure that the tools you use are from reputable sources and have been verified for authenticity.

Change Management: Similar to tracking changes in your toolkit, implement a change management process for scanning tools and processes. Document any modifications, updates, or additions to your toolkit to maintain transparency and control.

Logging and Monitoring: Imagine having a surveillance system in your fortress. Implement robust logging and monitoring for scanning activities. This allows you to track who is using the tools, when they are used, and for what purpose. Set up alerts for suspicious or unauthorized activities.

Secure Communication: Just as you'd secure your castle's walls, protect communication between scanning tools and the target systems. Use secure protocols like HTTPS and SSH to ensure that data exchanged during assessments is encrypted and cannot be intercepted by malicious actors.

Training and Awareness: Consider this as educating your team on how to use your tools safely. Provide training and awareness programs for your security team to ensure they understand the proper use of scanning tools and follow security best practices.

Secure Disposal: When retiring old tools, think of it as disposing of worn-out equipment safely. Properly decommission scanning tools and securely delete any sensitive data associated with them. Ensure that no residual data remains on retired systems.

Legal and Ethical Considerations: Understand the legal and ethical aspects of using scanning tools. Ensure that your security team operates within the boundaries of relevant laws and regulations. Obtain explicit permission before conducting security assessments, especially when testing external systems.

Incident Response Plan: Just as you'd have a plan for handling emergencies in your fortress, establish an incident response plan for security assessments. Define procedures for handling unexpected issues, such as accidental denial-of-service situations or unexpected impacts on target systems.

Documentation and Reporting: Think of this as maintaining records of your tools and how they are used. Keep detailed documentation of scanning activities, including scan configurations, results, and any actions taken. This documentation serves as a valuable resource for audits and reporting.

Regular Audits and Reviews: Conduct regular audits and reviews of your scanning tools and processes. Evaluate whether they align with security policies and best practices. Identify and address any weaknesses or vulnerabilities in your security assessment infrastructure.

Vendor and Third-Party Assessments: When acquiring new scanning tools or services, vet vendors and third-party providers for security and trustworthiness. Consider their security practices, data handling policies, and reputation in the cybersecurity community.

Secure Development Practices: If your organization develops custom scanning tools, follow secure coding practices to minimize vulnerabilities. Implement code reviews and security testing to ensure that the tools are robust and resistant to exploitation.

In summary, securing scanning tools and processes is a critical aspect of maintaining a strong cybersecurity posture. Just as you'd protect your toolkit from falling into the wrong hands, securing these tools and processes ensures that they serve their intended purpose of identifying vulnerabilities and strengthening security defenses. By following best practices, staying vigilant, and fostering a security-conscious culture, organizations can effectively manage and secure their scanning resources in today's dynamic threat landscape.

In the ever-expanding digital realm, user authentication and access control are like the gatekeepers of a well-guarded fortress, ensuring that only authorized individuals can enter and interact with sensitive information and resources. Picture this as a digital bouncer at the entrance, verifying the identity of those seeking access.

Let's embark on a journey to explore the essential concepts, mechanisms, and best practices of user authentication and access control in the world of cybersecurity.

At its core, user authentication is the process of verifying the identity of a user or entity attempting to access a system, application, or network. Think of it as presenting your identification card at the entrance of a secure facility. Authentication serves as the first line of defense against unauthorized access, ensuring that only legitimate users gain entry.

Authentication typically relies on something the user knows, something the user has, or something the user is. These are often referred to as the "factors" of authentication.

"Something you know" involves knowledge-based factors, such as passwords, PINs, or answers to security questions. It's like a secret passphrase that only you should know.

"Something you have" relates to possession-based factors, such as smart cards, hardware tokens, or mobile authentication apps. These are physical items that the user possesses, akin to a key that unlocks the digital door.

"Something you are" encompasses biometric factors, including fingerprint scans, facial recognition, or retina scans. These factors rely on unique physical or behavioral characteristics that are difficult to replicate, similar to a fingerprint that's exclusive to you.

Multi-factor authentication (MFA) combines two or more of these authentication factors to enhance security. Think of it as requiring both a key and a passphrase to unlock a secure vault. MFA adds an extra layer of protection by making it more challenging for attackers to impersonate legitimate users.

Now, let's delve into access control, which determines what actions an authenticated user is allowed to perform within a system or application. Access control is like the security personnel inside the fortress, ensuring that individuals are guided to the areas they are authorized to enter.

Access control mechanisms can be classified into three main types:

Discretionary Access Control (DAC): In this model, users have control over the access permissions of the resources they own. It's like giving residents of a shared community the authority to decide who can enter their individual homes. DAC is often used in file systems, where file owners can set permissions for their files and directories.

Mandatory Access Control (MAC): MAC is like a strict security clearance system. It enforces a hierarchical access model, where access permissions are determined by security labels or levels. Users have limited control over these labels, and access is granted based on security policies and clearances. Government and military environments commonly use MAC to protect classified information.

Role-Based Access Control (RBAC): RBAC is akin to assigning roles and responsibilities to individuals within an organization. Users are grouped into roles, and access permissions are associated with these roles. It simplifies access management by granting permissions based on job functions. For example, a system administrator role might have full access to system settings, while a regular user role has limited access.

Additionally, access control can be applied at various levels, including the operating system, network devices, applications, and databases. It's like having multiple layers of security within the fortress, each protecting different areas and resources.

Access control policies define who can access what and under what conditions. These policies are like the rules and regulations of the fortress, specifying who is allowed into specific areas and what actions they can perform. Policies are typically implemented through access control lists (ACLs), permissions, and rules.

Effective user authentication and access control involve several best practices and considerations:

Strong Password Policies: Encourage users to create strong, unique passwords and enforce password complexity rules. Regularly prompt users to change their passwords and avoid using easily guessable information.

Account Lockout Mechanisms: Implement account lockout mechanisms to protect against brute force attacks. After a certain number of failed login attempts, temporarily lock or suspend user accounts.

Secure Storage of Credentials: Safeguard user credentials by hashing and salting passwords before storing them. This ensures that even if the authentication database is compromised, attackers cannot easily decipher passwords.

Regular Access Reviews: Periodically review and audit user access rights. Ensure that users have only the permissions they need to perform their job functions, and revoke unnecessary access.

Least Privilege Principle: Follow the principle of least privilege (PoLP) by granting users the minimum level of access required to perform their tasks. Avoid assigning excessive permissions, which can lead to security vulnerabilities.

Monitoring and Logging: Implement robust monitoring and logging mechanisms to track user activities and access attempts. Analyze logs to detect suspicious behavior and potential security incidents.

Education and Awareness: Educate users about security best practices, including the importance of strong passwords, MFA, and recognizing phishing attempts. Foster a security-conscious culture within the organization.

Secure Remote Access: When allowing remote access, use secure protocols such as VPNs and secure remote desktop solutions. Implement MFA for remote authentication to enhance security.

Patch and Update Systems: Keep authentication and access control systems up to date with the latest security patches and updates to mitigate known vulnerabilities.

Incident Response Plan: Develop an incident response plan to address security incidents related to user authentication and access control. Define procedures for handling unauthorized access attempts and data breaches.

Third-Party and Vendor Access: When working with third-party vendors or service providers, establish secure methods for granting access. Ensure that these entities adhere to your access control and authentication policies.

In summary, user authentication and access control are fundamental components of cybersecurity, serving as the gatekeepers to digital resources and information.

Chapter 10: Building a Career in Cybersecurity

Embarking on a journey into the world of cybersecurity career paths is like setting out on an exciting adventure, full of opportunities, challenges, and the promise of safeguarding the digital realm. Whether you're a seasoned professional or just starting your career, the field of cybersecurity offers a wide range of roles, each with its unique focus and responsibilities.

Let's begin our exploration by understanding the diverse landscape of cybersecurity career paths and the essential skills and knowledge areas that can help you thrive in this dynamic field.

At the heart of cybersecurity careers lies the mission to protect digital assets, data, and information from a multitude of threats. Think of it as being the guardian of a digital kingdom, where your expertise and vigilance are the keys to fortifying the kingdom's defenses.

The cybersecurity field is often categorized into several key areas, each addressing specific aspects of digital security. Let's take a closer look at some of these career paths:

Information Security Analyst: Information security analysts are the detectives of the cybersecurity world. They investigate security breaches, analyze vulnerabilities, and implement security measures to protect an organization's data and systems. Think of them as digital crime scene investigators.

Network Security Engineer: Network security engineers are like the architects and builders of secure networks. They design and implement network security measures, including firewalls, intrusion detection systems, and virtual private networks (VPNs), to safeguard data in transit.

Penetration Tester (Ethical Hacker): Penetration testers are the ethical hackers who simulate cyberattacks to identify vulnerabilities and weaknesses in an organization's security defenses. They use their skills to find and fix security flaws before malicious hackers can exploit them.

Security Consultant: Security consultants provide expert advice and guidance to organizations on cybersecurity strategies and best practices. They assess security risks, develop security policies, and help organizations strengthen their security posture.

Incident Responder: Incident responders are like the first responders to a digital emergency. They investigate and manage security incidents, such as data breaches and malware infections, to minimize the impact and recover from the incident.

Security Architect: Security architects are the master builders of secure systems and applications. They design and implement security solutions, considering factors like data encryption, access control, and threat modeling to create robust security frameworks.

Security Administrator: Security administrators are responsible for managing and maintaining security systems, such as firewalls, antivirus software, and access control systems. They ensure that these tools are configured correctly and operate smoothly.

Cybersecurity Analyst: Cybersecurity analysts monitor and analyze security data to detect and respond to security threats. They use security information and event management (SIEM) tools to identify suspicious activities and take appropriate actions.

Security Compliance Analyst: Compliance analysts ensure that organizations adhere to industry-specific cybersecurity regulations and standards. They conduct audits, assess compliance, and help organizations meet legal and regulatory requirements.

Cryptographer: Cryptographers are like the mathematicians and codebreakers of the digital world. They design and analyze cryptographic algorithms to secure data and communications.

Security Awareness Trainer: Security awareness trainers educate employees and users about cybersecurity best practices. They develop training programs and materials to raise awareness and reduce the risk of human-related security breaches, such as phishing.

Now, you might wonder, what does it take to embark on a successful cybersecurity career journey? What skills and knowledge areas are essential to thrive in this field?

Technical Proficiency: Cybersecurity is a technical field, so having a strong foundation in information technology is crucial. Understanding networking, operating systems, and programming languages can be highly beneficial.

Cybersecurity Certifications: Obtaining relevant certifications can boost your credentials and demonstrate your expertise to potential employers. Certifications like Certified Information Systems Security Professional (CISSP), Certified Ethical Hacker (CEH), and Certified Information Security Manager (CISM) are highly regarded in the industry.

Continuous Learning: Cybersecurity is an ever-evolving field, with new threats and technologies emerging regularly. It's essential to stay up-to-date with the latest developments and continuously enhance your knowledge and skills.

Problem-Solving Skills: Cybersecurity professionals often face complex challenges that require creative problem-solving. Being able to analyze security incidents, assess vulnerabilities, and devise effective solutions is critical.

Communication Skills: Effective communication is key in cybersecurity roles, as you'll often need to explain security concepts to non-technical stakeholders and collaborate with colleagues in various departments.

Ethical Mindset: Ethical behavior and a commitment to upholding ethical standards are essential in cybersecurity, particularly for roles like penetration testers and security consultants.

Attention to Detail: Cyber threats can hide in the smallest details. Paying close attention to logs, alerts, and system configurations is essential for identifying and mitigating security risks.

Teamwork and Collaboration: Many cybersecurity challenges require teamwork and collaboration with colleagues in IT, legal, and other departments. Being able to work effectively in a team is a valuable skill.

Security Awareness: Understanding the psychology and tactics of cybercriminals is crucial for roles focused on user awareness and incident response.

In addition to these skills and knowledge areas, it's important to choose a cybersecurity career path that aligns with your interests and strengths. Whether you're passionate about ethical hacking, network security, or security policy and compliance, there's a cybersecurity role that can provide a fulfilling and rewarding career.

Skill development and certification in the realm of cybersecurity are like building blocks in constructing a strong and reputable career. In this chapter, we'll explore the importance of honing your skills, the value of certifications, and how these elements can help you thrive in the ever-evolving world of cybersecurity.

Imagine skill development as the process of sharpening your tools for the journey ahead. In cybersecurity, your skills are your tools, and they need to be constantly honed and upgraded to meet the challenges of an ever-changing threat landscape.

Let's start by examining why skill development is essential in the cybersecurity field. Picture it as the foundation upon which your career is built. Cyber threats are dynamic and evolving, and as a cybersecurity professional, you need to stay ahead of the curve. This means continuously enhancing your skills to understand new attack vectors, vulnerabilities, and defense mechanisms.

But where do you begin with skill development? Think of it as embarking on a learning adventure with numerous paths to explore. Here are some key areas to focus on:

Technical Proficiency: The cornerstone of cybersecurity is technical knowledge. You should have a strong understanding of networking, operating systems, and programming languages. Think of it as the language you need to speak fluently to communicate with digital systems and security tools.

Security Fundamentals: Building a solid foundation in security fundamentals is essential. This includes understanding concepts like encryption, authentication, access control, and security protocols. These fundamentals are like the building blocks of your cybersecurity knowledge.

Hands-on Experience: Practical experience is invaluable. Think of it as the laboratory where you apply your knowledge. Setting up virtual labs, conducting security experiments, and participating in Capture The Flag (CTF) challenges can provide valuable hands-on experience.

Cybersecurity Tools: Familiarize yourself with the tools and technologies commonly used in cybersecurity. These tools are like your instruments for diagnosing and addressing security issues. Learn how to use security scanners, intrusion detection systems, and forensic analysis tools effectively.

Programming and Scripting: Developing coding skills is a valuable asset in cybersecurity. It allows you to automate tasks, analyze security data, and create custom security tools. Think of it as having the ability to craft your own solutions when needed.

Incident Response: Understanding how to respond to security incidents is crucial. Think of it as having a well-prepared emergency kit for unexpected situations. Familiarize yourself with incident response procedures, forensic analysis techniques, and recovery processes.

Security Policies and Compliance: Knowledge of security policies and regulatory compliance is essential, especially if you're interested in roles related to security governance and risk management. Think of it as understanding the rules and regulations governing your cybersecurity kingdom.

Ethical Hacking: If you're inclined towards offensive security, consider exploring ethical hacking. Think of it as donning the hat of a digital detective tasked with uncovering vulnerabilities and testing security defenses.

Security Awareness: Understanding the psychology of cybercriminals and human behavior is vital for roles focused on user awareness and social engineering defense. Think of it as learning to read the signs of potential threats.

Now that we've laid the groundwork for skill development, let's delve into the world of certifications. Certifications are like badges of honor that validate your expertise and proficiency in specific areas of cybersecurity. Think of them as your credentials to showcase your knowledge and skills to potential employers.

Here are some reasons why certifications are valuable in the cybersecurity field:

Validation of Expertise: Certifications serve as tangible evidence of your knowledge and skills. They demonstrate to employers and peers that you have met specific standards and have the expertise required for the job.

Career Advancement: Certifications can open doors to career advancement. Think of them as keys that unlock higher-paying roles and more significant responsibilities. Many organizations require or prefer candidates with relevant certifications for senior positions.

Industry Recognition: Certain certifications are widely recognized and respected in the cybersecurity industry. They are like badges of trust that indicate your credibility and commitment to the field.

Professional Development: Preparing for certifications is a learning journey in itself. It encourages continuous learning and keeps you up-to-date with the latest industry trends and best practices.

Competitive Edge: In a competitive job market, certifications can give you a competitive edge. Think of them as your unique selling points (USPs) that set you apart from other candidates.

Now, let's explore some popular cybersecurity certifications and their relevance in the field:

Certified Information Systems Security Professional (CISSP): CISSP is like the gold standard in cybersecurity certifications. It covers a broad range of security domains and is highly regarded for roles in security management and leadership.

Certified Ethical Hacker (CEH): CEH is like the badge of an ethical hacker. It's ideal for those interested in penetration testing and ethical hacking roles.

Certified Information Security Manager (CISM): CISM is like a compass for security governance and risk management. It's suitable for professionals aspiring to lead security initiatives and manage security programs.

CompTIA Security+: Security+ is like the foundation stone of cybersecurity certifications. It's an entry-level certification that provides a solid understanding of security principles and practices.

Certified Information Systems Auditor (CISA): CISA is like the certification for auditing and control. It's ideal for professionals involved in auditing, control, and assurance roles.

Certified Cloud Security Professional (CCSP): CCSP is like the certification for cloud security experts. It's relevant for those working with cloud technologies and services.

Certified Information Security Technician (CIST): CIST is like the junior sibling of CISSP, designed for entry-level professionals seeking to build a career in information security.

Certified Wireless Security Professional (CWSP): CWSP is like the badge for wireless security experts. It's valuable for professionals working with wireless networks and devices.

Certified in Risk and Information Systems Control (CRISC): CRISC is like the certification for risk management professionals. It's suitable for those focused on risk assessment and mitigation.

Certified Cloud Computing Professional (CCCP): CCCP is like the certification for cloud architects and professionals involved in cloud design and implementation.

When choosing certifications, consider your career goals, interests, and the specific skills you want to develop. Additionally, research the market demand for certain certifications in your region or the industries you aim to work in.

It's important to note that certifications are not a one-size-fits-all solution. They complement your existing skills and experience and should align with your career trajectory. Think of them as milestones on your learning journey, each adding value and recognition to your cybersecurity career.

In summary, skill development and certification are integral components of a successful cybersecurity career. By continuously honing your skills and obtaining relevant certifications, you can build a strong foundation, demonstrate your expertise, and open doors to exciting opportunities in the ever-evolving world of cybersecurity.

BOOK 2
INTERMEDIATE GRAY HAT TACTICS
PENETRATION TESTING DEMYSTIFIED

ROB BOTWRIGHT

Chapter 1: Advanced Penetration Testing Overview

The world of cybersecurity is a complex battleground, and advanced penetration testing plays a crucial role in fortifying the defenses of organizations against an ever-evolving array of threats. Think of it as a skilled scout who ventures into the unknown to identify vulnerabilities before malicious actors can exploit them.

Advanced penetration testing is the next level of ethical hacking, going beyond the basics to uncover intricate security weaknesses and assess an organization's resilience to sophisticated attacks. It's akin to exploring the hidden passages and secret doors within a fortress to ensure that no vulnerability goes unnoticed.

At its core, penetration testing is about simulating real-world cyberattacks to assess the security posture of an organization. Advanced penetration testing takes this concept to a higher plane, focusing on intricate methodologies, cutting-edge techniques, and a deeper understanding of the digital landscape.

Let's embark on a journey to unravel the role and significance of advanced penetration testing in modern cybersecurity.

Expert-Level Ethical Hacking Overview: Advanced penetration testing begins with an expert-level understanding of ethical hacking. Picture it as the foundation upon which all advanced techniques and strategies are built. Ethical hackers, often referred to as "white hat" hackers, are the digital detectives who wield their skills for the greater good, identifying vulnerabilities and strengthening defenses.

Planning and Scoping Penetration Tests: Advanced penetration testing doesn't happen haphazardly. It's a meticulously planned operation, akin to a military campaign.

Before the testing begins, careful planning and scoping are essential. Think of it as charting the course and objectives for a mission. The testing team defines the goals, identifies the target systems and networks, and outlines the rules of engagement.

Information Gathering and Enumeration: Once the scope is defined, advanced penetration testers engage in thorough information gathering. Think of this as collecting intelligence about the target, similar to reconnaissance in a military operation. They seek to understand the organization's infrastructure, network topology, application architecture, and potential vulnerabilities.

Vulnerability Assessment and Exploitation: This is where advanced penetration testing truly shines. Testers use their expertise to identify and exploit vulnerabilities in the target environment. Think of it as finding the weak points in a fortress and exploiting them to gain access. Advanced testers leverage not only known vulnerabilities but also zero-day exploits—security flaws that are not yet publicly known.

Exploiting Web Applications: With the proliferation of web-based applications, securing them has become paramount. Advanced penetration testers specialize in exploiting web application vulnerabilities. Think of it as navigating the labyrinth of web applications to find hidden weaknesses, such as SQL injection, cross-site scripting (XSS), and remote code execution vulnerabilities.

Wireless Network Penetration Testing: As wireless technology continues to advance, so do the risks associated with wireless networks. Advanced penetration testers assess the security of wireless networks, identifying vulnerabilities in Wi-Fi protocols and encryption mechanisms. Think of it as ensuring that the digital fortress extends its defenses to the airwaves.

Post-Exploitation Techniques: Advanced penetration testing goes beyond just gaining initial access. It involves post-exploitation activities, akin to establishing a foothold within the target. Testers aim to maintain persistence, escalate privileges, and move laterally through the network. Think of it as the digital equivalent of setting up a hidden base within an enemy's stronghold.

Evading Detection and Covering Tracks: In the world of advanced penetration testing, stealth is a prized skill. Testers employ techniques to evade detection by security monitoring systems and cover their tracks to maintain anonymity. Think of it as leaving no trace behind, just like a ghost in the digital realm.

Expanding the Attack Surface: As organizations expand their digital footprint, advanced penetration testers adapt by expanding the attack surface. They assess not only traditional networks but also cloud environments, IoT devices, and even physical security systems. Think of it as guarding against threats from every possible angle.

Penetration Testing Reporting and Remediation: Advanced penetration testing culminates in a comprehensive report. This report details the vulnerabilities discovered, the impact of potential exploits, and recommendations for remediation. Think of it as the battle report that provides insights into the state of the digital defenses and a roadmap for improvement.

Advanced penetration testing is not a one-time endeavor. It's an ongoing process that adapts to the evolving threat landscape. Organizations that invest in advanced penetration testing gain several key benefits:

Identifying Hidden Vulnerabilities: Advanced penetration testing uncovers vulnerabilities that may remain undetected by traditional security assessments, ensuring that no stone is left unturned.

Mitigating Zero-Day Exploits: By proactively identifying and addressing zero-day vulnerabilities, organizations reduce the risk of falling victim to unknown threats.

Testing Incident Response: Advanced penetration testing also assesses an organization's incident response capabilities. Think of it as a fire drill for cybersecurity incidents, helping organizations refine their response procedures.

Enhancing Security Awareness: The process of advanced penetration testing raises security awareness among employees and stakeholders. It's like a collective sharpening of the organization's cybersecurity senses.

In summary, advanced penetration testing is the vanguard of cybersecurity, a critical element in safeguarding digital assets from relentless threats. It combines expertise, planning, and cutting-edge techniques to ensure that organizations are well-prepared to defend against the most sophisticated adversaries. Think of it as the guardian who tirelessly patrols the digital realm, making it safer for all who dwell within.

Imagine a world where digital fortresses are constantly under siege by cunning adversaries, and the defenders of these fortresses are skilled warriors armed with advanced penetration testing knowledge. In this chapter, we'll delve into the fascinating realm of real-world case studies in advanced penetration testing, where we explore actual incidents, challenges, and triumphs in the ongoing battle for digital security.

These case studies serve as a window into the dynamic and ever-evolving field of cybersecurity, providing insights into the strategies and tactics used by advanced penetration testers to safeguard organizations against relentless cyber threats.

The Tale of the Insider Threat: In this case, a multinational corporation fell victim to an insider threat, one of the most challenging adversaries to detect. The organization's advanced penetration testing team was called upon to simulate the actions of a disgruntled employee with privileged access. Think of it as a digital mole that had infiltrated the ranks. The team meticulously recreated the insider's actions, identifying vulnerabilities in access controls, privilege escalation procedures, and data exfiltration prevention measures. The outcome was a comprehensive report that helped the organization strengthen its defenses against insider threats, emphasizing the importance of monitoring user activity and implementing robust access control mechanisms.

The Zero-Day Showdown: In a world where zero-day vulnerabilities are coveted by cybercriminals, an e-commerce giant faced a significant challenge. The organization's advanced penetration testing team embarked on a mission to identify and mitigate these elusive threats. Picture it as a high-stakes poker game where the testers played the role of both attacker and defender. They employed cutting-edge techniques to discover zero-day vulnerabilities in the organization's web applications, focusing on areas like input validation and server-side security. The result was a race against time to patch these vulnerabilities before they could be exploited by malicious actors. This case study highlights the importance of proactive security measures, including patch management and secure coding practices.

The Cloud Conundrum: As organizations migrate their operations to the cloud, new security challenges arise. A tech startup found itself in a precarious position, with its cloud infrastructure exposed to potential threats. The advanced penetration testing team took on the role of cloud security specialists, simulating attacks on the organization's cloud resources. Think of it as a journey into the digital cloudscape, where the testers identified misconfigurations, insecure API endpoints, and vulnerabilities in the shared responsibility model. The organization received a detailed report outlining best practices for securing cloud environments and ensuring that data in the cloud remains protected. This case study underscores the need for specialized expertise in cloud security and the shared responsibility between cloud service providers and their customers.

The IoT Intrigue: With the proliferation of Internet of Things (IoT) devices, a healthcare provider faced a unique challenge—securing a vast network of connected medical devices. The advanced penetration testing team assumed the role of IoT security experts, assessing the security of these life-critical devices. Think of it as exploring the digital frontier of healthcare. They uncovered vulnerabilities in device firmware, communication protocols, and inadequate authentication mechanisms. The organization received recommendations for improving device security and implementing network segmentation to isolate IoT devices from critical infrastructure. This case study sheds light on the importance of securing IoT ecosystems, especially in sectors where lives are at stake.

The Red Team Challenge: In a scenario reminiscent of a high-stakes espionage thriller, a financial institution engaged an advanced penetration testing team to conduct a red team exercise. The objective was to test the organization's incident response capabilities and defenses against sophisticated attacks. Think of it as a battle of wits between the defenders and the red team, where the testers mimicked the tactics of nation-state actors. They launched coordinated attacks involving social engineering, advanced malware, and lateral movement within the network. The organization's incident response team was put to the test, and their performance was assessed. This case study highlights the value of red team exercises in preparing organizations for real-world cyber threats and the importance of a robust incident response plan.

The Supply Chain Sabotage: A manufacturing conglomerate faced a critical challenge—a breach in its supply chain could have devastating consequences. The advanced penetration testing team took on the role of supply chain security specialists, assessing the organization's vendors and partners. Think of it as a journey through a complex ecosystem of suppliers and subcontractors. They identified vulnerabilities in vendor communication, weak authentication mechanisms, and potential points of compromise. The organization received recommendations for securing the supply chain, emphasizing the need for vendor risk assessment and stringent contractual agreements. This case study underscores the interconnectedness of cybersecurity and the importance of extending security measures beyond the organization's boundaries.

These real-world case studies illustrate the dynamic nature of advanced penetration testing and its pivotal role in securing organizations against a wide range of threats. They showcase the diverse skills and expertise required in this field, from insider threat detection to cloud security, IoT protection, red teaming, and supply chain security.

Advanced penetration testing is not merely a technical exercise; it's a strategic approach to safeguarding digital assets and preserving the trust of stakeholders. These case studies provide a glimpse into the challenges and victories of cybersecurity professionals who tirelessly defend the digital realm against an ever-evolving adversary.

Chapter 2: Planning and Scoping Penetration Tests

Imagine you're setting sail on an uncharted sea. You have a ship, a crew, and a destination in mind, but before you embark on this adventure, you need to define the boundaries of your journey and the goals you aim to achieve. This concept of setting boundaries and objectives is at the heart of defining scope and objectives in any project, including advanced penetration testing.

In the world of advanced penetration testing, defining scope and objectives is akin to charting your course and specifying your mission. It's about clarifying what you will and won't explore, what you aim to accomplish, and the rules of engagement for your digital expedition.

Scoping the Mission: Think of scope as the map that outlines the geographical limits of your exploration. In advanced penetration testing, scoping is the process of clearly defining the boundaries of what will be tested and assessed. It's about deciding which systems, networks, applications, and assets are within the purview of the testing and which are excluded. For example, in a web application penetration test, you might define the scope as specific web applications, URLs, and functionalities to be tested, excluding others.

Identifying Targets: Once the scope is set, it's time to identify the targets of the testing. Picture it as selecting the islands you want to explore on your sea voyage. In advanced penetration testing, targets can range from individual servers and network segments to specific web applications, IoT devices, and cloud resources. Identifying the targets ensures that the testing team knows precisely where to direct their efforts.

Establishing Objectives: Every journey has a purpose, and every advanced penetration test has objectives. Think of objectives as the treasures you aim to discover during your exploration. These objectives define what you want to achieve through the testing. Objectives can include identifying vulnerabilities, assessing the effectiveness of security controls, evaluating incident response procedures, or testing the organization's defenses against specific attack scenarios.

Defining Rules of Engagement: Just as you establish rules for your voyage, you need rules of engagement for your penetration test. These rules specify how the testing will be conducted, what techniques and tactics are allowed, and any constraints or limitations. Rules of engagement help ensure that the testing aligns with legal and ethical standards. For example, rules might dictate that testers should not disrupt critical services or access sensitive customer data during the test.

Setting Timeframes: Like any journey, a penetration test has a timeframe. Think of it as the duration of your adventure. Setting timeframes ensures that the testing team knows when to start, how long the testing will last, and when it should conclude. Timeframes are crucial for planning and coordination, allowing stakeholders to allocate resources and schedule activities accordingly.

Identifying Constraints: In some cases, constraints may impact the testing process. Constraints can be resource limitations, compliance requirements, or other factors that affect how the testing is conducted. For example, an organization may have specific compliance regulations that must be adhered to during the test, influencing the testing approach and reporting.

Communication and Collaboration: Effective communication and collaboration are essential during the scoping process. Think of it as assembling your crew and ensuring everyone understands their roles. The testing team, along with stakeholders, should collaborate to define scope and objectives accurately. Clear communication helps prevent misunderstandings and ensures that expectations are aligned.

Documentation: Documenting the scope and objectives is a critical step. Think of it as creating a navigational chart for your journey. Proper documentation serves as a reference point throughout the testing process and provides a record of the agreed-upon terms. It helps maintain transparency and accountability.

Why is defining scope and objectives so crucial in advanced penetration testing?

Focus and Precision: By clearly defining scope and objectives, you ensure that the testing effort is focused and precise. It prevents testers from wandering into uncharted territories and helps them concentrate their efforts on the most critical areas.

Alignment with Goals: Defining objectives ensures that the testing aligns with the goals and priorities of the organization. It ensures that the testing provides actionable insights and addresses specific security concerns.

Risk Management: Scope and objectives also play a vital role in risk management. They help organizations identify and prioritize areas of concern, allowing them to allocate resources effectively to mitigate the most significant risks.

Ethical and Legal Compliance: Clear rules of engagement and constraints ensure that the testing is conducted ethically and within the bounds of the law. It helps organizations avoid unintended disruptions or legal complications.

Efficiency: Well-defined scope and objectives streamline the testing process, making it more efficient. Testers can focus their efforts on high-priority areas, maximizing the impact of the testing.

Transparency and Accountability: Documentation of scope and objectives promotes transparency and accountability. It provides a record that stakeholders can refer to throughout the testing engagement, reducing the likelihood of disputes or misunderstandings.

In advanced penetration testing, the process of defining scope and objectives is not a mere formality but a critical foundation for the entire testing effort. It ensures that the testing team and the organization are on the same page, guiding them toward a successful and meaningful exploration of the digital landscape. Think of it as setting sail with a well-charted map, clear objectives, and a united crew, ready to face the challenges and discoveries that lie ahead.

In the world of advanced penetration testing, understanding the landscape of risks and threats is akin to being a detective who meticulously examines clues to solve a complex case. Before embarking on the journey of testing an organization's security, it's essential to conduct a comprehensive risk assessment and threat modeling to identify potential vulnerabilities, scenarios, and attack vectors.

Risk Assessment - Uncovering Vulnerabilities: Think of risk assessment as peeling back the layers of an onion. It involves a systematic examination of an organization's infrastructure, applications, and assets to identify vulnerabilities. These vulnerabilities could be software flaws, misconfigurations, or weaknesses in security controls. The goal is to create a catalog of potential entry points for attackers. Imagine it as creating a list of possible hiding spots for a mischievous intruder.

Prioritizing Risks - The Threat Hierarchy: Not all vulnerabilities are created equal. Some pose a higher risk to an organization's security than others. Imagine this as assigning different threat levels to potential hiding spots—the ones in the most vulnerable locations are of utmost concern. Risk prioritization involves evaluating the impact and likelihood of exploitation for each vulnerability. High-impact, high-likelihood vulnerabilities are the top priority, while low-impact, low-likelihood ones may be of lesser concern.

Understanding the Threat Landscape: Threat modeling is like developing a profile of potential intruders. It's about understanding the motives, capabilities, and methods of potential attackers. This includes identifying the types of adversaries an organization may face, whether they are script kiddies, hacktivists, cybercriminals, or nation-state actors. Think of it as creating a character sketch for the intruder in your detective story.

Attack Scenarios - The Plot Unfolds: Threat modeling involves developing attack scenarios based on the identified vulnerabilities and the capabilities of potential adversaries. Think of this as crafting the narrative for your cybersecurity story. Each scenario outlines how an attacker could exploit a specific vulnerability and what the potential consequences might be. These scenarios help testers simulate real-world attack scenarios during penetration testing.

Mitigation Strategies - Strengthening the Defenses: Just as a detective devises strategies to catch the intruder, threat modeling results in the development of mitigation strategies. These strategies are like setting traps and security measures to thwart potential attackers. They involve recommending countermeasures, security controls, and best practices to mitigate identified risks. It's akin to fortifying the vulnerable areas of a building to prevent break-ins.

Evaluating Impact - The Detective's Dilemma: Advanced penetration testers must assess the impact of potential attacks on an organization's operations, reputation, and compliance. Imagine it as weighing the consequences of a crime. Testers determine the severity of each attack scenario by considering factors such as data loss, service disruption, financial impact, and legal implications. This assessment helps organizations understand the real-world implications of identified vulnerabilities.

Testing Against Threat Models - The Simulation: Once threat models and attack scenarios are developed, advanced penetration testers simulate these scenarios during testing. It's like enacting a crime scene to understand how an intruder operates. Testers attempt to exploit vulnerabilities based on the threat models, and their findings provide valuable insights into an organization's security posture.

Feedback Loop - The Ongoing Detective Work: Risk assessment and threat modeling are not one-time activities but ongoing detective work. Just as a detective gathers new evidence, testers continuously update threat models based on evolving threats and vulnerabilities. This iterative process ensures that an organization's security measures remain aligned with the changing threat landscape.

Risk Communication - Sharing the Findings: Effective communication of risk assessment findings is crucial. It's like presenting evidence in a courtroom. Organizations need to understand the risks they face and the potential consequences of vulnerabilities. Testers provide clear and actionable reports that enable stakeholders to make informed decisions about security investments and improvements.

Regulatory Compliance - Playing by the Rules: In many industries, compliance with regulations and standards is mandatory. Risk assessment and threat modeling help organizations identify gaps in compliance. Think of this as ensuring that the detective's actions follow the law. Testers assess whether an organization's security measures align with industry-specific regulations and standards, helping them avoid legal and regulatory penalties.

In summary, risk assessment and threat modeling are the detective work that lays the groundwork for advanced penetration testing. They provide the insights and strategies needed to simulate real-world attacks, identify vulnerabilities, and strengthen an organization's security posture. It's a dynamic process that evolves with the ever-changing threat landscape, ensuring that organizations stay one step ahead of potential intruders in the ongoing cybersecurity story.

Chapter 3: Information Gathering and Enumeration

Imagine you're a digital detective, and your mission is to gather crucial information about a potential adversary. In the world of advanced penetration testing, information gathering is the first step in unraveling the mysteries of an organization's digital landscape. It's like peering through a magnifying glass to uncover hidden clues that could lead to a breakthrough in your investigation.

Open Source Intelligence (OSINT) - The Digital Detective's Toolkit: OSINT is your trusty toolkit, filled with online resources and techniques to collect publicly available information about your target. It involves scouring the internet for details such as domain names, email addresses, employee names, social media profiles, and even leaked data. It's akin to building a character profile for the potential adversary, gathering clues from various sources.

Whois and DNS Records - The Digital Trail: Think of domain Whois records as your digital breadcrumbs left behind by organizations. These records provide valuable insights into the ownership and registration of domains. DNS (Domain Name System) records, on the other hand, reveal the network infrastructure associated with a domain. It's like tracing the footprints of your adversary in the digital realm, discovering the pathways they use.

Enumeration and Scanning - Finding Hidden Assets: Enumeration and scanning techniques are your tools for discovering hidden assets and services. Imagine it as knocking on every door to see who answers. You probe the target's network to identify open ports, services running on those ports, and potential vulnerabilities. It's like finding secret entrances and backdoors in a fortress.

Subdomain Enumeration - Expanding the Map: Subdomains are like hidden chambers within a castle. They often represent overlooked entry points for attackers. Advanced penetration testers use subdomain enumeration tools and techniques to identify all subdomains associated with a domain. This reveals additional attack surfaces and potential vulnerabilities.

Search Engine Hacking - Mining for Nuggets: Search engines are treasure troves of information. Advanced testers employ search engine hacking techniques to extract sensitive data, such as login credentials, exposed databases, and configuration files. It's like sifting through a haystack to find the needle of critical information.

Exploiting Misconfigurations - The Weak Links: Misconfigurations are the weak links in an organization's security. Testers search for misconfigured services, cloud resources, and applications that may expose sensitive data or provide unauthorized access. It's like finding an unlocked door in an otherwise secure building.

Social Engineering - Manipulating the Human Element: Humans are often the weakest link in cybersecurity. Social engineering techniques involve manipulating individuals to divulge sensitive information or perform actions that benefit the attacker. It's like convincing the gatekeeper to grant you access to the fortress by using psychological tricks.

Credential Harvesting - Stealing the Keys: Credentials are the keys to the kingdom. Testers use various techniques to harvest usernames and passwords, including phishing, credential stuffing, and password spraying attacks. It's like stealing the master key to unlock the fortress gates.

Shodan and IoT Scanning - Unveiling the Internet of Things: Shodan is your detective's magnifying glass for the Internet of Things (IoT). It's a search engine that scans the internet for connected devices. Testers use Shodan to identify vulnerable IoT devices, such as webcams, routers, and industrial control systems. It's like discovering hidden vulnerabilities in a smart home or industrial facility.

Deep Web and Dark Web Research - Descending into the Shadows: The deep web and dark web are the shadowy corners of the internet where anonymity prevails. Testers may venture into these realms to gather intelligence on potential threats, leaked data, or underground forums where cybercriminals congregate. It's like delving into the underworld to uncover the secrets of digital adversaries.

Active Reconnaissance - Testing the Waters: In some cases, testers may perform active reconnaissance, which involves probing the target's systems and networks to gather information. This may include techniques like port scanning, vulnerability scanning, and network mapping. It's like dipping your toes in the water to gauge its depth before diving in.

Honeypots and Deception - Playing Mind Games: Honeypots and deception techniques are the mind games testers play with potential adversaries. These strategies involve creating fake assets or lures to divert attackers' attention and gather information about their tactics. It's like setting traps within the fortress to catch intruders.

In summary, advanced information gathering techniques are the foundation of successful penetration testing. They enable testers to gather critical intelligence, understand the target's digital landscape, and identify potential vulnerabilities and attack vectors. Think of it as donning the mantle of a digital detective, piecing together clues, and staying one step ahead of potential adversaries in the ever-evolving world of cybersecurity.

Picture yourself as an explorer in the digital realm, armed with tools and techniques to uncover hidden treasures within a vast and complex network landscape. In the world of advanced penetration testing, enumerating network resources and services is akin to creating a detailed map of an uncharted territory, where every server, service, and protocol is a potential landmark waiting to be discovered.

Port Scanning - Knocking on Digital Doors: Port scanning is your way of knocking on digital doors to see which ones open. Think of it as walking through a neighborhood, checking the front doors of houses. Advanced testers use port scanning tools to identify open ports on target systems. Each open port represents a potential entry point into the system.

Service Identification - Finding the Inhabitants: Once you've discovered open ports, it's time to identify the services running on those ports. Imagine it as learning about the inhabitants of a house once you've entered. Service identification techniques reveal the nature of services, such as web servers, email servers, or database servers. This information helps testers understand the functionality of the target systems.

Banner Grabbing - Gathering Clues: Banner grabbing is like reading the welcome sign on the door of a house. Testers collect banners and service banners, which are messages sent by services upon connection. These banners often contain version information and other clues that assist testers in identifying the specific software and its version running on a service.

Operating System Fingerprinting - Identifying the Owner: Just as a detective can deduce the owner of a house by its style and features, testers use operating system fingerprinting techniques to identify the underlying operating system of a target system. This knowledge helps testers tailor their attack strategies to the specific OS, as different operating systems may have varying vulnerabilities and behaviors.

Vulnerability Scanning - Finding Weak Spots: Vulnerability scanning is like inspecting a building for structural weaknesses. Testers use vulnerability scanning tools to identify known vulnerabilities in the services and software running on target systems. This process helps testers pinpoint potential weak spots that could be exploited by attackers.

Network Mapping - Creating a Blueprint: Network mapping is akin to creating a blueprint of a building. It involves discovering and documenting the structure of the target network, including the relationships between systems, subnets, and network devices. Mapping the network provides testers with a comprehensive view of the target environment.

SNMP Enumeration - Tapping into Network Management: SNMP (Simple Network Management Protocol) enumeration is like gaining access to the building's security system. Testers use SNMP enumeration techniques to retrieve information about network devices, configurations, and performance metrics. This data can be valuable for understanding the network infrastructure.

DNS Enumeration - Decoding Domain Names: DNS enumeration is like decoding the names of streets and neighborhoods in a city. Testers use DNS enumeration techniques to gather information about domain names, subdomains, and associated IP addresses. This helps testers identify additional targets and services.

NetBIOS Enumeration - Exploring Windows Networks: NetBIOS enumeration is your key to exploring Windows-based networks. Testers use NetBIOS enumeration techniques to gather information about Windows systems, shares, user accounts, and network resources. This knowledge is essential for understanding the Windows environment and potential attack vectors.

SMTP Enumeration - Unveiling Email Services: SMTP enumeration is like uncovering the post office in a town. Testers use SMTP enumeration techniques to gather information about email services, including email addresses, users, and mail server configurations. This information can be useful for email-based attacks and social engineering.

Enumeration of Web Applications - Delving into the Web: Web application enumeration involves exploring web applications to identify their functionalities, directories, and endpoints. It's like exploring different sections of a building to find hidden rooms. Testers use web application enumeration techniques to discover potential vulnerabilities and areas for further testing.

Brute Force Attacks - Testing All the Keys: Brute force attacks are like trying every possible key to unlock a door. Testers may use brute force techniques to guess credentials, passwords, or encryption keys. This approach can be time-consuming but effective if weak or default credentials are in use.

In summary, enumerating network resources and services is the essential first step in advanced penetration testing. It's the process of uncovering the digital landscape, understanding the network's structure, identifying potential vulnerabilities, and gathering critical information about target systems. Think of it as becoming a digital cartographer, mapping out the terrain before embarking on your journey through the intricate world of cybersecurity.

Chapter 4: Vulnerability Assessment and Exploitation

Imagine you're a vigilant guardian standing at the gates of a fortress, carefully examining every nook and cranny for potential weaknesses. In the realm of advanced vulnerability scanning and assessment, this role of a diligent sentinel is precisely what you play. It's about going beyond the surface and diving deep into an organization's digital infrastructure to identify vulnerabilities that could be exploited by adversaries.

The Art of Scanning - Unveiling the Digital Landscape: Advanced vulnerability scanning is akin to spreading out a detailed map of the fortress grounds. It involves using scanning tools and techniques to systematically probe every corner of a network, revealing the layout, vulnerabilities, and potential entry points. This meticulous process helps testers understand the organization's digital landscape.

Network Discovery - Mapping the Castle: Network discovery is your first step in the scanning adventure. It's like exploring the outer perimeter of the fortress to find all the entrances. Testers use tools to identify all the devices, servers, and systems connected to the network. This mapping provides an overview of the attack surface.

Port Scanning - Knocking on Doors: Port scanning is like knocking on the doors of the fortress to see which ones open. Testers send packets to target systems to check for open ports. Each open port represents a potential entry point for attackers. Understanding the available services helps testers assess their security.

Service Enumeration - Understanding the Inhabitants: Once you've found open doors, it's time to understand who lives inside. Service enumeration techniques reveal the services running on those ports. Imagine it as getting to know the inhabitants of different rooms within the fortress. Testers identify the software and versions in use, which is crucial for assessing vulnerabilities.

Banner Grabbing - Collecting Clues: Banner grabbing is like reading the welcome signs on the doors you've opened. Testers collect banners or service banners, which are messages sent by services upon connection. These banners often contain version information and other clues that assist testers in identifying the specific software running on a service.

Operating System Fingerprinting - Identifying the Owner: Advanced testers use operating system fingerprinting techniques to identify the underlying operating system of target systems. Think of it as determining the architectural style of the fortress. Understanding the OS is vital because different operating systems may have varying vulnerabilities and security configurations.

Vulnerability Scanning - Spotting Weaknesses: Vulnerability scanning is your treasure hunt for weak points in the fortress's defenses. Testers use vulnerability scanning tools to identify known vulnerabilities in the services and software running on target systems. This process helps testers pinpoint potential weaknesses that could be exploited by attackers.

Authentication Testing - Cracking the Safe: Authentication testing is like attempting to crack the safe within the fortress. Testers try to authenticate to services and systems using various techniques, such as password guessing or brute force attacks. It helps assess the strength of authentication mechanisms and the risk of unauthorized access.

Web Application Scanning - Exploring the Inner Chambers: Web application scanning is akin to exploring the inner chambers of the fortress. Testers use specialized tools to examine web applications, identifying vulnerabilities like SQL injection, cross-site scripting (XSS), and security misconfigurations. These vulnerabilities can provide adversaries with entry points into critical systems.

Wireless Network Scanning - Assessing the Castle Grounds: Just as the fortress may have extensive grounds, organizations often have wireless networks extending beyond their physical offices. Testers perform wireless network scanning to identify and assess the security of wireless access points. It's like exploring the castle grounds to ensure there are no hidden entrances.

IoT Device Scanning - Watching the Outposts: The modern fortress extends to IoT devices that control smart homes, industrial systems, and more. Testers scan for IoT devices to assess their security. Think of it as keeping an eye on outposts and watchtowers to ensure they are well-defended.

Custom Scripting - Tailoring the Attack: In some cases, testers may need to craft custom scripts and tools to uncover vulnerabilities that automated scanning tools might miss. Custom scripting is like fashioning a unique key to open a secret door within the fortress.

False Positive Analysis - Separating Wheat from Chaff: Scanning may yield false alarms or non-exploitable findings. Testers perform false positive analysis to separate genuine vulnerabilities from false alarms. It's like distinguishing real threats from noise in the digital landscape.

Continuous Monitoring - Guarding the Fortress: Vulnerability scanning and assessment aren't one-time activities; they are part of ongoing vigilance. Organizations need to continuously monitor their digital defenses, regularly scanning for new vulnerabilities and assessing the impact of changes in their environment. In summary, advanced vulnerability scanning and assessment are the keys to fortifying the digital fortress. It's about systematically uncovering weaknesses, understanding the landscape, and assessing the security of the organization's assets. Think of it as being the vigilant guardian, ensuring that the fortress remains well-defended against potential adversaries in the ever-evolving world of cybersecurity. Imagine you're an intrepid explorer in the world of cybersecurity, embarking on a quest to uncover the secrets hidden deep within a digital fortress. As you venture further, you encounter complex vulnerabilities—those elusive, multi-layered weaknesses that require intricate techniques to exploit. In this chapter, we'll delve into the art of exploitation, where we'll unlock the doors of these complex vulnerabilities and shed light on the methods used by advanced penetration testers.

Understanding Complex Vulnerabilities - Unraveling the Puzzle: Complex vulnerabilities are like intricate puzzles within the fortress. They often involve multiple layers of misconfigurations, logic flaws, or intricate software interactions. Understanding these vulnerabilities requires a keen eye for detail and a deep understanding of the target's architecture.

Privilege Escalation - Ascending the Ranks: Privilege escalation is akin to gaining access to higher levels within the fortress. When an attacker starts with limited privileges, exploiting vulnerabilities to escalate their access is crucial. Techniques such as privilege escalation exploits, misconfigured permissions, and insecure service configurations are the keys to ascending the ranks.

Buffer Overflow Exploits - Breaking the Barrier: Buffer overflow exploits are like breaching the fortress's walls. These vulnerabilities occur when a program writes data beyond the boundaries of a designated buffer, potentially allowing attackers to execute malicious code. Crafting and executing buffer overflow exploits require a deep understanding of memory management and assembly language.

Code Injection Attacks - Manipulating the Script: Code injection attacks are like manipulating the scripts that control the fortress's defenses. SQL injection, Command injection, and Cross-Site Scripting (XSS) are examples of these techniques. Attackers inject malicious code into vulnerable applications, causing them to execute unintended actions.

Exploiting Zero-Day Vulnerabilities - The Element of Surprise: Zero-day vulnerabilities are like secret passages in the fortress unknown to its defenders. These are vulnerabilities for which no patch or mitigation is available, making them highly sought after by attackers. Exploiting zero-days requires in-depth knowledge of the vulnerability and the target environment.

Privilege Escalation via Kernel Exploits - Becoming the Commander: Kernel exploits are like gaining control over the fortress's central command center. These exploits target vulnerabilities in the operating system's kernel, allowing attackers to gain full control over the system. They are among the most potent and complex exploits, often requiring advanced knowledge of low-level system internals.

Binary Exploitation - Mastering the Code: Binary exploitation is like deciphering the fortress's secret code. Testers analyze and manipulate compiled programs to discover vulnerabilities that can be exploited. Techniques include reverse engineering, debugging, and crafting exploits tailored to the target application's binary code.

Cryptographic Attacks - Cracking the Code: Cryptographic attacks are like cracking the codes that protect the fortress's secrets. Testers exploit weaknesses in cryptographic algorithms, protocols, or implementations to reveal sensitive information or forge digital signatures. Techniques include cryptographic flaws, protocol vulnerabilities, and side-channel attacks.

Web Application Exploitation - Breaching the Digital Gates: Web application exploitation is like breaching the digital gates of the fortress. Testers use a range of techniques, including SQL injection, Cross-Site Scripting (XSS), and Remote Code Execution (RCE), to compromise web applications and gain access to sensitive data or control over the server.

Memory Corruption Exploits - Disturbing the Balance: Memory corruption exploits are like disturbing the delicate balance within the fortress's defenses. Techniques like stack overflows, heap overflows, and use-after-free vulnerabilities target memory allocation and manipulation, potentially leading to code execution.

Exploiting Logic Flaws - Outsmarting the System: Logic flaws are like outsmarting the security systems within the fortress. Testers identify vulnerabilities where the intended logic of an application or system fails to account for certain scenarios, allowing unintended actions. Exploiting logic flaws often involves crafting intricate attack scenarios.

Client-Side Attacks - Manipulating the User: Client-side attacks are like manipulating the users within the fortress to open the gates themselves. Techniques like phishing, malicious attachments, and drive-by downloads target end-user devices to gain access or compromise their data.

Bypassing Security Controls - Skirting the Guards: Bypassing security controls is like finding ways to skirt the guards at the fortress's entrances. Testers seek vulnerabilities that allow them to bypass authentication, authorization, or other security measures to gain unauthorized access.

Abusing Misconfigurations - Exploiting Oversight: Misconfigurations are like exploiting the fortress's vulnerable entry points due to oversight. Testers actively look for misconfigured settings or weak security configurations that can be exploited to achieve their objectives In summary, advanced exploitation techniques are the keys to unlocking the secrets hidden within complex vulnerabilities. It's about delving deep into the fortress, understanding its inner workings, and manipulating weaknesses to achieve specific goals. Think of it as becoming a master locksmith, using intricate techniques to open doors that others may overlook in the ever-evolving landscape of cybersecurity.

Chapter 5: Exploiting Web Applications

Navigating the vast realm of web application security can often feel like embarking on a grand adventure, where you're both the explorer and the guardian of digital domains. In this chapter, we'll uncover the essential frameworks that guide you through this journey, helping you assess web applications with precision and confidence.

Understanding the Landscape - Your Digital Playground: Before delving into the frameworks, it's crucial to grasp the digital landscape you're about to explore. Web applications are the interactive gateways to a world of data, services, and user experiences. They can be as simple as a blog or as complex as an e-commerce platform, each with its unique set of vulnerabilities.

OWASP - Your Trusted Companion: The Open Web Application Security Project (OWASP) is your trusted companion in the realm of web application security. Think of OWASP as your guidebook, offering a comprehensive list of the most critical web application security risks. It outlines the top vulnerabilities, such as Injection, Cross-Site Scripting (XSS), and Broken Authentication, empowering you to prioritize your assessments.

OWASP Top Ten - The Essentials: Within the OWASP guidebook, the OWASP Top Ten is like your map to the most treacherous regions. It highlights the ten most critical web application security risks, providing a starting point for your assessments. These include issues like SQL injection, sensitive data exposure, and security misconfigurations.

CWE - The Vulnerability Dictionary: The Common Weakness Enumeration (CWE) is your dictionary of vulnerabilities. Think of it as a comprehensive lexicon that categorizes and describes common security weaknesses in software. CWE helps you speak the language of vulnerabilities, making it easier to communicate your findings and understand the risks associated with web applications.

The Reconnaissance Phase - Surveying the Terrain: Imagine you're surveying the terrain before embarking on your adventure. The reconnaissance phase involves gathering information about the web application, its architecture, and its potential weaknesses. Tools like Burp Suite, Nmap, and OWASP Amass can assist you in this initial exploration.

Mapping the Attack Surface - Defining the Boundaries: Just as explorers map out the boundaries of their adventure, you'll need to map the attack surface of the web application. This involves identifying all entry points, endpoints, and user interactions within the application. Tools like OWASP ZAP and Burp Suite's Spider feature help you discover these areas.

Scanning for Vulnerabilities - Unveiling Hidden Dangers: Vulnerability scanning is your treasure hunt within the application. Automated scanners, such as Nessus, Acunetix, and OWASP Dependency-Check, comb through the application to identify known vulnerabilities. They check for issues like outdated libraries, misconfigurations, and common coding mistakes.

Manual Testing - The Hands-On Approach: While automated scanners are valuable, manual testing is like getting your hands dirty on the adventure. This involves actively interacting with the web application, attempting to exploit vulnerabilities, and uncovering issues that automated tools might miss. Techniques like manual code review, parameter tampering, and session fixation testing come into play.

Reporting and Documentation - Your Adventure Journal: Just as explorers document their journeys, you'll need to create a detailed adventure journal in the form of reports. These reports not only outline the vulnerabilities discovered but also provide recommendations for remediation. Tools like Dradis and OWASP Defectdojo help in organizing and generating these reports.

Testing Methodologies - Your Expedition Plan: Just as expeditions require a well-thought-out plan, web application assessments follow testing methodologies. OWASP offers the Application Security Verification Standard (ASVS) and the Testing Guide, which provide step-by-step instructions for thorough assessments. Following these methodologies ensures a structured and comprehensive approach.

Custom Testing - Tailoring Your Adventure: Sometimes, the terrain of web applications is unique, and off-the-shelf tools and frameworks might not cover it entirely. That's when you'll need to tailor your approach, crafting custom tests and scripts to address specific vulnerabilities or functionalities.

Bug Bounty Programs - Collaborative Exploration: Bug bounty programs are like collaborative adventures with the application's creators. Many organizations offer rewards for security researchers who discover and responsibly disclose vulnerabilities. Platforms like HackerOne and Bugcrowd facilitate these partnerships.

Continuous Monitoring - Safeguarding Your Digital Territory: Just as guardians protect their territories, continuous monitoring ensures the ongoing security of web applications. Tools like OWASP Dependency-Check and OWASP Dependency-Track help you monitor for new vulnerabilities in the libraries and components your application relies on.

In summary, web application assessment frameworks are your guiding stars in the vast digital landscape of cybersecurity. They provide structure, methodology, and a common language for exploring and safeguarding web applications. Think of them as your compass and maps, empowering you to navigate the intricate terrain and uncover vulnerabilities with confidence on your cybersecurity adventure.

Welcome to the exhilarating world of web application security, where we'll dive deep into the realm of advanced vulnerabilities and the art of exploiting them. Picture yourself as an intrepid digital explorer, navigating the complex terrain of web applications, each with its unique vulnerabilities waiting to be uncovered.

Understanding the Web Application Landscape: Before we embark on this journey, let's grasp the terrain we're about to traverse. Web applications are the dynamic, interactive gateways to an organization's digital presence, ranging from e-commerce platforms to social media sites. Each presents its own set of challenges and vulnerabilities.

Injection Attacks - Poking Holes in the Castle Walls: Injection attacks are like poking holes in the castle walls. Techniques such as SQL injection and NoSQL injection exploit vulnerabilities that allow attackers to inject malicious code into application inputs, potentially gaining access to databases or executing arbitrary commands.

Cross-Site Scripting (XSS) - Planting Mischief in the Garden: XSS is like planting mischief in the digital garden. It involves injecting malicious scripts into web pages, which are then executed by unsuspecting users' browsers. This can lead to theft of sensitive information or the hijacking of user sessions.

Cross-Site Request Forgery (CSRF) - Manipulating User Actions: CSRF is akin to manipulating the actions of users within the fortress. Attackers trick users into performing actions on a web application without their consent, potentially causing unintended actions or data manipulation.

Security Misconfigurations - Unlocked Gates and Open Doors: Security misconfigurations are like finding unlocked gates and open doors within the fortress. These vulnerabilities occur when developers overlook security settings, leaving sensitive data exposed or granting unintended access. Exploiting them can provide a direct path to unauthorized areas.

XML External Entity (XXE) - Unveiling Hidden Scripts: XXE attacks are like unveiling hidden scripts within the fortress's documents. Attackers exploit weaknesses in XML processing, causing the application to parse malicious XML files that disclose sensitive data or execute arbitrary code.

Insecure Deserialization - Reconstructing the Trojan Horse: Insecure deserialization is akin to reconstructing the Trojan Horse. Attackers manipulate serialized data to execute code or gain unauthorized access when the application deserializes the data.

Server-Side Request Forgery (SSRF) - Controlling the Messenger: SSRF is like controlling the fortress's messengers. Attackers trick the application into making requests to internal or external resources, potentially exposing sensitive information or facilitating attacks on internal systems.

Broken Authentication - Disguising as an Insider: Broken authentication is akin to disguising oneself as an insider. Attackers exploit flaws in authentication mechanisms to impersonate legitimate users, gain unauthorized access, or perform actions on their behalf.

Session Management Issues - Stealing the Key to the Treasure Chest: Session management vulnerabilities are like stealing the key to the treasure chest. Attackers exploit weaknesses in how sessions are managed, potentially hijacking user sessions or gaining unauthorized access to accounts.

Business Logic Flaws - Outsmarting the Guards: Business logic flaws are like outsmarting the guards within the fortress. These vulnerabilities occur when attackers manipulate the expected flow of an application's business logic to their advantage, potentially bypassing security controls or causing unintended actions.

API Vulnerabilities - Breaching the Backend: API vulnerabilities are akin to breaching the fortress's backend systems. Attackers exploit weaknesses in the APIs that power web applications, potentially accessing sensitive data or causing disruptions.

File Upload Vulnerabilities - Sneaking in Through the Backdoor: File upload vulnerabilities are like sneaking in through the fortress's backdoor. Attackers manipulate file upload functionalities to upload malicious files, potentially gaining control over the server or executing arbitrary code.

Content Security Policy (CSP) Bypass - Circumventing the Guards: CSP bypass is akin to circumventing the guards placed by the fortress. Attackers find ways to bypass the security policies intended to restrict the execution of scripts, potentially launching XSS attacks.

DOM-Based Vulnerabilities - Manipulating the Mindset: DOM-based vulnerabilities involve manipulating the Document Object Model (DOM) within a web page to execute malicious actions. Attackers can change the page's behavior, steal data, or hijack user sessions.

Client-Side Attacks - Deceiving the User: Client-side attacks are like deceiving the users within the fortress. Attackers craft malicious content or scripts that execute in users' browsers, potentially compromising their data or sessions.

Browser Exploitation - Subverting the Gatekeeper: Browser exploitation is akin to subverting the fortress's gatekeeper. Attackers target vulnerabilities in web browsers themselves to gain control over the user's device or steal sensitive information.

API Abuse - Playing by Your Own Rules: API abuse involves manipulating and misusing an application's APIs for unintended purposes. Attackers may scrape data, overload resources, or orchestrate attacks by leveraging APIs.

Web Services Vulnerabilities - Weak Links in the Chain: Web services vulnerabilities are like identifying weak links in a chain connecting different components of the fortress. Attackers exploit weaknesses in the APIs and services that web applications rely on, potentially causing disruptions or data breaches.

Continuous Vigilance - Guarding Your Digital Territory: Just as guardians protect their territory, continuous vigilance is essential in web application security. Organizations must remain vigilant, regularly assessing, patching, and updating their applications to defend against evolving threats.

In summary, exploring and exploiting advanced web application vulnerabilities is both a thrilling adventure and a critical cybersecurity practice. It's about understanding the weaknesses in the digital fortresses we rely on daily and fortifying them to withstand the ever-evolving landscape of threats. Think of it as being the hero who uncovers vulnerabilities to make the digital world safer for all.

Chapter 6: Wireless Network Penetration Testing

Imagine yourself as a digital detective, equipped with tools and techniques to uncover hidden secrets within the realm of wireless networks. In this chapter, we'll explore the world of wireless network assessment tools, your trusty companions on the journey to secure Wi-Fi environments and ensure that they remain impenetrable fortresses against potential threats.

Understanding Wireless Networks - Your Digital Ecosystem: Before we delve into the tools at your disposal, let's first understand the ecosystem we're dealing with. Wireless networks are the lifeblood of our modern connected world. They enable our devices to communicate without cumbersome wires, but they also introduce vulnerabilities that need vigilant protection.

Wi-Fi Protocols - The Languages of the Air: Wi-Fi networks communicate using various protocols, such as 802.11b, 802.11g, 802.11n, and the latest, 802.11ax (Wi-Fi 6). These protocols define how devices connect, transmit data, and encrypt communications. Assessing these protocols is crucial to identify vulnerabilities.

Wireless Network Assessment - Scanning the Airwaves: Think of wireless network assessment as scanning the airwaves for hidden treasures and potential threats. Assessment tools are like your metal detectors, helping you uncover hidden Wi-Fi networks, identify access points, and map their coverage areas.

Wi-Fi Scanners - Your Digital Compass: Wi-Fi scanners, such as NetSpot, inSSIDer, and Acrylic Wi-Fi, act as your digital compass. They detect and display nearby Wi-Fi networks, including their names, signal strengths, and encryption types. This information helps you understand the wireless landscape.

Wireless Sniffers - Eavesdropping on Conversations: Wireless sniffers like Wireshark are like eavesdropping devices for the digital world. They capture and analyze wireless traffic, allowing you to inspect data packets and gain insights into network behavior. This is valuable for identifying potential vulnerabilities or abnormal activity.

Channel Analyzers - Finding the Quiet Spots: Channel analyzers, such as Wi-Fi Analyzer and inSSIDer, help you find the quiet spots in the crowded airwaves. They provide information about Wi-Fi channel congestion, helping you select the best channels for your network to avoid interference.

Access Point Detection - Uncovering Hidden Gems: Access point detection tools are like treasure maps that help you uncover hidden gems. They identify rogue access points, unauthorized devices, or misconfigured hardware that could compromise your network's security.

SSID Enumeration - Discovering Hidden Networks: SSID enumeration tools are like secret-revealing spells. They can discover hidden (non-broadcasted) SSIDs, which might be intentionally concealed but could still be vulnerable to attacks.

WEP/WPA/WPA2/WPA3 Cracking - Breaking the Code: Cracking tools like Aircrack-ng and Hashcat are akin to locksmiths breaking the code. They attempt to crack the encryption keys used to secure Wi-Fi networks, revealing the passphrase and potentially gaining unauthorized access.

Deauthentication and Disassociation Attacks - Kicking Intruders Out: Deauthentication and disassociation attacks are like eviction notices for unwanted guests. Tools like aireplay-ng can send deauthentication or disassociation packets to disconnect devices from a Wi-Fi network, a useful defensive tactic against potential attackers.

Evil Twin and Rogue AP Detection - Spotting Impostors: Evil twin and rogue AP detection tools are like detectives sniffing out impostors. They identify malicious access points that mimic legitimate networks, often used in phishing or man-in-the-middle attacks.

Packet Injection - Testing for Weaknesses: Packet injection tools like mdk3 and Scapy are like testers that probe network defenses. They send crafted packets to test how a network reacts to various attacks, helping identify vulnerabilities or weaknesses.

Wireless Intrusion Detection Systems (WIDS) - The Watchful Guards: WIDS are like the watchful guards of your fortress. They continuously monitor wireless traffic for suspicious behavior and known attack patterns. Tools like Snort and Suricata can be configured as WIDS to protect your network.

Captive Portal Testing - Gateway to the Unknown: Captive portal testing tools are like keys to gates leading to the unknown. They help assess the security of authentication portals often used in public Wi-Fi networks, ensuring they don't pose risks to users' data.

Wi-Fi Password Auditing - Strengthening Your Defenses: Wi-Fi password auditing tools help strengthen your defenses by identifying weak or commonly used passphrases. Tools like Hydra and John the Ripper can assist in auditing the strength of your Wi-Fi passwords.

Reporting and Documentation - Your Adventure Journal: Just as explorers document their journeys, it's essential to keep a detailed adventure journal in the form of reports. These reports not only outline the vulnerabilities discovered but also provide recommendations for remediation. Tools like Wi-Fi Pineapple and Kismet can assist in generating reports.

Wireless Security Auditing Methodologies - Your Expedition Plan: Just as expeditions require a well-thought-out plan, wireless security audits follow methodologies. The Wireless Security Assessment Methodology (WSAM) and OWASP Wireless Security Testing Guide offer structured approaches for comprehensive assessments.

Continuous Monitoring - Safeguarding Your Digital Territory: Just as guardians protect their territories, continuous monitoring ensures the ongoing security of your wireless networks. Tools like IDS/IPS systems, network monitoring solutions, and WIDS help you guard against evolving threats.

In summary, wireless network assessment tools are your trusted companions in the realm of Wi-Fi security. They equip you with the knowledge and tools needed to navigate the wireless landscape, uncover vulnerabilities, and ensure that your digital fortress remains impervious to potential threats. Think of it as a thrilling adventure where you're both the explorer and the guardian, safeguarding the digital world one network at a time.

Welcome to the exciting realm of wireless network vulnerabilities, where we'll embark on a journey to understand and exploit weaknesses in Wi-Fi networks. Think of this adventure as unraveling the secrets of wireless communication, much like deciphering an ancient treasure map.

The Intricate Web of Wireless Communication: Imagine Wi-Fi networks as a complex web of digital communication, connecting devices wirelessly and enabling seamless connectivity. To exploit vulnerabilities, we need to comprehend this intricate network.

Vulnerabilities - The Hidden Weaknesses: Vulnerabilities are like hidden doors in a fortress, waiting to be discovered. In wireless networks, they come in various forms, from insecure configurations to outdated encryption protocols.

Unauthorized Access - The Silent Intruder: Unauthorized access is akin to a silent intruder sneaking into a secured castle. When attackers exploit vulnerabilities, they can gain unauthorized access to Wi-Fi networks, potentially compromising sensitive data.

Weak Encryption - The Cracked Code: Weak encryption is like a code waiting to be cracked. When Wi-Fi networks use outdated or easily breakable encryption protocols, attackers can intercept and decrypt transmitted data.

WEP and Its Vulnerabilities - The Weak Sentinel: Wired Equivalent Privacy (WEP) was once the guardian of Wi-Fi networks, but it has numerous vulnerabilities. Attackers can exploit these weaknesses to crack WEP keys and gain access.

WPA/WPA2 and Their Weaknesses - The Chink in the Armor: Wi-Fi Protected Access (WPA) and its successor, WPA2, are like fortresses with chinks in their armor. While more secure than WEP, they have vulnerabilities that attackers can exploit to crack passwords or launch attacks.

WPA3 - The New Guardian: WPA3 is like the new guardian of the fortress, addressing many vulnerabilities of its predecessors. However, it's not invulnerable, and as technology evolves, new weaknesses may emerge.

Router Misconfigurations - The Open Gateways: Router misconfigurations are like open gateways in the fortress walls. When routers are poorly configured, they can expose Wi-Fi networks to attacks, allowing intruders to enter without much effort.

Default Credentials - The Unchanged Lock: Default credentials are like locks that remain unchanged. Many routers come with default usernames and passwords that attackers can easily guess or find online.

Rogue Access Points - The Impostors: Rogue access points are like impostors lurking in the fortress. Attackers can set up rogue Wi-Fi networks with similar names to legitimate ones, tricking users into connecting and potentially compromising their data.

Evil Twin Attacks - The Deceptive Twins: Evil twin attacks are like deceptive twins trying to fool users. Attackers create malicious Wi-Fi networks that mimic legitimate ones, intercepting data or launching attacks on connected devices.

Krack Attacks - The Key Reinstallation Flaw: Krack attacks are like cunning thieves exploiting a flaw in the fortress's key management. Attackers can intercept and manipulate data by exploiting vulnerabilities in the WPA and WPA2 key-handshake process.

Deauthentication Attacks - The Silent Ejection: Deauthentication attacks are like silent ejections from the fortress. Attackers send deauthentication packets to disconnect devices from a Wi-Fi network, disrupting connectivity or forcing users onto malicious networks.

MAC Address Spoofing - The Identity Theft: MAC address spoofing is like identity theft in the digital world. Attackers can impersonate trusted devices by spoofing their MAC addresses, potentially gaining access to Wi-Fi networks.

Brute Force Attacks - The Persistent Intruder: Brute force attacks are like persistent intruders trying every possible key combination. Attackers use these attacks to guess Wi-Fi passwords, requiring time and computational power.

Dictionary Attacks - The Word Sleuths: Dictionary attacks are like word sleuths searching for the right passphrase. Attackers use lists of common passwords or words to guess Wi-Fi passwords, exploiting weak passphrases.

WPS Vulnerabilities - The Shortcut Exploits: Wi-Fi Protected Setup (WPS) vulnerabilities are like shortcuts that attackers can exploit. Weaknesses in WPS can allow attackers to quickly guess or obtain the Wi-Fi password.

Guest Network Risks - The Open Door: Guest networks can be like open doors in a fortress. When improperly configured, they can provide unauthorized access to the main network or expose guests to potential attacks.

Hidden SSID Vulnerabilities - The Concealed Weaknesses: Hidden SSID vulnerabilities are like concealed weaknesses that attackers can uncover. While hiding the network's name may seem secure, attackers can still discover and exploit hidden SSIDs.

Continuous Vigilance - Guarding Your Digital Territory: Just as guardians protect their territory, continuous vigilance is essential in wireless network security. Regularly updating firmware, configuring strong passwords, and monitoring for unusual activity are vital for safeguarding Wi-Fi networks.

In summary, exploiting wireless network vulnerabilities is both a captivating journey and a critical aspect of cybersecurity. It involves understanding the weaknesses within the digital fortresses we rely on for connectivity and taking measures to fortify them. Think of it as being the digital detective who uncovers vulnerabilities to ensure that Wi-Fi networks remain secure and resilient against potential threats.

Chapter 7: Post-Exploitation Techniques

Welcome to the intriguing world of advanced privilege escalation in the realm of cybersecurity. In this chapter, we'll embark on a journey to explore the techniques and tactics that adversaries employ to elevate their privileges within a system or network. Think of it as deciphering the art of accessing the inner sanctum of a digital fortress, where valuable secrets and control await those who can find a way in.

Understanding Privilege Escalation - The Quest for Elevated Access: Privilege escalation is like seeking the keys to the kingdom. It involves gaining higher levels of access or permissions on a system or network, often beyond what's initially granted to a user or application.

Types of Privileges - The Digital Hierarchy: Privileges come in various forms, like the hierarchy within a fortress. There are user-level privileges, which grant access to resources, and system-level privileges, which control the overall functioning of the system.

User-Level Privilege Escalation - Climbing the Ladder: User-level privilege escalation is akin to climbing the ladder within the fortress. Attackers exploit vulnerabilities or misconfigurations to gain additional access rights, allowing them to perform actions they were not initially permitted to do.

Vertical Privilege Escalation - Upward Mobility: Vertical privilege escalation is like moving up the chain of command within the fortress. Attackers aim to gain higher-level access, such as administrative or root privileges, by exploiting vulnerabilities.

Horizontal Privilege Escalation - Changing Roles: Horizontal privilege escalation is like changing roles within the fortress.

Attackers try to gain access to resources or accounts of other users with the same privilege level, potentially accessing sensitive data or impersonating them.

System-Level Privilege Escalation - Mastering the Control: System-level privilege escalation is akin to mastering control of the entire fortress. Attackers target vulnerabilities or weaknesses that grant them access to critical system functions or administrative privileges.

Privilege Escalation Techniques - The Tools of the Trade: Privilege escalation techniques are like the tools that skilled infiltrators use. These techniques include exploiting software vulnerabilities, misconfigurations, or weaknesses in the authentication process to gain higher privileges.

Exploiting Software Vulnerabilities - Weakness in the Fortress Walls: Exploiting software vulnerabilities is like finding a crack in the fortress walls. Attackers identify and leverage vulnerabilities in software or applications to execute malicious code and escalate privileges.

Kernel Exploitation - The Heart of the System: Kernel exploitation is like targeting the heart of the fortress—the operating system kernel. Attackers seek to exploit vulnerabilities in the kernel, gaining the highest level of control over the system.

Rootkits - The Stealthy Invaders: Rootkits are like stealthy invaders who infiltrate the fortress undetected. These malicious tools are designed to maintain privileged access by hiding their presence and actions on the system.

Password Cracking - Unlocking Doors: Password cracking is like unlocking doors within the fortress. Attackers use various techniques, such as brute force or dictionary attacks, to guess or crack passwords and gain access to accounts with higher privileges.

Privilege Escalation via Misconfigurations - Doors Left Ajar: Privilege escalation through misconfigurations is like exploiting doors left ajar in the fortress. Attackers identify and exploit misconfigured settings or permissions to elevate their access.

Abusing Trust Relationships - Impersonation Tactics: Abusing trust relationships is akin to impersonating a trusted figure within the fortress. Attackers exploit trust relationships between systems or domains to gain elevated privileges.

DLL Injection - Manipulating the Guards: DLL injection is like manipulating the fortress guards. Attackers inject malicious dynamic link libraries (DLLs) into processes, potentially gaining control and escalating privileges.

Bypassing User Account Control (UAC) - Scaling the Ramparts: Bypassing User Account Control is like scaling the fortress ramparts. Attackers employ techniques to bypass UAC restrictions on Windows systems, gaining administrative privileges.

Privilege Escalation on Linux - The Unix Kingdom: Privilege escalation on Linux systems is like navigating the Unix kingdom. Attackers exploit vulnerabilities or misconfigurations in Linux systems to gain elevated privileges.

Persistence Mechanisms - Maintaining Control: Persistence mechanisms are like maintaining control within the fortress. Attackers establish methods to ensure their continued access and privileges even after initial compromise.

Defensive Strategies - Fortifying the Defenses: Defensive strategies are like fortifying the defenses of the fortress. Organizations employ measures such as patch management, least privilege access, and monitoring to mitigate privilege escalation threats.

Detection and Response - The Watchful Guardians: Detection and response are like the watchful guardians of the fortress. Organizations use security tools and practices to detect and respond to privilege escalation attempts, minimizing the impact of successful attacks.

Continuous Vigilance - Safeguarding Your Digital Territory: Just as guardians protect their territory, continuous vigilance is essential in privilege escalation prevention. Organizations must continuously assess and strengthen their defenses to safeguard against evolving threats.

In summary, advanced privilege escalation is both a captivating exploration of digital vulnerabilities and a critical aspect of cybersecurity defense. It involves understanding the weaknesses within digital fortresses and taking measures to fortify defenses against potential adversaries seeking elevated access.

Welcome to the intriguing realm of data exfiltration and persistence, where we'll uncover the art of stealing information from digital fortresses and ensuring that access remains covert and long-lasting. Think of it as unraveling the secrets of digital espionage, where stealth and ingenuity are key.

Understanding Data Exfiltration - The Art of Stealing: Data exfiltration is like the art of stealing secrets from a fortress. It involves covertly transferring sensitive information from a target system or network to a location controlled by an attacker.

Types of Data Exfiltration - The Stolen Treasures: Data exfiltration comes in various forms, much like the stolen treasures from a fortress. It can include stealing files, credentials, financial data, or intellectual property.

Covert Channels - The Secret Passageways: Covert channels are like secret passageways within a fortress. Attackers create hidden communication channels within a network to transmit data undetected.

Exfiltration Techniques - The Tools of the Trade: Exfiltration techniques are like the tools of skilled spies. These techniques include disguising data, using encrypted tunnels, or exploiting vulnerabilities to siphon information.

File Transfer Protocols - The Silent Couriers: File transfer protocols are like silent couriers who transport stolen documents. Attackers may use protocols like FTP, HTTP, or SMB to exfiltrate files without raising suspicion.

Data Compression - Shrinking the Payload: Data compression is like shrinking the payload to fit through narrow passages. Attackers compress data before exfiltration to reduce its size and avoid detection.

Encryption - Concealing the Contents: Encryption is like sealing stolen letters in an envelope. Attackers encrypt exfiltrated data to conceal its contents from prying eyes.

Steganography - Hiding in Plain Sight: Steganography is like hiding secrets within plain sight. Attackers embed data within images, audio files, or other media, making it difficult to detect.

DNS Tunneling - Smuggling Data: DNS tunneling is like smuggling data through a covert route. Attackers use DNS requests and responses to exfiltrate data, bypassing traditional security measures.

Exfiltration Over Encrypted Channels - Covert Communication: Exfiltrating data over encrypted channels is like speaking in code. Attackers may use HTTPS or other encrypted protocols to transmit stolen information without arousing suspicion.

Exfiltration Through Email - Sending Secrets: Exfiltrating data through email is like sending secret messages. Attackers may attach stolen files or use email as a covert channel to send sensitive information.

Persistence - The Art of Staying Hidden: Persistence is like remaining hidden within the fortress after stealing secrets. Attackers establish mechanisms to maintain access and control over compromised systems.

Backdoors - The Hidden Entrances: Backdoors are like hidden entrances left ajar within the fortress. Attackers create these secret pathways for future access, evading detection.

Trojans - The Infiltrators: Trojans are like infiltrators who disguise themselves. Attackers plant malicious software that provides remote access to compromised systems, ensuring persistent control.

Rootkits - The Silent Invaders: Rootkits are like silent invaders who conceal their presence. These malicious tools hide within the operating system, allowing attackers to maintain control without detection.

Persistence in Memory - Transient Control: Persistence in memory is like maintaining transient control within the fortress. Attackers inject code into running processes, ensuring access even if the system reboots.

Scheduled Tasks - Covert Actions: Scheduled tasks are like covert actions within the fortress. Attackers create tasks that run at specific times, ensuring regular access to compromised systems.

Registry Modifications - Stealthy Changes: Registry modifications are like stealthy changes made to the fortress layout. Attackers alter the Windows Registry to maintain control over compromised systems.

Persistence on Mobile Devices - The Pocket Espionage: Persistence on mobile devices is like pocket-sized espionage. Attackers employ techniques to ensure ongoing access to smartphones and tablets.

Defense and Detection - The Guardians of Secrets: Defense and detection are like the guardians protecting stolen treasures. Organizations implement security measures and tools to detect data exfiltration and prevent persistence.

Continuous Vigilance - Safeguarding Your Digital Territory: Just as guardians protect their territory, continuous vigilance is essential in defending against data exfiltration and persistence. Organizations must remain vigilant, update security measures, and monitor for unusual activities to safeguard their digital fortresses.

In summary, data exfiltration and persistence are both intriguing aspects of cybersecurity—a delicate dance between attackers and defenders. Understanding these techniques is essential for organizations to protect their valuable assets and secrets from covert theft and persistent threats. Think of it as being the digital detective who unravels the secrets of espionage to ensure that the treasures of your digital fortress remain safely locked away.

Chapter 8: Evading Detection and Covering Tracks

Welcome to the intriguing world of anti-forensics and evasion strategies, where we'll explore the art of covering your tracks and avoiding detection in the digital landscape. Think of it as learning the techniques used by digital ninjas to slip through the cracks and leave no trace behind.

Understanding Anti-Forensics - The Art of Concealment: Anti-forensics is like the art of concealing your tracks in the digital realm. It involves techniques and strategies to make it difficult for forensic analysts to recover information or trace your activities.

Importance of Evasion - Staying in the Shadows: Evasion is like staying in the shadows to avoid detection. Whether you're a cybercriminal or a security professional testing a network, evasion techniques can be crucial to achieving your objectives.

Anti-Forensic Techniques - The Disguises: Anti-forensic techniques are like disguises that conceal your digital footprint. These methods include data wiping, file obfuscation, and data fragmentation to make it challenging for investigators to reconstruct your actions.

Data Deletion - Erasing Your Presence: Data deletion is like erasing your presence from a crime scene. Attackers use secure deletion tools to remove traces of their activities, making it difficult for forensic experts to recover information.

File Shredding - Digital Destruction: File shredding is like digital destruction. It involves overwriting files with random data, ensuring that even specialized tools cannot recover the original contents.

File Hiding - Concealing Clues: File hiding is like concealing clues in a treasure hunt. Attackers hide files within other files, making it less likely for forensic analysts to identify and extract valuable information.

Data Encryption - Locking the Secrets: Data encryption is like locking your secrets in a digital vault. Attackers use encryption to protect sensitive data, rendering it unreadable without the decryption key.

Disk Encryption - Securing the Evidence: Disk encryption is like securing the evidence in a safe. Attackers encrypt entire disks to prevent investigators from accessing stored data.

Steganography - Hiding in Plain Sight: Steganography is like hiding in plain sight. Attackers embed data within images, audio files, or other media, making it nearly impossible for forensic experts to detect.

Memory Forensics - Uncovering Hidden Clues: Memory forensics is like uncovering hidden clues within a crime scene. Forensic analysts examine a computer's volatile memory to find traces of malicious activity.

Log Manipulation - Altering the Records: Log manipulation is like altering the records at a crime scene. Attackers modify log files to remove evidence of their actions, making it challenging for investigators to reconstruct events.

Time Manipulation - Altering the Clock: Time manipulation is like altering the clock to confuse investigators. Attackers change timestamps on files and system logs to mislead forensic analysts.

Network Evasion - Dodging Digital Surveillance: Network evasion is like dodging digital surveillance cameras. Attackers use techniques such as VPNs, proxies, and Tor to hide their online activities.

IP Spoofing - Impersonating Others: IP spoofing is like impersonating someone else in a crowded room. Attackers forge IP addresses to hide their identity and location, making it difficult to trace their actions.

DNS Tunneling - Smuggling Data: DNS tunneling is like smuggling data through a hidden route. Attackers use DNS requests and responses to exfiltrate data and bypass network security measures.

Traffic Encryption - Securing Communication: Traffic encryption is like speaking in code. Attackers encrypt their network traffic to prevent eavesdropping and interception.

Evasion in Web Attacks - Dodging Detection: Evasion in web attacks is like dodging security cameras in a heist. Attackers use techniques like obfuscation and encoding to evade detection in web-based attacks.

Anti-Forensic Tools - The Ninja Arsenal: Anti-forensic tools are like the arsenal of a digital ninja. These software and techniques help attackers cover their tracks and avoid leaving evidence behind.

Digital Footprint Minimization - Walking Lightly: Minimizing your digital footprint is like walking lightly to avoid leaving tracks. Security-conscious individuals and organizations employ strategies to reduce their online presence.

Defense Against Anti-Forensics - The Digital Detectives: Defense against anti-forensics is like being a digital detective. Forensic analysts and security professionals use countermeasures and advanced tools to uncover hidden traces and prevent evasion.

Ethical Use - The Righteous Path: Ethical use of anti-forensics techniques is like using your skills for good. Security professionals and ethical hackers employ these strategies to test and improve the resilience of systems and networks.

Continuous Vigilance - Safeguarding Your Digital Territory: Just as guardians protect their territory, continuous vigilance is essential in defending against anti-forensics and evasion tactics. Organizations must stay ahead of attackers, employing robust security measures and staying informed about emerging threats.

In summary, anti-forensics and evasion strategies are both fascinating and essential aspects of cybersecurity. Whether you're a digital ninja seeking to protect your privacy or a digital detective defending against cybercriminals, understanding these techniques is crucial in the ever-evolving landscape of digital security. Think of it as being the master of disguise, ensuring that your digital presence remains concealed and your tracks remain hidden from prying eyes.

Welcome to the fascinating world of covering digital tracks effectively, where we'll delve into the art of maintaining privacy and discretion in an increasingly interconnected digital landscape. Think of it as a journey into the realm of online invisibility, where you become the master of your digital presence.

Understanding Digital Tracks - Your Online Trail: Digital tracks are like footprints in the digital sand, left behind as you navigate the online world. They encompass your online activities, communications, and interactions.

Importance of Privacy - Guarding Your Digital Self: Privacy is like a shield that protects your digital self. It's the ability to control what information you share and who has access to it in the vast digital realm.

Data Footprints - The Traces You Leave: Data footprints are like the traces you leave behind in the digital wilderness. They include your browsing history, social media posts, emails, and more.

Social Media Privacy - Safeguarding Your Online Persona: Social media privacy is like setting boundaries for your digital life. It involves configuring your profiles, managing visibility, and being mindful of the content you share.

Online Anonymity - Becoming a Digital Ghost: Online anonymity is like becoming a digital ghost, hiding your true identity from prying eyes. Tools like VPNs and Tor enable you to browse the web without revealing your IP address.

Private Browsing - Stealth Mode: Private browsing is like going into stealth mode. It prevents your browser from storing your history, cookies, and other data, enhancing your online privacy.

Secure Messaging - Encrypted Conversations: Secure messaging is like having a private conversation in a crowded room. End-to-end encryption ensures that only you and the intended recipient can read your messages.

Email Privacy - Locking Your Inbox: Email privacy is like securing your mailbox. Encrypted email services protect your messages from being intercepted and read by unauthorized parties.

Password Management - The Key to Security: Password management is like safeguarding the keys to your digital kingdom. Password managers help you create and store strong, unique passwords for each online account.

Two-Factor Authentication (2FA) - Double Locks: Two-factor authentication is like adding a second lock to your door. It provides an extra layer of security by requiring something you know (password) and something you have (e.g., a code from your phone) to access your accounts.

Incognito Mode - Discreet Browsing: Incognito mode is like browsing discreetly. It prevents your browsing history and cookies from being saved on your device.

Virtual Private Networks (VPNs) - Digital Tunnels: VPNs are like digital tunnels that protect your online activities. They encrypt your internet connection, making it difficult for third parties to monitor your online behavior.

TOR Network - The Onion Router: The TOR network is like a labyrinth of tunnels within the digital world. It anonymizes your online activities by routing your traffic through multiple servers, concealing your IP address.

Ad Blockers - Reducing Digital Noise: Ad blockers are like noise-canceling headphones for the web. They not only remove intrusive ads but also block tracking scripts that monitor your online behavior.

Browser Extensions - Digital Assistants: Browser extensions are like digital assistants that enhance your online privacy. They can block trackers, secure your connections, and offer additional privacy features.

Search Engines - Privacy-Focused Choices: Privacy-focused search engines are like treasure maps for the web. They prioritize your privacy by not storing your search history or tracking your queries.

Digital Hygiene - Clean Online Habits: Digital hygiene is like maintaining cleanliness in your online space. It involves regularly reviewing your digital tracks and taking steps to minimize exposure.

Location Privacy - Where Are You?: Location privacy is like a cloak of invisibility. Disabling location services on your devices prevents them from constantly tracking and sharing your whereabouts.

Online Reputation Management - Your Digital Persona: Online reputation management is like curating your digital persona. It involves monitoring and shaping how you appear online, both personally and professionally.

Educating Others - Spreading the Knowledge: Educating others about digital privacy is like lighting a path through the digital wilderness. Sharing your knowledge helps friends and family protect themselves online.

Ethical Considerations - Respecting Others' Privacy: Ethical considerations are like the golden rule of the digital world—

treat others' privacy as you would want yours treated. Respect boundaries and seek consent when sharing information about others.

Continuous Vigilance - Safeguarding Your Digital Territory: Just as guardians protect their territory, continuous vigilance is essential in maintaining your digital privacy. Stay informed about emerging threats, and adapt your privacy practices accordingly.

In summary, covering digital tracks effectively is both a skill and a mindset—a journey towards reclaiming control over your online presence. Whether you're navigating the vast online landscape or simply seeking to protect your personal information, these strategies empower you to be the guardian of your digital territory, ensuring that your digital footprints remain discreet and your online identity remains yours to control.

Chapter 9: Expanding the Attack Surface

Welcome to the intriguing world of leveraging external attack vectors, where we'll explore the art of exploiting weaknesses beyond the traditional boundaries of a network or system. Think of it as embarking on a digital adventure, where we uncover the hidden pathways that attackers use to breach the defenses of organizations and individuals alike.

Understanding External Attack Vectors - The Digital Battlefield: External attack vectors are like secret entrances to a digital fortress. They are the pathways that adversaries exploit from outside the target's perimeter to gain unauthorized access or compromise systems.

Importance of External Attack Vectors - Expanding the Battlefield: External attack vectors play a crucial role in modern cybersecurity. As organizations strengthen their internal defenses, attackers are increasingly turning to external avenues to find vulnerabilities.

Web-Based Attacks - The Open Gates: Web-based attacks are like open gates inviting intruders. Attackers target web applications, websites, and web servers to exploit vulnerabilities and gain access to sensitive data.

Phishing - Luring the Unwary: Phishing is like a deceptive fishing expedition. Attackers use convincing emails, messages, or websites to trick individuals into revealing confidential information, such as login credentials or financial details.

Spear Phishing - Precision Strikes: Spear phishing is like a targeted missile. Attackers craft highly personalized messages to deceive specific individuals or organizations, often with the aim of gaining access to sensitive systems or information.

Malware Delivery - The Trojan Horse: Malware delivery is like introducing a Trojan horse into a city. Attackers use malicious software to infect devices and establish backdoors, providing them with ongoing access and control.

Drive-By Downloads - Silent Infection: Drive-by downloads are like stealthy intruders. Attackers exploit vulnerabilities in web browsers or plugins to silently install malware on users' devices.

Watering Hole Attacks - Ambush Tactics: Watering hole attacks are like ambush tactics. Attackers compromise websites frequently visited by their target audience, infecting visitors with malware.

Ransomware - The Digital Extortionist: Ransomware is like a digital extortionist. Attackers encrypt victims' data and demand a ransom for its release, often causing significant disruptions and financial losses.

Supply Chain Attacks - Infiltrating the Source: Supply chain attacks are like infiltrating the source. Attackers compromise suppliers, vendors, or service providers to infiltrate their target's network through trusted connections.

Third-Party Software Vulnerabilities - Weakest Links: Third-party software vulnerabilities are like the weakest links in a chain. Attackers seek out security flaws in software used by the target, exploiting them to gain access.

DNS Attacks - Manipulating Signposts: DNS attacks are like manipulating signposts on the internet highway. Attackers tamper with the Domain Name System to redirect users to malicious websites or intercept communications.

IoT Vulnerabilities - The Internet of Targets: IoT vulnerabilities are like a multitude of targets waiting to be exploited. Attackers compromise insecure Internet of Things devices to launch attacks or gain a foothold on a network.

Remote Desktop Protocol (RDP) Exploits - Remote Entry Points: RDP exploits are like remote entry points into a fortress. Attackers target RDP vulnerabilities to gain remote access to systems and networks.

Brute Force Attacks - The Persistent Intruder: Brute force attacks are like a persistent intruder trying every key in the lock. Attackers systematically guess passwords or encryption keys until they gain access.

Credential Stuffing - Reusing Keys: Credential stuffing is like using stolen keys from one lock to open others. Attackers reuse leaked or stolen credentials to access multiple accounts, exploiting individuals' tendency to reuse passwords.

Distributed Denial of Service (DDoS) Attacks - Flooding the Gates: DDoS attacks are like a flood overwhelming the gates of a fortress. Attackers use botnets to flood a target's resources, rendering them unavailable to legitimate users.

Botnets - The Army of Compromised Devices: Botnets are like an army of compromised devices. Attackers control networks of infected computers, often using them to launch coordinated attacks or carry out malicious activities.

Social Engineering - Manipulating the Human Element: Social engineering is like manipulating the human element of security. Attackers use psychological tactics to deceive individuals into divulging sensitive information or taking harmful actions.

Mobile Device Exploits - The Pocket Threat: Mobile device exploits are like threats lurking in your pocket. Attackers target vulnerabilities in smartphones and tablets to compromise personal or corporate data.

Defensive Measures - Fortifying the Perimeter: Defensive measures are like fortifying the perimeter of a digital fortress. Organizations deploy firewalls, intrusion detection systems, and security policies to protect against external attacks.

Continuous Vigilance - Guarding the Gates: Just as guardians protect the gates of a fortress, continuous vigilance is essential in defending against external attack vectors. Organizations and individuals must stay informed about emerging threats and adapt their defenses accordingly.

Welcome to the world of exploiting third-party services and integrations, a realm where the boundaries of digital security extend beyond an organization's own infrastructure. Think of it as an expedition into the intricate web of interconnected technologies, where we'll unravel the intricacies of leveraging third-party services to achieve malicious objectives.

Understanding Third-Party Services and Integrations - The Digital Ecosystem: Third-party services and integrations are like bridges between islands in a vast digital archipelago. They enable organizations to extend functionality, but they also introduce potential vulnerabilities.

Importance of Third-Party Security - Strengthening the Chain: Third-party security is like reinforcing a chain; it's only as strong as its weakest link. Neglecting the security of these services can compromise an organization's entire ecosystem.

API Vulnerabilities - Keys to the Castle: API vulnerabilities are like keys to a digital castle. Attackers exploit flaws in Application Programming Interfaces to gain access, manipulate data, or carry out unauthorized actions.

OAuth and OpenID Connect Vulnerabilities - Access Control Breaches: OAuth and OpenID Connect vulnerabilities are like breaches in the access control system. Attackers exploit flaws in these authentication and authorization protocols to gain unauthorized access.

Server-Side Request Forgery (SSRF) - Manipulating Requests: SSRF is like a magician's trick, manipulating requests from a server to access internal resources or services, potentially bypassing security measures.

Cross-Site Request Forgery (CSRF) - Forging User Actions: CSRF is like impersonating a user's actions. Attackers trick users into performing unintended actions on a third-party service, potentially causing harm.

Insecure Deserialization - Unpacking a Malicious Gift: Insecure deserialization is like opening a potentially harmful gift. Attackers exploit weaknesses in how data is unpacked to execute arbitrary code.

Data Leaks through Misconfigured Integrations - Unintended Disclosures: Data leaks through misconfigured integrations are like accidentally sending confidential documents to the wrong recipient. Attackers can access sensitive data if integrations are not properly configured.

Supply Chain Attacks - Tainting the Ingredients: Supply chain attacks are like tainting the ingredients of a trusted recipe. Attackers compromise third-party suppliers or dependencies, spreading malicious code or vulnerabilities.

Exploiting Cloud Services - Shifting the Battlefield: Exploiting cloud services is like shifting the battlefield to an opponent's territory. Attackers target misconfigured cloud resources or services to compromise data or infrastructure.

Malicious Plugins and Extensions - Trojan Horses: Malicious plugins and extensions are like Trojan horses hiding in plain sight. Attackers create seemingly useful add-ons that contain malicious code, compromising user data or system integrity.

Data Interception in Transit - Eavesdropping on the Conversation: Data interception in transit is like eavesdropping on a conversation. Attackers intercept data exchanged between a user and a third-party service, potentially accessing sensitive information.

Data Exfiltration through Integrations - Unauthorized Data Flow: Data exfiltration through integrations is like an unauthorized data flow. Attackers use integrations to siphon off data to external destinations without detection.

API Rate Limiting Bypass - Overwhelming Defenses: API rate limiting bypass is like overwhelming a security guard. Attackers manipulate API requests to bypass rate limits and flood services with malicious traffic.

Credential Harvesting - Gathering Keys: Credential harvesting is like gathering keys to a treasure chest. Attackers trick users or third-party services into revealing usernames and passwords.

Integration Vulnerability Scanning - Detecting Weak Links: Integration vulnerability scanning is like a security patrol. Organizations use tools to identify vulnerabilities in third-party integrations and services.

Authentication and Authorization Reviews - Gatekeeping Inspection: Authentication and authorization reviews are like inspecting gatekeepers. Organizations assess how third-party services handle access control and permissions.

Continuous Monitoring - Guarding the Perimeter: Continuous monitoring is like standing guard at the perimeter. Organizations vigilantly watch third-party integrations and services for signs of compromise.

Incident Response Planning - Swift Action: Incident response planning is like a well-rehearsed emergency protocol. Organizations prepare to respond swiftly to security incidents involving third-party services.

Ethical Hacking - Proactive Defense: Ethical hacking is like hiring a friendly intruder. Organizations conduct authorized penetration testing to identify vulnerabilities in their third-party services.

Vendor Risk Management - Partnering with Security: Vendor risk management is like ensuring your allies are battle-ready. Organizations assess and manage the security posture of third-party service providers.

Collaboration for Security - United Defense: Collaboration for security is like forming alliances. Organizations work with third-party providers to strengthen mutual defenses against common threats.

In summary, exploiting third-party services and integrations is a complex dance between security and convenience. Understanding the intricacies of these digital connections is vital, as they can be both the keys to unlocking new capabilities and the vulnerabilities that attackers seek to exploit. Organizations must navigate this landscape carefully, maintaining a strong defense while reaping the benefits of a connected digital ecosystem.

Chapter 10: Penetration Testing Reporting and Remediation

Welcome to the world of comprehensive report writing, where we will delve into the art of conveying the intricacies of cybersecurity assessments effectively. Think of report writing as the bridge that connects the technical details of your assessments with the understanding of stakeholders who need to make informed decisions.

The Purpose of Cybersecurity Reports - Crafting a Narrative: Cybersecurity reports serve as a narrative, translating complex technical findings into actionable insights for decision-makers.

Understanding Your Audience - Tailoring the Message: To write a comprehensive report, you must understand your audience, whether they are technical experts, executives, or compliance officers.

Report Structure - Building a Foundation: A well-structured report is like a well-constructed building, with each section serving a specific purpose in conveying your assessment's findings.

Executive Summary - The Bird's-Eye View: The executive summary is like the bird's-eye view of a landscape, providing a concise overview of the assessment's key findings, risks, and recommendations.

Methodology - Unveiling the Process: The methodology section is like a map of your journey, explaining how the assessment was conducted, the tools and techniques used, and the scope of the assessment.

Scope and Objectives - Defining Boundaries: Defining the scope and objectives is like setting the boundaries of a game;

it helps stakeholders understand what was assessed and what wasn't.

Findings and Vulnerabilities - The Heart of the Matter: The findings and vulnerabilities section is like the heart of your report, detailing the security weaknesses, misconfigurations, and vulnerabilities discovered during the assessment.

Risk Assessment - Gauging Impact and Likelihood: Risk assessment is like predicting the weather; it combines the potential impact and likelihood of vulnerabilities to provide a risk score.

Recommendations - Providing Solutions: Recommendations are like offering an umbrella on a rainy day; they provide actionable steps to mitigate identified risks and improve security.

Technical Details - For the Experts: Technical details are like the inner workings of a machine; they provide in-depth information for technical teams on how to reproduce and remediate vulnerabilities.

Appendices - Supporting Evidence: Appendices are like the reference section of a book; they contain supporting evidence, such as logs, screenshots, or additional documentation.

Visual Aids - Clarifying Complexity: Visual aids, like diagrams and charts, are the illustrators of your report, making complex concepts easier to understand.

Writing Style - Clear and Concise: The writing style should be clear and concise, avoiding jargon or overly technical language to ensure that the report is accessible to all stakeholders.

Grammar and Proofreading - Polishing Your Work: Just as you would polish a gemstone, grammar and proofreading ensure that your report is free from errors and inconsistencies.

Timeliness - A Matter of Urgency: Timeliness is crucial in report writing, as delivering the report promptly ensures that stakeholders can take immediate action to address security issues.

Feedback and Iteration - Continuous Improvement: Gathering feedback and iteratively improving your report-writing skills is like honing a craft; it leads to more effective communication.

Legal and Ethical Considerations - Navigating the Waters: Reporting vulnerabilities and security issues must be done in a legal and ethical manner, following responsible disclosure practices.

Reporting Standards - Meeting Expectations: Adhering to reporting standards, such as those outlined by industry bodies or regulatory agencies, ensures that your reports meet expectations.

Post-Assessment Communication - Beyond the Report: Effective communication after delivering the report is essential, as it allows for clarification, additional context, and addressing any questions.

Follow-Up and Remediation - Ensuring Action: Following up on the report's recommendations and verifying that remediation efforts are underway is crucial for closing the loop.

Documentation Retention - A Record of Actions: Maintaining records of the assessment and report is like keeping a diary of your journey; it provides a historical perspective and documentation of actions taken.

Continuous Learning - Evolving Skills: Report writing is a skill that evolves over time; staying up-to-date with the latest best practices and learning from each assessment is essential.

In summary, comprehensive report writing is not just about conveying technical findings; it's about translating those findings into a language that stakeholders can understand and act upon. It's a crucial skill in the world of cybersecurity, where effective communication can make the difference between addressing vulnerabilities and leaving them unattended.

Welcome to the realm of effective remediation strategies, a critical component of cybersecurity that's all about turning vulnerabilities into strengths. Imagine it as the process of fortifying a castle after discovering weaknesses in its defenses—only in this case, the castle is your digital infrastructure, and the vulnerabilities are the chinks in your armor.

Effective remediation starts with a thorough understanding of the vulnerabilities you've uncovered during your security assessments. These vulnerabilities are like cracks in the walls of your castle, and to defend against potential attacks, you need to address them strategically.

Prioritization is Key: Not all vulnerabilities are created equal. Some are more critical than others, and prioritizing them is like sorting your tasks by importance. You need to tackle the most critical vulnerabilities first to mitigate the highest risks.

Patch Management: Patching vulnerabilities is like fixing those cracks in the castle walls. Applying security patches and updates to your systems and software is one of the most effective ways to remediate known vulnerabilities.

Configuration Management: Properly configuring your systems and applications is like reinforcing your castle's defenses. Misconfigurations can create vulnerabilities, so ensuring that everything is set up securely is crucial.

Change Control: Implementing change control processes is like guarding the castle gates. Unauthorized changes can introduce vulnerabilities, so having strict controls in place is essential.

Password Management: Strengthening password policies is like fortifying the castle's password-protected gates. Weak or easily guessable passwords can lead to unauthorized access.

User Education and Awareness: Educating your users about security best practices is like training your castle's guards. Users play a crucial role in security, and they need to be aware of potential risks.

Access Control: Restricting access to sensitive data and systems is like putting locks on the most valuable treasures in your castle. Only authorized personnel should have access to critical resources.

Network Segmentation: Segmenting your network is like creating different layers of defense within your castle. If an attacker breaches one segment, they shouldn't have free access to the entire network.

Vulnerability Scanning and Assessment: Regularly scanning for vulnerabilities is like sending scouts to check for weaknesses. Continuous assessment helps you stay aware of potential vulnerabilities as they arise.

Penetration Testing: Performing penetration tests is like simulating an attack on your castle. It helps you identify vulnerabilities that might not be apparent through automated scans.

Incident Response Planning: Having an incident response plan in place is like having a blueprint for how to react when your castle is under attack. It ensures that you can respond swiftly and effectively to security incidents.

Security Policies and Procedures: Establishing security policies and procedures is like creating a code of conduct for your castle's residents. Everyone should know the rules and how to follow them.

Monitoring and Logging: Monitoring your systems and keeping logs is like having surveillance cameras in your castle. It allows you to detect and investigate suspicious activities.

Endpoint Security: Ensuring that endpoint devices are secure is like securing all the doors and windows of your castle. Endpoints are common targets for attackers.

Data Encryption: Encrypting sensitive data is like putting your treasures in a locked safe. Even if an attacker gains access, they can't easily decipher the information.

Backup and Disaster Recovery: Having backup and disaster recovery plans in place is like having a contingency plan for when your castle faces a catastrophe. It ensures you can recover from data loss or system failures.

Third-Party Risk Management: Managing the security of third-party vendors is like ensuring your castle's allies are trustworthy. You need to assess and monitor their security practices.

Security Awareness Training: Providing security awareness training for your staff is like teaching them how to use their weapons effectively. They need to know how to defend against threats.

Regular Security Audits: Conducting regular security audits is like periodically inspecting your castle's defenses. It helps you identify vulnerabilities and weaknesses that may have been missed.

Regulatory Compliance: Meeting regulatory compliance requirements is like adhering to the laws of the land where your castle is located. Non-compliance can result in penalties.

Continuous Improvement: Just as you would fortify your castle over time to adapt to new threats, continuous improvement is key in cybersecurity. Stay up-to-date with the latest threats and remediation strategies.

Documentation and Reporting: Documenting your remediation efforts and reporting on your progress is like keeping a journal of your castle's security history. It helps you track your successes and areas for improvement.

In summary, effective remediation strategies are the actions you take to strengthen your cybersecurity defenses after identifying vulnerabilities. It's an ongoing process that requires vigilance and adaptability, much like maintaining a castle in a changing world. By prioritizing, planning, and executing these strategies, you can significantly reduce your organization's security risks and better protect your digital assets.

BOOK 3
ADVANCED GRAY HAT EXPLOITS
BEYOND THE BASICS

ROB BOTWRIGHT

Chapter 1: Mastering Zero-Day Exploits

Welcome to the intriguing world of zero-day exploits, where we dive deep into the very cutting edge of cybersecurity vulnerabilities and attacks. Zero-day exploits are like the secret passages and hidden traps within the labyrinth of digital systems, and understanding them is like holding the key to unlocking these hidden mysteries.

To begin, let's demystify what a zero-day exploit truly is. Think of it as a secret recipe for a potent potion in the world of hacking. A zero-day exploit targets a vulnerability in software or hardware that is not known to the vendor or the public. This means it's a vulnerability that has zero days of protection, hence the name.

Now, why are zero-day exploits so coveted in the world of cyber attackers? Picture them as prized treasures in a treasure hunt. Possessing a zero-day exploit gives attackers a significant advantage because they can target systems that are unaware of the vulnerability, making them incredibly difficult to defend against.

The life cycle of a zero-day exploit begins with its discovery. It's like finding a rare gem in the vast world of software. Hackers or security researchers stumble upon these vulnerabilities through extensive testing or by sheer luck.

Once a zero-day vulnerability is identified, it's like having a secret weapon at your disposal. The discoverer can choose to exploit it for malicious purposes, sell it on the black market, or, in an ethical context, report it to the software vendor for patching.

The term "zero-day" doesn't imply that the vulnerability will remain a secret forever. Think of it more like an eclipse; there's a brief period when the vulnerability is in the shadows before it's revealed to the world. During this time, it's a potent weapon in the wrong hands.

The process of crafting a zero-day exploit is akin to an artisan creating a masterpiece. It involves deep knowledge of the vulnerable software or hardware, as well as the operating system it runs on. Attackers meticulously craft their exploit code to target the specific vulnerability.

To deliver a zero-day exploit, attackers often use clever tactics, like sending phishing emails or exploiting other known vulnerabilities to gain initial access. It's like an art thief sneaking into a museum to steal a masterpiece.

Once the attacker gains access, they unleash the zero-day exploit. It's like the grand reveal of a magician's trick. The exploit code takes advantage of the vulnerability, granting the attacker control over the system.

From there, it's like the attacker having a key to the kingdom. They can steal sensitive data, plant malware, or move laterally through a network, all while remaining undetected because the vulnerability is unknown to defenders.

Zero-day exploits can have far-reaching consequences. Picture it like a single spark that ignites a forest fire. Attacks using zero-days can lead to data breaches, financial losses, and even national security threats.

Defending against zero-day exploits is akin to fortifying a castle with unknown vulnerabilities. Organizations employ various strategies, including robust patch management, intrusion detection systems, and threat intelligence, to minimize their exposure.

Ethical hackers also play a crucial role in this ecosystem. They hunt for zero-day vulnerabilities in a responsible manner, disclosing them to vendors for patching. It's like a group of friendly treasure hunters helping secure the digital landscape.

The cat-and-mouse game between attackers and defenders in the realm of zero-day exploits is unending. Hackers continue to search for undiscovered vulnerabilities, while defenders work tirelessly to stay one step ahead.

In summary, zero-day exploits are the enigmatic jewels of the cybercriminal underworld. They represent the ever-evolving nature of cybersecurity, where both attackers and defenders strive to outwit each other in an ongoing battle for digital supremacy. Understanding the fundamentals of zero-day exploits is a crucial step in this complex and ever-changing landscape.

Welcome to the fascinating world of zero-day exploit development and mitigation, where we explore the intricate art of crafting digital weaponry and the measures taken to shield our digital realms from these invisible threats. Imagine it as a grand chess match in the cyber domain, where attackers and defenders strategize their moves meticulously. Zero-day exploits, as we've previously discussed, are like the crown jewels of the hacking realm. They target vulnerabilities in software or hardware that are unknown to the public, granting attackers unprecedented access and control. Now, let's delve deeper into the two sides of this coin: development and mitigation.

Developing a zero-day exploit is akin to being a blacksmith forging a sword. It requires a deep understanding of the target software or hardware, as well as the vulnerability itself. Hackers must meticulously craft their exploit code to take advantage of this hidden weakness.

The process begins with vulnerability discovery. It's like finding a hidden passage in a castle's labyrinth. Hackers, security researchers, or even state-sponsored actors invest time and effort into locating these digital chinks in the armor.

Once a vulnerability is unearthed, it's like discovering buried treasure. The exploit developer holds a powerful secret, but the ethical path is to report it to the software vendor for patching. However, not all choose this path, and some decide to harness this newfound power for nefarious purposes.

Crafting an exploit is akin to composing a symphony. It involves writing code that can trigger the vulnerability and allow the attacker to gain control over the targeted system. This code must be stealthy, reliable, and tailored to the specific vulnerability.

The next step is delivery, much like a magician's trick. Attackers must find a way to get their exploit onto the victim's system. This often involves social engineering, phishing emails, or exploiting other known vulnerabilities as entry points.

Once the exploit is unleashed, it's like opening Pandora's box. The attacker gains a foothold on the victim's system and can execute malicious actions, all while remaining hidden in the shadows.

Now, let's shift our focus to mitigation, the defender's side of the equation. Picture it as a fortress defending against an invisible, ever-evolving threat.

The first line of defense is awareness. Organizations must constantly scan for vulnerabilities within their digital walls. It's like having watchtowers that keep an eye on the horizon for potential threats.

Patch management is crucial, much like repairing cracks in a castle's walls. Software vendors release patches to fix known vulnerabilities. Promptly applying these patches is the digital equivalent of shoring up defenses.

Intrusion detection systems act as sentinels, watching for any signs of intrusion. They're like vigilant guards patrolling the castle grounds, ready to sound the alarm at the slightest hint of danger.

Threat intelligence is the knowledge gathered from the frontlines of the digital battlefield. It's like having spies in the enemy's camp, providing valuable information about emerging threats and tactics.

User education is essential, just as knights must be trained to wield their swords. Teaching employees about security best practices and how to spot potential threats helps fortify the human element of defense.

Access control is like guarding the castle gates. Restricting access to sensitive areas ensures that only those with proper authorization can enter.

Network segmentation divides the digital realm into distinct zones, much like creating layers of defense within the castle walls. If one area is breached, it doesn't necessarily grant access to the entire network.

Encryption is like locking valuable treasures in a vault. Even if an attacker gains access, the information remains unreadable without the encryption key.

Incident response plans are the blueprints for reacting to an attack. They're like having a well-drilled army ready to defend the castle in times of crisis.

Security audits are akin to conducting regular inspections of the castle's defenses. They help identify vulnerabilities and weaknesses that may have been overlooked.

The ever-evolving landscape of zero-day exploits requires constant vigilance. It's like defending a castle against an enemy that adapts and evolves with each assault.

Ethical hackers play a crucial role in this ongoing battle. They're like friendly spies who hunt for vulnerabilities and report them to help fortify the castle's defenses.

In summary, zero-day exploit development and mitigation represent a high-stakes game in the world of cybersecurity.

It's a dance between those who craft these potent weapons and those who strive to protect our digital realms from harm. Understanding the intricacies of both sides is vital in this ever-evolving cyber landscape.

Chapter 2: Advanced Reverse Engineering Techniques

In the realm of cybersecurity, advanced binary analysis methods are like the detective work of the digital world. They involve delving deep into the core of software programs and examining their binary code to uncover hidden secrets and vulnerabilities.

Binary code is the language that computers understand, consisting of a series of zeros and ones. It's like the DNA of software, containing instructions that dictate how a program should operate.

Advanced binary analysis is the art of dissecting this code, understanding its inner workings, and, in some cases, manipulating it to achieve specific goals. It's akin to a skilled surgeon operating on the inner mechanisms of a machine.

One fundamental technique in binary analysis is reverse engineering. Think of it as taking apart a complex machine to understand how it functions, without access to its blueprints. Reverse engineers dissect binary code to unravel the program's logic, data structures, and algorithms.

Static analysis is a critical method in this process. It's like examining the pieces of a puzzle before putting them together. Static analysis tools inspect the binary code without executing it, searching for patterns and vulnerabilities.

Dynamic analysis, on the other hand, is like observing the puzzle pieces in action. Dynamic analysis tools run the binary code in a controlled environment, monitoring its behavior and interactions with the system. This helps identify runtime issues and vulnerabilities that may not be evident through static analysis alone.

Symbolic execution takes binary analysis to a more advanced level. It's like exploring a maze by creating a map as you go.

Symbolic execution tools follow the code's execution path symbolically, deriving possible inputs and exploring various execution scenarios.

Binary instrumentation is a technique that injects code into the binary to monitor its behavior or manipulate its execution. It's like adding sensors to a machine to observe its operation. This method allows researchers to gain deeper insights into the binary's behavior.

Fuzz testing is a creative approach to binary analysis. It's like bombarding a machine with a barrage of random inputs to see how it reacts. Fuzz testers generate a wide range of inputs and observe how the binary responds, uncovering potential vulnerabilities and crashes. Another critical aspect of binary analysis is vulnerability discovery. It's like finding hidden traps in a maze. Researchers search for vulnerabilities within the binary code, aiming to identify weaknesses that could be exploited by malicious actors.

Exploit development is a fascinating branch of binary analysis. It's like crafting a key to unlock a specific door within the maze. Exploit developers create software that leverages vulnerabilities to gain unauthorized access or control over a system.

Code obfuscation is a defensive strategy that adds complexity to binary code. It's like constructing intricate riddles to protect valuable information. Obfuscation makes reverse engineering and analysis more challenging, acting as a deterrent to potential attackers.

Binary patching involves modifying binary code to fix vulnerabilities or add new features. It's like performing surgery on a living organism to improve its functionality. Patching can be a crucial step in securing software that cannot be easily updated.

Malware analysis is a specialized field within binary analysis. It's like dissecting a mysterious organism to understand its behavior and purpose. Malware analysts examine malicious binaries to uncover their functionality and potential impact.

Intrusion detection systems rely on advanced binary analysis methods to identify suspicious behavior in real-time. They're like vigilant guards who can spot subtle signs of intrusion within a digital environment.

Binary analysis plays a pivotal role in software security. It's like having a team of detectives who examine every nook and cranny of a program to ensure it's free from vulnerabilities and weaknesses.

Ethical hackers often use advanced binary analysis techniques to identify and patch vulnerabilities before malicious actors can exploit them. They're like digital superheroes, protecting the digital world from potential threats.

In summary, advanced binary analysis methods are the tools and techniques that allow us to peer into the inner workings of software, uncover vulnerabilities, and strengthen our defenses. It's a fascinating journey through the intricate world of zeros and ones, where every line of code tells a story waiting to be discovered.

Imagine you're handed a complex machine with no instruction manual, and your task is to figure out how it works - that's the essence of reverse engineering. In the realm of cybersecurity, reverse engineering is a powerful technique used to unravel the inner workings of software and hardware, ultimately to discover vulnerabilities and weaknesses that could be exploited by malicious actors.

At its core, reverse engineering is akin to solving a puzzle, where the pieces are scattered across lines of code, binary data, and machine instructions. It's the process of dissecting a software program or hardware device to gain a deep understanding of its functionality, design, and underlying vulnerabilities.

The journey often begins with binary code, the fundamental language of computers consisting of zeros and ones. Imagine this code as the DNA of software, encoding every instruction and data structure that governs a program's behavior. Reverse engineers start by examining this binary code, hoping to uncover the program's secrets.

Static analysis is a crucial technique in this process. It's like examining each puzzle piece individually before trying to fit them together. Static analysis tools scrutinize the binary code without executing it, searching for patterns, vulnerabilities, and potential weaknesses.

Dynamic analysis, on the other hand, is akin to observing the puzzle pieces in action. Dynamic analysis tools run the binary code in a controlled environment, closely monitoring its behavior and interactions with the system. This approach helps identify runtime issues and vulnerabilities that may not be evident through static analysis alone.

Symbolic execution takes reverse engineering to a more advanced level. It's like exploring a maze by creating a map as you go. Symbolic execution tools follow the code's execution path symbolically, deriving possible inputs and exploring various execution scenarios. This technique is particularly valuable for uncovering complex vulnerabilities.

Binary instrumentation is another fascinating approach in reverse engineering. It's like adding sensors to a machine to observe its operation. Binary instrumentation involves injecting code into the binary to monitor its behavior or manipulate its execution, providing researchers with deeper insights into the binary's behavior.

Fuzz testing introduces an element of creativity to the process. It's like bombarding a machine with a barrage of random inputs to see how it reacts. Fuzz testers generate a wide range of inputs and observe how the binary responds, often uncovering potential vulnerabilities, crashes, or unexpected behavior.

Reverse engineering isn't limited to uncovering vulnerabilities. It also encompasses the art of understanding a program's functionality, which is invaluable in various contexts. It's like dissecting a complex clockwork mechanism to comprehend how each gear and spring contributes to the overall function.

Code analysis tools play a pivotal role in reverse engineering. They're like a set of specialized tools in a mechanic's workshop, each serving a distinct purpose. These tools can disassemble binary code, reconstruct high-level representations, and help reverse engineers navigate through the complexity of software.

Reversing malware is a specific domain within reverse engineering. It's like examining a mysterious organism to understand its behavior and purpose. Malware analysts delve into malicious binaries, dissecting their functionality and potential impact, often with the goal of developing countermeasures.

Reverse engineering also extends to hardware devices. Imagine trying to understand the intricate components of an electronic gadget or a microchip. Hardware reverse engineers explore the physical design and the embedded software, seeking vulnerabilities or ways to modify the device's behavior.

Intrusion detection systems rely on advanced reverse engineering techniques to identify suspicious behavior in real-time. It's like having vigilant guards who can decipher the digital footprints of potential intruders within a network.

The role of reverse engineering is not limited to discovering vulnerabilities; it's also about understanding how systems and applications work. It's like peering behind the curtains of a magic show to understand the mechanics of the tricks.

Ethical hackers often employ reverse engineering to identify vulnerabilities in software or hardware before malicious actors can exploit them. They play a crucial role in fortifying digital defenses and ensuring that systems are resilient against potential threats.

In summary, reverse engineering is a fascinating journey into the heart of digital technology. It's the art of deciphering the hidden language of computers, uncovering vulnerabilities, and understanding how the digital world operates. Whether for discovering weaknesses or unraveling the mysteries of software and hardware, reverse engineering is a powerful tool in the arsenal of cybersecurity professionals.

Chapter 3: Rootkit Development and Deployment

Rootkit design and architecture are essential topics in the realm of cybersecurity, as they delve into the intricate world of covert software that seeks to evade detection and maintain unauthorized access to a computer or network.

Imagine rootkits as the stealthy spies of the digital world, lurking in the shadows of a system, and manipulating its behavior without the user's knowledge or consent. Understanding their design and architecture is akin to deciphering the blueprints of a hidden passage within a fortress.

Rootkits often operate at a deep level within an operating system, taking advantage of their privileged position to remain hidden and exert control. It's like infiltrating the inner chambers of a castle to control its defenses from within.

Kernel-level rootkits are among the most sophisticated, as they embed themselves within the core of the operating system, known as the kernel. They manipulate system calls and intercept data at a fundamental level. Think of them as secret agents with direct access to the king's council.

User-mode rootkits operate at a higher layer, manipulating application program interfaces (APIs) and system libraries. They're like spies who gather information from the courtiers and servants, subtly influencing the king's decisions.

Rootkits are often categorized based on their persistence mechanisms. Some rootkits are memory-resident, meaning they exist only in the volatile memory of a computer and vanish upon reboot, leaving no trace. They're like ghosts that haunt the system temporarily.

File-based rootkits, on the other hand, embed themselves within system files or replace legitimate files with malicious counterparts. They're like impostors who disguise themselves as trusted advisors to the king.

Library rootkits manipulate system libraries and dynamic link libraries (DLLs) to alter the behavior of applications. They're like forgers who create counterfeit documents, fooling the king's bureaucracy.

In terms of architecture, rootkits often follow a modular approach. They consist of multiple components, each with a specific function. These components work together like a well-coordinated spy network.

The loader component is like the mastermind who initiates the rootkit's installation and activation. It's responsible for injecting the rootkit into the system.

The cloaking component is the expert in disguise. It's like the spy who dons different identities to move undetected. The cloaking component conceals the rootkit's presence, altering system data structures and API calls to hide its activities.

The communication component is the messenger, allowing the rootkit to send and receive instructions covertly. It's like the secret agent who communicates with the enemy without raising suspicion.

The payload component carries out the rootkit's main mission, whether it's data theft, unauthorized access, or some other malicious activity. It's like the spy who executes the actual operation behind enemy lines.

The rootkit's architecture is often designed with flexibility in mind, allowing it to adapt to different environments and evade detection. It's like a chameleon that changes its appearance to blend into various surroundings.

Rootkits can employ various techniques to maintain persistence. They may hide in the master boot record (MBR) of a hard drive, ensuring that they are loaded into memory every time the system starts, like a secret agent with a hidden entrance to the castle.

Some rootkits manipulate the system's boot process by replacing or modifying system files or boot loaders. They're like infiltrators who control the castle gates.

Rootkits can also use techniques such as "hooking," where they intercept and redirect system calls or API functions. This manipulation allows them to manipulate the behavior of applications and the operating system itself, all while remaining hidden.

In some cases, rootkits employ advanced evasion techniques, such as direct kernel object manipulation (DKOM), which involves altering data structures within the kernel to cover their tracks. It's like the spy who leaves false footprints to confuse pursuers.

Rootkits often have the ability to disable or circumvent security mechanisms like firewalls and antivirus software. They can manipulate these tools to prevent detection and removal, much like a spy who infiltrates the enemy's security apparatus.

Understanding rootkit design and architecture is crucial for cybersecurity professionals and ethical hackers. It's like learning the tactics of spies to defend against espionage. By comprehending how rootkits operate and the tricks they employ, defenders can develop countermeasures and protect their systems from these covert threats.

In summary, rootkits are the clandestine agents of the digital world, designed with intricate architectures to infiltrate and manipulate computer systems. Whether operating at the kernel level or in user mode, these stealthy programs remain a persistent threat. Studying their design and architecture is essential for those tasked with defending against their covert activities.

Rootkit deployment and evasion tactics are like the art of setting up a hidden base in enemy territory and making sure it stays concealed. These topics delve into the strategies and techniques used by cyber attackers to infiltrate systems, embed rootkits, and avoid detection.

Imagine a secret agent who needs to establish a covert presence in a foreign country. Rootkit deployment is similar, where attackers aim to establish a hidden foothold in a target system. This foothold provides them with a gateway to conduct malicious activities.

One common method of rootkit deployment is through malicious software or malware. Attackers may trick users into downloading and executing malicious files, often disguised as legitimate software or email attachments. Once executed, these files can install the rootkit discreetly, much like a spy who infiltrates an enemy organization under a false identity.

Social engineering plays a crucial role in rootkit deployment. Attackers may manipulate users through deceptive emails, enticing downloads, or convincing them to visit compromised websites. By exploiting human psychology and trust, they gain access to systems, much like a skilled manipulator who gains access to confidential information through charm and persuasion.

Another method of deployment involves exploiting software vulnerabilities. Attackers search for weaknesses in operating systems, applications, or plugins that can serve as entry points. Once identified, they use exploits to inject the rootkit into the system. This is akin to a burglar finding a hidden entrance into a building and exploiting it to gain access.

Rootkit deployment can also occur through the compromise of legitimate user accounts. Attackers may steal or crack user credentials, gaining access to systems without raising suspicion. Once inside, they can install rootkits, leveraging the trust associated with the compromised accounts.

The evasion aspect of rootkit deployment is where things get truly covert. Once a rootkit is in place, it's critical for attackers to ensure it remains hidden from security measures and detection efforts.

One evasion technique involves altering system calls and API functions. Rootkits can intercept these calls and modify their behavior, allowing them to hide their activities. This is like a spy who intercepts messages between enemy agents and sends misleading information.

Rootkits often employ cloaking techniques to evade detection. They manipulate system data structures and memory, making it appear as if everything is normal. This is akin to a master of disguise who blends seamlessly into a crowd, making it impossible to identify them.

To avoid detection, rootkits may employ polymorphism, a technique that changes their code and appearance each time they execute. This makes it incredibly challenging for security solutions to recognize them, like a spy who constantly changes their appearance to avoid being recognized.

Rootkits can also use encryption to hide their communications and activities. Much like encrypting secret messages, this technique makes it nearly impossible for defenders to decipher the rootkit's intentions.

Stealth mechanisms are crucial for rootkits. They often employ techniques like "rootkit hooks" to intercept and manipulate low-level system functions, ensuring they maintain control without being noticed. It's like having an insider at the highest levels of an organization, pulling strings from behind the scenes.

Rootkits can even manipulate the behavior of security software. They may disable or manipulate antivirus programs, firewalls, or intrusion detection systems to avoid triggering alarms. This is like a spy infiltrating an enemy's security apparatus and disabling their surveillance.

Rootkit evasion extends to memory-resident rootkits, which exist only in volatile memory and vanish upon system reboot. These rootkits ensure they leave no trace, like a ghost that disappears after completing its mission.

Virtual machine detection is another evasion tactic. Rootkits can check if they're running within a virtualized environment, which is often used for security testing. If detected, they may behave differently to avoid analysis, much like a spy who changes tactics when they suspect they're under surveillance.

In summary, rootkit deployment and evasion tactics are like the strategies employed by covert agents in the world of cyberattacks. Attackers use various methods to install rootkits, from exploiting vulnerabilities to social engineering. Once deployed, rootkits employ sophisticated techniques to remain hidden from security measures, much like spies who constantly adapt and evade detection. Understanding these tactics is essential for cybersecurity professionals defending against rootkit threats.

Chapter 4: Privilege Escalation Strategies

Privilege escalation techniques are akin to the strategies employed by a determined individual seeking to gain access to restricted areas within a fortress, moving from the outer chambers to the inner sanctum. In the realm of cybersecurity, these techniques revolve around exploiting vulnerabilities and weaknesses within a computer system or network to elevate one's privileges and gain unauthorized access.

Picture a castle with multiple layers of security. The lowest level, or the outermost chamber, is where regular users dwell. They have limited access and privileges, much like common citizens in a kingdom. Privilege escalation aims to break through these barriers and reach the inner chambers, where the most valuable assets and information are stored.

One common privilege escalation technique involves exploiting software vulnerabilities. Just like finding a hidden passage in the castle walls, attackers search for weaknesses in operating systems, applications, or plugins. Once they identify these vulnerabilities, they employ exploits to bypass security measures and gain elevated privileges.

User misconfiguration is another entry point. Attackers may exploit mistakes made by users, such as weak passwords or improperly configured access controls. It's similar to an intruder finding an unlocked door or a guard who accidentally leaves a gate open.

Social engineering plays a crucial role in privilege escalation. Attackers often manipulate individuals within an organization, convincing them to reveal sensitive information or perform actions that grant elevated privileges. This is like a skilled con artist who gains access to exclusive areas by deceiving the guards.

Privilege escalation can also involve exploiting misconfigured or vulnerable hardware devices. These devices might include routers, switches, or network appliances. By compromising these devices, attackers can manipulate network traffic and gain unauthorized access, just as a spy might manipulate the mechanisms controlling access to secret passages.

Once attackers gain initial access, they seek to elevate their privileges within the system. One method is to exploit privilege escalation vulnerabilities. These are flaws in the operating system or software that, when manipulated, allow an attacker to gain higher levels of access. It's like finding a hidden lever that opens a secret door to a more privileged area of the castle.

Kernel-level privilege escalation is among the most sophisticated techniques. It involves gaining control of the operating system's kernel, which is at the core of system operations. This is akin to infiltrating the king's inner circle, with direct influence over key decisions and access to highly sensitive information.

Another technique is DLL (Dynamic Link Library) injection, which allows attackers to load malicious code into legitimate processes, effectively giving them elevated privileges within those processes. It's like planting a spy within the council chambers, with the ability to influence decisions from within.

Privilege escalation can also involve manipulating access control lists (ACLs) and permissions. Attackers may modify these settings to grant themselves higher privileges or access to restricted areas. This is like a spy who forges documents to gain entry into highly secure zones.

Exploiting weak or misconfigured service accounts is another approach. Attackers may use these accounts to move laterally within a network, elevating their privileges along the way. It's like a spy infiltrating different departments of an organization, steadily gaining access to more sensitive information.

Privilege escalation techniques are not limited to a single method. Attackers often combine multiple approaches to achieve their goals. Just as a skilled infiltrator uses a variety of techniques to navigate through a complex fortress, cybercriminals employ different methods to bypass security layers and reach their objectives.

As defenders, understanding these privilege escalation techniques is paramount. It's akin to fortifying the castle's defenses, shoring up vulnerabilities, and training guards to recognize and thwart intruders. By staying vigilant and implementing robust security measures, organizations can better protect themselves against these determined attackers.

In summary, privilege escalation techniques are the digital equivalent of breaching the inner chambers of a fortress. Attackers exploit vulnerabilities, misconfigurations, and social engineering to gain elevated privileges within a computer system or network. Understanding these techniques is crucial for cybersecurity professionals tasked with defending against such intrusions. Bypassing privilege isolation mechanisms is akin to navigating through a highly secure facility, where each room is more restricted than the last. In the realm of cybersecurity, these mechanisms are the safeguards that prevent unauthorized users or malicious software from accessing privileged resources and data.

Imagine a facility with multiple levels of access control. The outermost layer represents ordinary users, while the inner layers are increasingly secure, with restricted access to sensitive information and critical systems. Bypassing privilege isolation mechanisms aims to break through these layers, gaining access to privileged resources.

One common way to bypass these mechanisms is through exploiting software vulnerabilities. Just as a crafty intruder might find a hidden passage or tunnel into a secure building, cyber attackers seek weaknesses in software, operating systems, or applications. Once identified, they use exploits to circumvent security measures and elevate their privileges.

User misconfiguration is another entry point. Attackers may take advantage of mistakes made by users, such as weak passwords, improper access controls, or misconfigured security settings. It's like an intruder exploiting a lapse in security protocols or finding an unlocked door within the facility.

Social engineering plays a significant role in bypassing privilege isolation mechanisms. Attackers manipulate individuals within an organization, convincing them to divulge sensitive information or perform actions that grant elevated privileges. This is similar to an infiltrator deceiving security personnel or insiders into granting access.

Once initial access is gained, attackers seek to escalate their privileges within the system. One method is exploiting privilege escalation vulnerabilities. These are flaws in the operating system or software that, when manipulated, allow an attacker to gain higher levels of access. It's like finding a hidden lever that opens a door to a more privileged area within the facility.

Kernel-level privilege escalation is among the most sophisticated techniques. It involves gaining control of the operating system's kernel, which is at the core of system operations. This is akin to infiltrating the facility's central control room, with the ability to influence decisions and access critical resources.

Another technique is DLL (Dynamic Link Library) injection, which allows attackers to inject malicious code into legitimate processes, effectively granting them elevated privileges within those processes. It's like planting an undercover agent within the innermost chambers, with the capability to influence decisions from within.

Privilege escalation can also involve manipulating access control lists (ACLs) and permissions. Attackers may modify these settings to grant themselves higher privileges or access to restricted areas. This is similar to infiltrating a secure facility and tampering with access control systems.

Exploiting weak or misconfigured service accounts is another approach. Attackers may use these accounts to move laterally within a network, elevating their privileges along the way. It's like an intruder infiltrating different sections of the facility, gradually gaining access to more sensitive areas.

Bypassing privilege isolation mechanisms is not limited to a single method. Attackers often combine multiple approaches to achieve their goals. Just as a determined intruder uses various techniques to navigate through a secure facility, cybercriminals employ different methods to bypass security layers and reach their objectives.

As defenders, understanding these privilege isolation bypass techniques is crucial. It's akin to reinforcing the layers of security within the facility, identifying vulnerabilities, and training security personnel to recognize and thwart intruders. By staying vigilant and implementing robust security measures, organizations can better protect themselves against these determined attackers.

In summary, bypassing privilege isolation mechanisms is the digital equivalent of breaking through secure layers within a facility. Attackers exploit vulnerabilities, misconfigurations, and social engineering to gain elevated privileges and access privileged resources. Understanding these techniques is essential for cybersecurity professionals tasked with defending against such intrusions.

Chapter 5: Exploiting Advanced Web Application Vulnerabilities

In-depth web application vulnerability analysis is like peeling back the layers of an onion to reveal its innermost core. When it comes to cybersecurity, this process involves a meticulous examination of a web application's code, architecture, and functionalities to identify and mitigate vulnerabilities that could be exploited by malicious actors.

Think of a web application as a complex, interconnected system, much like a well-designed machine with numerous moving parts. These parts are the code, databases, server configurations, and user interfaces that make the application work. Just as an engineer would thoroughly inspect a machine to ensure its optimal performance, cybersecurity professionals delve deep into web applications to find and fix potential security flaws.

The first step in this process is a comprehensive understanding of the web application. It's like studying the blueprint of a machine to understand how it's designed and how its components interact. Security experts scrutinize the application's architecture, data flow, and functionality to gain insights into its inner workings.

Next comes the examination of the code. This is akin to inspecting the intricate machinery within the machine. Security professionals review the source code of the web application to identify vulnerabilities such as SQL injection, cross-site scripting (XSS), and other common issues. They look for coding errors, insecure dependencies, and potential entry points for attackers.

Authentication mechanisms are a critical focus during web application vulnerability analysis. Just as the safety features of a machine must be checked to ensure they work as intended, cybersecurity experts verify that user authentication and authorization processes are robust. They assess whether the application properly verifies user identities, enforces access controls, and prevents unauthorized access.

Data storage and handling within the application are also examined closely. This is like scrutinizing the storage and handling of materials within a machine. Security experts assess how sensitive data, such as user credentials and personal information, is stored, transmitted, and protected. They look for encryption practices and assess the resilience of data against breaches.

Input validation is a crucial aspect of web application vulnerability analysis. Just as a machine's input mechanisms must be inspected for defects, cybersecurity professionals assess how the application handles user inputs. They scrutinize how the application sanitizes and validates input data to prevent attacks like SQL injection and XSS.

Web application security experts also pay attention to session management. This is similar to monitoring the controls that manage and regulate the operation of a machine. They examine how user sessions are established, maintained, and terminated, ensuring that session tokens are secure and cannot be hijacked.

Web APIs (Application Programming Interfaces) are integral components of many modern web applications. Just as the interfaces of a machine must be checked for vulnerabilities, cybersecurity professionals assess the security of APIs. They look for improper authentication, access control issues, and data exposure through APIs.

The threat landscape is dynamic, and new vulnerabilities emerge regularly. Security experts stay updated on the latest security threats and vulnerabilities, similar to keeping an eye on evolving challenges in maintaining a machine's functionality. They apply patches and updates to address known vulnerabilities and proactively identify and mitigate emerging risks.

During in-depth web application vulnerability analysis, security professionals often use automated scanning tools, like X-ray machines for inspecting internal components of a machine. These tools help identify common vulnerabilities quickly, but manual inspection is also crucial to catch nuanced issues that automated tools might miss.

Finally, documentation and reporting are essential components of the analysis process. Just as a machine's maintenance records are maintained, cybersecurity experts document their findings, vulnerabilities discovered, and recommendations for remediation. This documentation helps developers and organizations address security issues effectively.

In summary, in-depth web application vulnerability analysis involves a meticulous examination of a web application's code, architecture, and functionality to identify and mitigate potential vulnerabilities. It is a process that resembles the careful inspection of a complex machine, with a focus on understanding, securing, and maintaining the application's security posture.

Exploring advanced techniques for web application exploitation is like embarking on a journey into the heart of cyberspace, where the battle between defenders and attackers plays out in the digital realm. These advanced techniques go beyond the basics and require a deeper understanding of web application vulnerabilities, coding intricacies, and the art of exploiting weaknesses.

Imagine web applications as intricate puzzles, each with unique vulnerabilities waiting to be discovered and manipulated. Advanced web application exploitation is about mastering the skills to solve these puzzles efficiently and effectively, uncovering the hidden treasures of information or control.

At the heart of advanced web application exploitation lies an in-depth knowledge of common vulnerabilities, such as SQL injection, Cross-Site Scripting (XSS), and Cross-Site Request Forgery (CSRF). These vulnerabilities serve as entry points into the application's inner workings, much like secret passages into a fortress.

SQL injection, for instance, involves manipulating the application's database queries to gain unauthorized access to sensitive data. Advanced practitioners go beyond the basic 'OR 1=1' payloads and delve into blind SQL injection, time-based attacks, and out-of-band techniques, like exploiting DNS queries, to extract data stealthily.

Cross-Site Scripting (XSS) allows attackers to inject malicious scripts into web pages viewed by other users, potentially stealing their data or session tokens. Advanced exploitation involves crafting complex payloads, evading security filters, and leveraging DOM-based XSS to manipulate client-side scripts.

Cross-Site Request Forgery (CSRF) enables attackers to trick authenticated users into performing actions without their consent. Advanced techniques involve crafting convincing CSRF attacks, targeting specific functionality, and bypassing anti-CSRF tokens through various means.

Beyond these foundational vulnerabilities, advanced practitioners explore less common but equally potent attack vectors. File inclusion vulnerabilities, for instance, allow attackers to include malicious files or code on the server, potentially leading to full compromise. Exploiting these vulnerabilities requires a deep understanding of file system structures and application logic.

Similarly, XML External Entity (XXE) attacks target the parsing of XML input, potentially leading to information disclosure or remote code execution. Advanced exploitation involves crafting malicious XML payloads, evading filters, and leveraging external entities for data exfiltration.

Another advanced technique is Server-Side Request Forgery (SSRF), where attackers manipulate the server into making requests to internal or external resources. This can lead to data exposure, remote code execution, or reconnaissance of internal networks.

Authentication bypass techniques are crucial in advanced web application exploitation. Skilled attackers look for weak password policies, account lockout mechanisms, and session management flaws to gain unauthorized access. They may also exploit password reset functionality to compromise accounts.

Web application firewalls (WAFs) and other security measures often stand in the way of exploitation. Advanced practitioners employ evasion techniques, such as encoding payloads, obfuscating malicious code, and fragmenting requests, to bypass these defenses.

Client-side attacks, like DOM-based exploitation, require a deep understanding of JavaScript and browser behavior. Advanced practitioners craft sophisticated payloads, exploit complex DOM structures, and manipulate client-side logic to achieve their objectives.

Once access is gained, maintaining persistence within the compromised application is essential. Advanced attackers use techniques like backdoors, web shells, and privilege escalation to ensure continued access and control.

Social engineering and user interaction play a significant role in advanced web application exploitation. Attackers may trick users into performing actions that benefit the attacker, such as clicking on malicious links or downloading malicious files.

Beyond the technical aspects, advanced practitioners often engage in reconnaissance and information gathering to identify potential targets and vulnerabilities. This may involve OSINT (Open Source Intelligence) techniques, scanning for exposed services, and profiling target organizations.

Finally, responsible disclosure and ethical considerations are vital in advanced web application exploitation. Skilled practitioners understand the importance of reporting vulnerabilities to organizations and working collaboratively to address them.

In summary, advanced techniques for web application exploitation involve a deep understanding of vulnerabilities, coding intricacies, and the art of manipulating weaknesses. It's a journey into the complex world of cyber threats, where attackers continuously refine their skills to uncover hidden treasures of information or control within web applications.

Chapter 6: Advanced Network-Based Attacks

Advanced network reconnaissance is like becoming a digital detective, equipped with specialized tools and techniques to uncover hidden information about target networks and systems. It's a crucial phase in the world of cybersecurity, where thorough investigation and meticulous data gathering are key to understanding the terrain you're about to navigate.

Imagine network reconnaissance as the process of exploring an unfamiliar city before planning your journey. It involves gathering valuable information about the target network, such as its structure, connected devices, and potential vulnerabilities. This phase allows cybersecurity professionals to make informed decisions and develop effective strategies for securing or penetrating the network.

One fundamental aspect of advanced network reconnaissance is passive reconnaissance. It's similar to quietly observing a city from a distance, without leaving any trace. In the digital realm, passive reconnaissance involves collecting publicly available information about the target network, such as domain names, IP addresses, and subdomains. This information is often found on websites, social media profiles, or in DNS records.

Active reconnaissance, on the other hand, is like sending out scouts to gather information more directly. This phase involves using various scanning tools and techniques to discover live hosts, open ports, and services running on the target network. It's like identifying the entry points and gates of a city by probing its infrastructure.

Port scanning is a critical aspect of active reconnaissance. It's akin to knocking on different doors in a city to see which ones are open. Cybersecurity professionals use port scanning tools to determine which ports on a target system are listening for incoming connections. This information helps them understand the services running on those ports, which can be crucial for identifying vulnerabilities.

Service enumeration goes hand in hand with port scanning. It's like learning about the businesses operating behind those doors you've identified. During service enumeration, security experts gather information about the specific services and their versions running on open ports. This knowledge is vital for pinpointing potential vulnerabilities or misconfigurations.

Operating system fingerprinting is another component of active reconnaissance. It's akin to identifying the native language spoken in the city. Cybersecurity professionals use fingerprinting techniques to determine the type and version of the operating system running on target systems. This information helps in tailoring attacks or defenses to the specific environment.

Beyond identifying hosts and services, advanced reconnaissance extends to vulnerability scanning. This phase is like inspecting the structural integrity of a city's buildings. Vulnerability scanners are employed to identify potential weaknesses in the target systems, such as missing patches, misconfigurations, or known vulnerabilities that could be exploited by attackers.

One critical aspect of advanced network reconnaissance is the gathering of network maps and topological information. It's like creating a detailed map of a city, highlighting its roads, intersections, and landmarks. Cybersecurity professionals aim to understand the layout of the target network, including its subnets, routers, and connected devices. This knowledge is invaluable for planning an attack or designing network defenses.

DNS enumeration is a crucial technique in reconnaissance, similar to understanding the street signs and addresses in a city. It involves querying DNS servers to gather information about the target network's domain names, subdomains, and associated IP addresses. This information can reveal additional entry points and assets.

Web reconnaissance focuses on gathering information related to web applications and services. It's like exploring the businesses and services offered in a city. Cybersecurity professionals search for web applications, directories, and hidden resources that may contain sensitive information or vulnerabilities. Techniques like spidering, directory brute-forcing, and web scraping are used to discover these assets.

Advanced reconnaissance also involves exploring cloud-based resources and third-party services. In the modern digital landscape, organizations often rely on cloud providers and external services. Cybersecurity professionals need to identify these dependencies and assess their security posture, as they can be potential points of entry or compromise.

Throughout the reconnaissance phase, it's essential to remain stealthy and avoid raising suspicion. Just as a detective would work undercover, cybersecurity professionals employ techniques to minimize their footprint, such as using proxy servers, rotating IP addresses, and conducting reconnaissance during off-peak hours.

In summary, advanced network reconnaissance is a meticulous process of gathering information about a target network, similar to exploring an unfamiliar city before planning a journey. It involves both passive and active techniques, such as port scanning, service enumeration, vulnerability scanning, and web reconnaissance. This phase is critical for cybersecurity professionals to understand the target's infrastructure, identify potential vulnerabilities, and make informed decisions in the ever-evolving landscape of digital threats. Advanced network exploitation techniques are akin to mastering the art of unlocking the doors to a fortress, where digital fortresses are networks protected by layers of security measures. In this realm of cybersecurity, experts delve deep into the intricate craft of exploiting vulnerabilities, infiltrating systems, and gaining unauthorized access to target networks.

Think of network exploitation as a digital cat-and-mouse game, where attackers continuously evolve their techniques while defenders fortify their systems. In this dynamic landscape, advanced practitioners are the ones who push the boundaries, thinking creatively and strategically to outsmart the defenses. One foundational aspect of advanced network exploitation is the understanding of common attack vectors. It's like learning the various techniques that can be used to breach a fortress, such as exploiting software vulnerabilities, manipulating user behavior, or bypassing authentication mechanisms.

Vulnerability exploitation is a core component of network exploitation. It's akin to finding a crack in the fortress wall and exploiting it to gain entry. Advanced practitioners meticulously analyze vulnerabilities in software, operating systems, or configurations and develop exploits that take advantage of these weaknesses. These exploits can range from simple buffer overflows to more sophisticated zero-day exploits. Privilege escalation is another critical area of network exploitation. It's like ascending from the lower levels of a fortress to its inner chambers. Advanced attackers seek ways to escalate their privileges on compromised systems, often starting with low-level access and aiming to gain administrative or root-level control. This can involve exploiting misconfigurations, weak permissions, or vulnerabilities in the privilege management system.

Lateral movement is a strategy akin to navigating the interconnected rooms and corridors of a fortress. Advanced attackers aim to move laterally within a network, searching for valuable assets or additional targets. Techniques like pass-the-hash, pass-the-ticket, or Kerberoasting are used to compromise other systems within the network.

Persistence is essential in advanced network exploitation. It's like leaving behind hidden passages within the fortress for future access. Skilled attackers employ various techniques to maintain their presence within compromised systems, such as implanting backdoors, creating user accounts, or setting up scheduled tasks for continued access.

Network exploitation often involves the manipulation of network traffic. It's like altering the signs and signals within the fortress to confuse defenders. Techniques like ARP spoofing, DNS spoofing, or man-in-the-middle attacks are used to intercept and manipulate network communications, potentially allowing attackers to eavesdrop, modify, or redirect traffic.

Social engineering plays a significant role in network exploitation. It's like convincing the guards at the fortress gates to let you in. Advanced attackers use social engineering techniques to manipulate human behavior, tricking users or administrators into revealing sensitive information, clicking on malicious links, or executing malicious code.

Advanced network exploitation is not limited to traditional networked systems. It extends to the cloud, where attackers target cloud-based resources, virtual environments, and containerized applications. Techniques like container breakout, cloud service misconfigurations, or exploiting weak access controls in cloud environments are part of this evolving landscape.

Zero-day exploits are the crown jewels of advanced network exploitation. These are like the secret keys to unlock previously unknown vulnerabilities in software or systems. Developing zero-day exploits requires deep technical expertise and an understanding of the inner workings of the target. Advanced attackers may discover and weaponize zero-days or acquire them from the thriving underground market.

Evasion and anti-forensics techniques are critical for advanced network exploitation. It's like leaving no trace of your presence in the fortress. Skilled attackers employ various tactics to evade detection by security tools and forensic investigators, such as obfuscating their code, cleaning logs, or encrypting communication.

Countermeasures and defensive strategies are continually evolving to thwart advanced network exploitation. Just as defenders strengthen the fortress's defenses, security professionals implement intrusion detection systems, endpoint protection, network segmentation, and security awareness training to mitigate the risks posed by advanced attackers.

In summary, advanced network exploitation is a dynamic and ever-evolving field within cybersecurity, where practitioners employ a wide range of techniques to exploit vulnerabilities, escalate privileges, move laterally, and maintain persistence within target networks. It's a high-stakes game of cat and mouse where attackers continuously adapt and innovate, while defenders work tirelessly to fortify their digital fortresses. Mastery of these techniques requires a deep understanding of cybersecurity, programming, system internals, and a creative mindset to navigate the complex and challenging landscape of network security.

Chapter 7: Advanced Post-Exploitation Techniques

Privilege escalation in post-exploitation is a fascinating and crucial aspect of cybersecurity that involves the art of elevating one's access rights and permissions within a compromised system or network. Imagine it as gaining access to the inner chambers of a well-guarded fortress, where you start with limited access but aim to acquire the keys to the kingdom.

When an attacker successfully breaches a system or network, they often begin with low-level privileges, which may grant them access to some resources but limit their ability to perform critical actions or access sensitive data. Privilege escalation is the process of circumventing these limitations and gaining higher-level access that allows the attacker to wield more power within the compromised environment.

One common method of privilege escalation involves exploiting vulnerabilities in the operating system or software running on the compromised system. Just like finding a hidden passage within the fortress, attackers search for weaknesses in the system's defenses. These weaknesses may include software vulnerabilities, misconfigurations, or insecure permissions that can be leveraged to escalate privileges.

Another avenue for privilege escalation is through the exploitation of application-level vulnerabilities. Think of it as finding a secret entrance through a specific room within the fortress. Web applications, for example, may contain vulnerabilities like SQL injection or insecure file uploads that attackers can exploit to gain higher privileges.

Privilege escalation often involves bypassing access controls. It's akin to tricking the guards at the fortress gate into granting you access to restricted areas. Attackers may manipulate access control mechanisms, such as permissions, access control lists, or role-based access controls, to elevate their privileges.

Kernel-level privilege escalation is a more advanced technique. It's like gaining control of the fortress's central command room. In this scenario, attackers exploit vulnerabilities in the operating system's kernel, the core component that manages system resources and hardware. Kernel-level exploits are highly sought after because they provide the highest level of control over the compromised system.

Once privilege escalation is achieved, attackers can perform a wide range of malicious actions. They can access sensitive files, execute arbitrary code, manipulate system settings, install backdoors, or even take full control of the compromised system. Just as an intruder within a fortress gains increasing control over its inner workings, attackers with elevated privileges can move laterally through the network, compromise additional systems, and persistently maintain their access.

Post-exploitation privilege escalation is not limited to traditional systems. It extends to cloud environments and virtualized infrastructure. Cloud providers often offer granular control over resources, and attackers seek ways to bypass these controls to gain unauthorized access to cloud-based resources.

Countermeasures against privilege escalation in post-exploitation are essential for defenders. Just as fortress defenders reinforce gates and walls, cybersecurity professionals implement measures such as least privilege access, continuous monitoring, vulnerability patching, and intrusion detection to detect and mitigate privilege escalation attempts.

Privilege escalation is a critical concept in red teaming and penetration testing, where ethical hackers simulate attacks to identify vulnerabilities and weaknesses within an organization's security posture. By emulating the tactics of real attackers, red teams help organizations strengthen their defenses.

In summary, privilege escalation in post-exploitation is a fascinating and pivotal aspect of cybersecurity, where attackers strive to elevate their access rights and permissions within compromised systems or networks. It involves exploiting vulnerabilities, bypassing access controls, and manipulating system configurations to gain higher-level access. Successful privilege escalation grants attackers more power to perform malicious actions and move laterally through the compromised environment. Defenders must implement robust security measures to detect and mitigate these escalation attempts and protect their digital fortresses from potential intruders.

Maintaining persistence and stealth in the realm of cybersecurity is akin to becoming a silent and invisible intruder within a well-guarded fortress. Once an attacker gains initial access to a system or network, the next challenge is to establish a foothold that allows them to maintain access, even in the face of defensive measures and security checks.

Persistence, in this context, refers to the ability of an attacker to maintain access and control over a compromised system or network over an extended period. It's like leaving secret passages and hidden chambers within the fortress that only you know how to access. Persistence is crucial because it enables attackers to return to the compromised environment at will, continue their malicious activities, and potentially move laterally to compromise additional systems.

To achieve persistence, attackers often employ various techniques and tactics, and these can be as creative and resourceful as the intruder seeking to bypass fortress defenses. One common method involves planting backdoors within the compromised system. Backdoors are like hidden keys that allow the attacker to unlock and regain access even after being temporarily evicted. These backdoors can be in the form of malicious scripts, hidden user accounts, or concealed processes.

Registry modifications are another technique for maintaining persistence. In a Windows environment, for example, attackers may alter the Windows Registry to ensure that their malicious code runs each time the system boots up. It's like secretly changing the layout of the fortress gates to make sure they swing open for you every morning.

Scheduled tasks and cron jobs can be manipulated to achieve persistence. Just as the fortress guards follow a strict schedule, attackers can set up automated tasks that execute their malicious code at specified intervals. This ensures that their access is regularly renewed, even if detected and removed temporarily.

File system modifications are a more covert way of maintaining persistence. Attackers may hide their tools and malicious code within the system's file structure, making it difficult for defenders to detect and remove them. These files can be disguised as legitimate system files or hidden within obscure directories.

Kernel-level rootkits are like secret societies operating within the fortress's governing body. Advanced attackers may go to great lengths to install rootkits within the operating system's kernel, allowing them to manipulate system calls and evade detection by security tools. Kernel-level rootkits are highly sophisticated and difficult to detect.

Data exfiltration channels are another aspect of maintaining persistence. Attackers often establish covert communication channels to exfiltrate data from the compromised environment without raising suspicion. These channels can include DNS tunnels, covert channels in network protocols, or even steganography, where data is hidden within seemingly innocent files or images.

Anti-forensics techniques are employed to erase or obscure digital footprints. Just as an intruder might sweep away their tracks within the fortress, attackers use methods like cleaning event logs, overwriting data, or encrypting their communications to avoid detection by forensic investigators.

Stealth is essential for maintaining persistence because it allows attackers to operate covertly and avoid triggering alarms or suspicion. Stealth involves blending in with the environment, remaining undetected, and behaving like a benign entity. It's like disguising yourself as a member of the fortress staff and going about your activities unnoticed.

One stealth technique is process injection, where malicious code is injected into legitimate processes. This makes the attacker's activities appear as part of normal system operations, making it challenging for security tools to distinguish between legitimate and malicious actions.

Another stealthy approach is "living off the land," where attackers use native system utilities and trusted applications to carry out their activities. By using built-in tools, attackers can avoid raising red flags associated with the use of unfamiliar or suspicious software.

Encryption and obfuscation play a role in maintaining stealth. Just as a skilled infiltrator might use codes and ciphers to communicate secretly, attackers encrypt their communications and obfuscate their code to evade detection. This makes it difficult for security solutions to analyze and identify malicious behavior.

Countermeasures against maintaining persistence and stealth are crucial for defenders. Security teams employ various techniques such as continuous monitoring, threat hunting, behavioral analysis, and anomaly detection to identify and remove persistent threats. Regular security assessments and vulnerability scanning also help uncover hidden backdoors and vulnerabilities.

In summary, maintaining persistence and stealth is a critical aspect of advanced cyberattacks, where attackers aim to establish a lasting foothold within compromised systems or networks. It involves various techniques, including backdoors, registry modifications, scheduled tasks, file system manipulation, rootkits, data exfiltration channels, and anti-forensics. Stealth is essential to avoid detection and blend in with the environment. Defenders must implement robust security measures and continuously monitor their systems to detect and mitigate persistent threats effectively. Just as a fortress must remain vigilant to guard against intruders, modern organizations must stay vigilant to protect their digital assets from determined and resourceful attackers.

Chapter 8: Advanced Evasion and Antiforensics

Evasive malware techniques represent a cat-and-mouse game in the world of cybersecurity, where malicious actors continually refine their tactics to avoid detection and removal. These techniques are akin to the strategies employed by covert agents to stay hidden and operate behind enemy lines without arousing suspicion.

One fundamental aspect of evasive malware is its ability to disguise itself. Malware often conceals its true nature by masquerading as legitimate software or adopting the appearance of benign files. This camouflage helps it bypass security checks, much like a spy slipping past enemy checkpoints in disguise.

Another evasive tactic is polymorphism, where malware changes its code structure each time it infects a new host. This constant mutation makes it challenging for antivirus programs to detect the malware based on known signatures, similar to a spy who adopts different personas to evade pursuit.

Obfuscation is a common technique used to make malware code unintelligible to security analysts. Like a secret code that only a select few can decipher, obfuscated malware code is designed to appear convoluted and meaningless, making it difficult to reverse-engineer and understand its true purpose.

Malware authors employ encryption to hide their malicious payloads. Just as spies encrypt their messages to prevent interception, malware encryption makes it nearly impossible for security tools to analyze the payload's contents without the decryption key.

Evasive malware is skilled at detecting virtual environments and sandboxes used for analysis. It behaves differently when executed in these controlled environments, remaining dormant or taking benign actions to avoid revealing its malicious intent until it reaches a real target.

Anti-emulation techniques are used to trick security tools into thinking they are dealing with legitimate software. Malware can include instructions that mimic normal user behavior, such as clicking on links or filling out forms, fooling the system into believing it is interacting with a human rather than malicious code.

Rootkit functionality is another layer of evasion. Malware may attempt to gain root access to a system, allowing it to hide within the operating system's core. This makes it challenging for security tools to detect and remove the malicious code, similar to how a spy operating within a foreign government's inner circle is difficult to identify.

Evasive malware often employs command and control (C2) servers to receive instructions and exfiltrate data. These servers are hidden within the dark corners of the internet, making it difficult for defenders to locate and disrupt them, much like secret rendezvous points for spies.

Zero-day exploits are often leveraged by evasive malware. These are previously unknown vulnerabilities in software that attackers can use to gain access and execute their code. Just as spies exploit weaknesses in a fortress's defenses, malware exploits weaknesses in software.

Once evasive malware gains access to a system, it seeks to establish persistence, ensuring that it remains active and undetected. This is achieved through techniques such as modifying system settings, creating hidden user accounts, and scheduling tasks to run at specific times, much like an infiltrator leaving secret passages within the fortress.

Evasive malware is also skilled at lateral movement within a network. It attempts to spread from one compromised system to others, much like a spy infiltrating different parts of a fortress. This lateral movement makes it challenging for defenders to contain and isolate the infection.

Defenders employ a range of techniques to detect and mitigate evasive malware. Behavioral analysis, anomaly detection, and heuristic scanning are used to identify unusual patterns and behavior that may indicate the presence of malware. Sandboxing and virtualization help researchers analyze and understand the malware's behavior without risking infection. Signature-based detection, although less effective against polymorphic malware, can still identify known threats.

Network segmentation and access controls are employed to limit the lateral movement of malware within a network, isolating infected systems and preventing further spread. Regular patching and vulnerability management are crucial to closing potential entry points for malware, such as those targeted by zero-day exploits.

In summary, evasive malware techniques are a constant challenge in the cybersecurity landscape. Malicious actors employ various tactics to hide, disguise, and persist within compromised systems and networks. Just as covert agents adapt to changing circumstances, malware evolves to evade detection and removal. Defenders must remain vigilant, employing a combination of detection, analysis, and prevention strategies to protect against these elusive threats.

Digital forensics countermeasures are essential in the ever-evolving landscape of cybercrime and digital investigations. These countermeasures are like the detective's toolkit, helping investigators uncover digital evidence while safeguarding the integrity of the process.

One critical aspect of digital forensics countermeasures is the preservation of evidence. Just as a detective secures a crime scene, digital investigators must ensure that digital evidence remains unchanged and intact. This involves creating forensic copies of data, known as "forensic images," to work from while leaving the original data undisturbed.

Chain of custody is another crucial consideration. Like a detective documenting the handling of physical evidence, digital investigators maintain a meticulous record of who accessed the digital evidence, when, and why. This chain of custody documentation is crucial to establishing the integrity of the evidence in court.

Encryption can pose a significant challenge in digital forensics. While encryption is a valuable tool for protecting sensitive data, it can hinder investigators' efforts to access and analyze information. To counter this, forensic experts use various techniques to decrypt data, working within legal and ethical boundaries.

Anti-forensic tools and techniques are employed by individuals seeking to evade digital investigation. These tools are akin to criminals attempting to cover their tracks or erase evidence. Digital forensic experts must be aware of anti-forensic tactics and work to counteract them.

Data hiding and steganography present further challenges. Just as spies encode messages within seemingly innocuous documents, individuals may hide data within files or disguise it using steganographic techniques. Digital investigators employ specialized tools and methods to detect and extract hidden data.

One significant countermeasure in digital forensics is the use of write blockers. These hardware or software devices prevent any write operations to the evidence media, ensuring that no changes are made during the investigation. Write blockers are essential to maintaining the integrity of the evidence.

Live forensics, also known as in situ analysis, involves examining a live, running system to gather evidence. This is similar to a detective collecting evidence at a crime scene before it can be tampered with. Live forensics tools allow investigators to capture volatile data from a running system without affecting its state.

Timeliness is critical in digital investigations. Just as detectives aim to gather evidence promptly, digital investigators must act swiftly to preserve and collect evidence before it can be altered, deleted, or lost. Delays in responding to an incident can compromise the integrity of the investigation.

Digital forensics countermeasures extend to the realm of mobile devices. Mobile forensics involves extracting and analyzing data from smartphones and tablets, much like detectives collecting evidence from personal belongings. Specialized tools and techniques are used to access and analyze mobile device data.

Cloud forensics addresses the challenges of investigating data stored in the cloud. Just as detectives must navigate complex crime scenes, digital investigators must navigate the cloud environment to access and analyze digital evidence. Cloud forensics tools and expertise are essential in this context. Memory forensics focuses on analyzing a system's volatile memory, much like a detective searching for clues at a crime scene. This can reveal valuable information about active processes, running applications, and recent user activity. Memory forensics tools are used to capture and analyze memory dumps.

Network forensics investigates data transmitted over networks, similar to detectives intercepting communication. Network packets and logs are analyzed to reconstruct events and identify potential threats or unauthorized activities.

Network forensics helps investigators understand how data was accessed and transmitted.

Digital forensics countermeasures also encompass the legal aspects of investigations. Just as detectives must adhere to legal procedures, digital investigators must follow strict rules of evidence collection and handling. Proper documentation and adherence to legal requirements are crucial in this regard. Certification and training are essential in the field of digital forensics. Just as detectives undergo specialized training, digital investigators pursue certifications such as Certified Information Systems Security Professional (CISSP) or Certified Forensic Computer Examiner (CFCE). These credentials validate their expertise.

Collaboration is key in digital investigations. Just as detectives may work with other law enforcement agencies, digital investigators often collaborate with various experts, including legal professionals, cybersecurity specialists, and law enforcement agencies. This multidisciplinary approach ensures a comprehensive investigation.

Continuous learning is vital in digital forensics. Just as detectives must stay updated on new investigative techniques, digital investigators must keep pace with evolving technology and cyber threats. Staying current with the latest tools and methodologies is essential to effective digital forensics.

In summary, digital forensics countermeasures play a critical role in the investigation of cybercrimes and digital incidents. These measures encompass a wide range of techniques and practices, from evidence preservation to decryption, and from mobile forensics to network analysis. Digital investigators, like detectives, must remain vigilant, adaptable, and well-trained to navigate the complex world of digital evidence.

Chapter 9: Weaponizing Exploits for Targeted Attacks

Targeted attack planning and execution are intricate processes that require meticulous preparation and careful consideration of multiple factors. Just as a master chess player thinks several moves ahead, those orchestrating targeted attacks must craft a detailed strategy. These attacks are not random; they are precise, deliberate, and often tailored to specific objectives.

The initial phase of targeted attack planning involves reconnaissance. Imagine it as a spy gathering intelligence before a mission. Attackers collect information about the target, such as its infrastructure, employees, technologies, and vulnerabilities. This reconnaissance phase often involves open-source intelligence (OSINT) gathering, which can reveal valuable details about the target.

Once attackers have gathered sufficient intelligence, they move on to the planning stage. This is where they develop a comprehensive strategy, much like a military general devising a battle plan. Attackers determine the best attack vectors, methods, and resources required to achieve their goals. They also assess potential risks and countermeasures that the target may have in place.

Social engineering is a common element of targeted attack planning. Attackers leverage psychological manipulation, often through deceptive emails, messages, or phone calls, to trick individuals within the target organization into revealing sensitive information or taking actions that benefit the attackers. Social engineering tactics can be highly effective when executed skillfully.

Attackers may also conduct reconnaissance on individuals within the target organization. Just as detectives investigate suspects, attackers gather information about key personnel, such as their roles, responsibilities, and personal interests. This knowledge allows attackers to tailor their social engineering attempts for maximum success.

The next step in targeted attack planning is the selection of attack vectors. Attackers choose the most suitable means to breach the target's defenses. This might involve exploiting software vulnerabilities, launching phishing campaigns, or employing more advanced techniques like zero-day exploits. The choice of attack vector depends on the target's weaknesses and the attackers' capabilities.

Zero-day exploits are particularly potent in targeted attacks. These are vulnerabilities in software or hardware that are unknown to the vendor and, therefore, lack patches or fixes. Attackers can use zero-day exploits to gain unauthorized access or control over a target system, making them valuable tools in targeted attacks.

Weaponizing exploits is an essential aspect of attack planning. Attackers develop or acquire exploits and malware capable of taking advantage of vulnerabilities. Just as a skilled blacksmith crafts weapons, attackers refine their tools to ensure they are effective, reliable, and difficult to detect by security solutions.

Attackers often use command and control (C2) infrastructure to maintain control over compromised systems. This infrastructure is like a communication network for their malicious activities. Attackers deploy C2 servers or botnets to manage compromised devices and exfiltrate data. Detecting and disrupting C2 infrastructure is a crucial defense against targeted attacks.

Payload delivery is a critical step in executing targeted attacks. Attackers must successfully deliver their malicious payloads to target systems. This can be achieved through email attachments, malicious websites, or other delivery methods. Just as a skilled archer aims for the bullseye, attackers aim to deliver their payloads precisely.

Exploitation is the moment of truth in a targeted attack. Attackers attempt to exploit vulnerabilities in the target's systems or software. Successful exploitation grants them access and control. This phase requires precision and timing, much like a skilled locksmith picking a lock.

Post-exploitation activities are where attackers establish persistence, move laterally within the network, and achieve their ultimate objectives. They may escalate privileges, exfiltrate sensitive data, or deploy additional malware. Like a strategist navigating a complex battlefield, attackers adapt to changing conditions and defenses.

Maintaining stealth is crucial throughout the attack. Attackers must avoid detection by security measures and monitoring systems. They use various evasion techniques, such as obfuscating code, encrypting communications, and mimicking legitimate traffic, to stay hidden. This cat-and-mouse game requires cunning and adaptability.

Exfiltration of stolen data is a primary goal in many targeted attacks. Attackers carefully plan how to remove sensitive information from the target environment without raising suspicion. This may involve exfiltrating data in small, covert batches or using covert channels to transmit information.

To cover their tracks effectively, attackers often engage in anti-forensic activities. They erase logs, alter timestamps, and employ other tactics to hinder digital investigations. These actions are akin to a fugitive attempting to erase their trail to evade capture.

Ultimately, targeted attack planning and execution require a deep understanding of cybersecurity, vulnerabilities, and human psychology. Attackers employ tactics that mimic the meticulous planning of intelligence agencies and the precision of military operations. Defending against targeted attacks demands a holistic security approach, including robust defenses, employee training, threat intelligence, and incident response capabilities.

Creating custom exploits for targeted campaigns is a sophisticated process that demands in-depth knowledge of software vulnerabilities, programming, and the target environment. It's akin to crafting a bespoke weapon specifically designed for a unique adversary. These tailored exploits are instrumental in achieving specific objectives within a targeted attack, making them a potent tool in the attacker's arsenal.

To embark on the journey of creating custom exploits, one must first identify a suitable vulnerability within the target's software or infrastructure. This vulnerability could be a previously unknown flaw, commonly referred to as a zero-day vulnerability, or an existing vulnerability that hasn't been patched by the target.

Zero-day vulnerabilities, in particular, are highly prized by attackers because they are unknown to the software vendor, and thus, there are no available patches or fixes. Identifying such vulnerabilities requires a combination of reverse engineering, vulnerability research, and advanced knowledge of the target's software stack.

Once a vulnerability is identified, the next step is to analyze it thoroughly. This entails understanding the root cause of the vulnerability, its potential impact on the target system, and the conditions necessary for its exploitation. This phase is akin to dissecting a complex puzzle to understand its inner workings.

The process of analyzing vulnerabilities often involves reverse engineering the target software. Reverse engineering is the art of dissecting software to understand its functionality, structure, and potential weaknesses. Skilled reverse engineers use tools and techniques to examine binary code and data structures, unraveling the software's secrets.

With a deep understanding of the vulnerability, the exploit developer can then proceed to create a proof-of-concept (PoC) exploit. A PoC exploit is a small piece of code that demonstrates the ability to trigger the vulnerability and gain control over the target system. It's like building a prototype of a complex machine to ensure it functions as intended.

Creating a PoC exploit involves crafting precise input data or code sequences that can trigger the vulnerability reliably. This requires a keen understanding of memory manipulation, stack and heap exploitation, and the intricacies of the target software's execution flow. It's akin to fine-tuning an intricate instrument for maximum performance.

Testing and refining the PoC exploit is a crucial phase in the exploit development process. Just as a skilled craftsman continually hones their creation, the exploit developer iterates on the code to ensure its reliability and effectiveness. This may involve addressing unforeseen challenges and edge cases.

Once the PoC exploit is perfected, the exploit developer can then work on weaponizing it for the targeted campaign. This involves adding functionality to the exploit to achieve specific goals, such as establishing a backdoor, escalating privileges, or exfiltrating data. It's like adding specialized attachments to a tool to make it more versatile.

Custom exploits often include evasion techniques to bypass security mechanisms and avoid detection. Attackers may employ various obfuscation methods to make the exploit code less recognizable to security solutions. This is akin to disguising a weapon to avoid detection at security checkpoints.

In the context of a targeted campaign, the exploit developer must also consider the delivery mechanism for the exploit. This involves crafting a phishing email or other means of enticing the target to execute the exploit. Social engineering tactics may be employed to manipulate the target into taking the desired action.

During the campaign, the custom exploit is deployed strategically. Just as a skilled archer aims for the bullseye, the attacker aims to deliver the exploit precisely when the target is vulnerable. Timing and precision are critical to success.

Once the exploit is executed, the attacker gains a foothold in the target's environment. This foothold can be leveraged to achieve the campaign's objectives, which may include data exfiltration, lateral movement within the network, or further compromise of other systems. It's akin to gaining access to a fortified castle and strategically advancing through its chambers.

Throughout the campaign, the attacker must maintain stealth and avoid detection. They may employ anti-forensic techniques to erase traces of their presence and cover their tracks effectively. This requires a deep understanding of digital forensics and the ability to counter investigative efforts.

Creating custom exploits for targeted campaigns is a complex and high-stakes endeavor. It requires a blend of skills, from vulnerability research and programming to social engineering and evasion tactics. Defenders must be equally adept at detecting and mitigating such exploits to safeguard their systems and data.

Chapter 10: The Future of Gray Hat Exploits

In the ever-evolving landscape of gray hat exploits and cybersecurity, staying ahead of emerging threats and trends is paramount. It's akin to navigating uncharted waters, where new dangers and opportunities constantly surface, shaping the future of hacking and cybersecurity practices.

One of the foremost emerging threats in the realm of gray hat exploits is the proliferation of sophisticated ransomware attacks. Attackers are increasingly targeting critical infrastructure, healthcare organizations, and municipalities with ransomware that encrypts valuable data, demanding hefty ransoms for decryption keys. These attacks have the potential to disrupt essential services and cause significant financial and reputational damage.

Another concerning trend is the rise of supply chain attacks. Rather than targeting a single organization, attackers are focusing on compromising software vendors and service providers, aiming to infect a multitude of downstream targets. This approach amplifies the impact of a single breach, potentially affecting countless organizations and their customers.

In the realm of vulnerability research, the discovery and exploitation of zero-day vulnerabilities remain a central theme. However, there's a growing market for these exploits, with governments and threat actors willing to pay substantial sums for exclusive access to these powerful weapons. This dynamic not only drives competition among researchers but also raises ethical questions about the responsible disclosure of vulnerabilities.

Web application security continues to be a battleground, with attackers increasingly focusing on exploiting advanced web application vulnerabilities. Cross-site scripting (XSS), SQL injection, and remote code execution vulnerabilities are still prevalent, but attackers are now leveraging more sophisticated techniques to evade detection and carry out data breaches or defacement attacks.

The Internet of Things (IoT) presents a burgeoning attack surface, as an increasing number of devices connect to the internet. These devices often lack robust security measures, making them susceptible to exploitation. Attacks targeting IoT devices have the potential to disrupt critical infrastructure, compromise personal privacy, and facilitate large-scale botnets for distributed denial-of-service (DDoS) attacks.

Machine learning and artificial intelligence (AI) are playing a dual role in the world of gray hat exploits. On one hand, attackers are harnessing these technologies to create more convincing phishing attacks and evasion tactics. On the other hand, defenders are employing AI-driven solutions for threat detection and response, resulting in a perpetual cat-and-mouse game between attackers and defenders.

Social engineering remains a potent weapon in the attacker's arsenal, with phishing attacks evolving to become increasingly convincing and personalized. Attackers leverage publicly available information from social media and other sources to craft highly targeted and persuasive lures, making it more challenging for individuals and organizations to discern malicious emails from legitimate ones.

In the realm of evasion and anti-forensics, attackers are continually refining their techniques to cover their digital tracks. This includes using advanced obfuscation methods, employing steganography to hide malicious code within seemingly innocuous files, and leveraging anti-analysis tactics to thwart security researchers and forensic investigators.

In response to these emerging threats and trends, the field of cybersecurity is witnessing a growing emphasis on threat intelligence sharing and collaboration. Information sharing among organizations, government agencies, and cybersecurity researchers is crucial for staying informed about evolving threats and devising effective defense strategies.

Moreover, ethical hacking and penetration testing are becoming integral components of organizations' cybersecurity strategies. By proactively identifying vulnerabilities and weaknesses in their systems, organizations can take preemptive measures to mitigate risks and enhance their security posture.

To navigate the ever-changing landscape of gray hat exploits, individuals and organizations must remain vigilant, adapt to emerging threats, and invest in the latest cybersecurity technologies and best practices. It's a dynamic and evolving field, where staying one step ahead of adversaries is the key to maintaining security and resilience in the digital age.

In today's rapidly evolving digital landscape, ethical hacking has become more essential than ever before. As technology advances at an unprecedented pace, so do the vulnerabilities and threats that organizations and individuals face. Ethical hackers, also known as white hat hackers, play a vital role in safeguarding digital assets, protecting sensitive data, and ensuring the security of interconnected systems.

The age of advanced technology has ushered in a new era of cybersecurity challenges. With the proliferation of internet-connected devices, the attack surface has expanded exponentially. Everything from smartphones and smart homes to critical infrastructure relies on complex software and networks, making them susceptible to a wide range of cyber threats.

One of the prominent challenges in this age is the rise of sophisticated cyberattacks. Cybercriminals and nation-state actors have access to powerful tools and techniques, enabling them to launch highly coordinated and persistent attacks. These threats go beyond simple malware and phishing; they include advanced persistent threats (APTs), zero-day exploits, and ransomware campaigns that can cripple organizations and hold their data hostage.

To combat these threats, ethical hackers must possess an in-depth understanding of the latest attack vectors and vulnerabilities. They continuously adapt their skills to stay ahead of cyber adversaries, embracing cutting-edge technologies and methodologies to assess and strengthen security measures. In this age, ethical hacking involves not only assessing network and application security but also addressing complex issues like cloud security, IoT security, and mobile security.

Cloud computing has transformed the way organizations operate, offering scalability and flexibility. However, it has also introduced unique security challenges. Ethical hackers must navigate the intricacies of cloud infrastructure, ensuring that data stored in the cloud remains secure. They assess cloud configurations, identify misconfigurations that could expose sensitive data, and help organizations implement robust security controls.

Internet of Things (IoT) devices have permeated every aspect of modern life, from smart thermostats in homes to industrial sensors in factories. While IoT offers convenience and automation, it also introduces vulnerabilities. Ethical hackers specialize in assessing the security of IoT devices, searching for weaknesses that could be exploited to gain unauthorized access or disrupt operations.

As organizations adopt DevOps practices to accelerate software development, security considerations must be integrated seamlessly into the process. Ethical hackers collaborate with development teams to implement security testing early in the software development lifecycle, ensuring that vulnerabilities are identified and remediated before they make it into production environments.

The proliferation of mobile devices has led to a surge in mobile application usage. Ethical hackers scrutinize mobile apps, searching for security flaws that could be exploited to compromise user data or device functionality. They evaluate the security of mobile operating systems and help organizations develop secure mobile app development practices.

In the age of advanced technology, ethical hacking is not limited to identifying vulnerabilities. It also involves threat hunting and incident response. Ethical hackers actively search for signs of compromise within an organization's network, assisting in the rapid detection and containment of security incidents. Their expertise in forensics and analysis helps organizations recover from breaches and strengthen their defenses against future attacks.

Collaboration and information sharing are essential in the battle against cyber threats. Ethical hackers often participate in cybersecurity communities, sharing knowledge, and insights about emerging threats and vulnerabilities. They contribute to the collective effort to protect digital assets and promote a safer online environment.

In summary, ethical hacking in the age of advanced technology is a dynamic and vital field. Ethical hackers serve as guardians of cybersecurity, leveraging their expertise to identify vulnerabilities, assess security measures, and proactively defend against cyber threats. Their role is pivotal in an era where technology is both a driver of progress and a source of security challenges. As technology continues to advance, ethical hacking will remain an indispensable component of cybersecurity, safeguarding digital ecosystems and ensuring the security and privacy of individuals and organizations alike.

BOOK 4
MASTERING GRAY HAT ETHICAL HACKING
EXPERT-LEVEL PENETRATION TESTING

ROB BOTWRIGHT

Chapter 1: Expert-Level Ethical Hacking Overview

In the realm of cybersecurity, an expert ethical hacker plays a multifaceted and indispensable role. Their mission extends far beyond conventional security measures, and it entails proactively probing systems, networks, and applications for vulnerabilities. These experts are akin to digital detectives, diligently investigating the ever-evolving threat landscape to safeguard the integrity, confidentiality, and availability of critical data.

To truly understand the role of an expert ethical hacker, it's essential to recognize that they wear multiple hats. They are defenders of digital fortresses, tasked with identifying weak points before malicious actors can exploit them. Their primary objective is to act as the vanguard of cybersecurity, staying one step ahead of cyber adversaries who constantly adapt their tactics and techniques.

Ethical hackers possess an in-depth understanding of the mindset and methodologies employed by cybercriminals. This knowledge allows them to anticipate potential attack vectors and vulnerabilities, helping organizations preemptively fortify their defenses. In essence, they think like hackers to protect against hackers, utilizing their expertise to maintain a robust security posture.

One of the key roles an expert ethical hacker assumes is that of a vulnerability assessor. They conduct comprehensive assessments of an organization's digital infrastructure, meticulously scrutinizing every nook and cranny for weaknesses. These assessments encompass a wide array of components, including web applications, network configurations, and even the human factor through social engineering assessments.

The ethical hacker employs a diverse toolkit of techniques and tools to uncover vulnerabilities. They utilize penetration testing to simulate real-world attacks, striving to replicate the tactics malicious actors might employ. This process involves identifying potential entry points, exploiting weaknesses, and gaining access to systems or data, all under controlled conditions. The ultimate goal is to uncover vulnerabilities before cybercriminals can exploit them, providing organizations with a critical window of opportunity to mitigate risks.

Beyond traditional penetration testing, expert ethical hackers also engage in red team operations. These simulated attacks, often conducted with the collaboration of the organization's security team, aim to assess the entire security infrastructure's resilience. The red team operates with a "no-holds-barred" mentality, employing every means at their disposal to breach defenses. This intense evaluation process helps organizations identify systemic weaknesses and areas that require immediate attention.

Expert ethical hackers are also masters of reconnaissance. They gather intelligence on potential threats and adversaries, monitoring the dark web, forums, and other online channels where cybercriminals congregate. This proactive approach enables them to stay informed about emerging threats and vulnerabilities, which is crucial in an ever-evolving digital landscape.

In addition to their technical prowess, ethical hackers excel at communication. They must convey complex technical findings to non-technical stakeholders in a clear and comprehensible manner. Effectively translating vulnerabilities and risks into actionable insights is a vital aspect of their role. This ensures that organizational leadership can make informed decisions about resource allocation and risk mitigation strategies.

Expert ethical hackers are champions of continuous improvement. They recognize that cybersecurity is an ongoing process, and they stay abreast of the latest developments in technology and threat landscapes. This commitment to professional growth enables them to remain effective in an environment where cyber threats evolve rapidly.

Furthermore, ethical hackers are instrumental in enhancing an organization's cybersecurity culture. They conduct security awareness training and provide guidance to employees on recognizing and mitigating common security threats, such as phishing attacks. By empowering the entire workforce to become more security-conscious, they strengthen the organization's overall security posture.

Ethical hackers also contribute to incident response efforts. In the unfortunate event of a security breach, their expertise is invaluable in identifying the extent of the compromise, assessing the damage, and devising a remediation plan. They collaborate closely with incident response teams, leveraging their knowledge to ensure swift and effective resolution.

Moreover, expert ethical hackers participate in the development and implementation of security policies and procedures. They help organizations establish robust security frameworks, ensuring that best practices are followed and regulatory compliance is maintained. This proactive approach not only bolsters defenses but also minimizes the risk of legal and reputational consequences.

In essence, the role of an expert ethical hacker is multifaceted, encompassing technical expertise, strategic thinking, and a commitment to safeguarding digital assets. They serve as proactive guardians of cybersecurity, continually striving to outsmart cyber adversaries and protect the digital realm. Their work is pivotal in an age where digital threats loom large, and their dedication to maintaining digital safety is a beacon of hope in the ever-evolving world of cybersecurity.

Ethical hacking, in the context of today's dynamic and ever-evolving threat landscape, serves as a vital pillar in the defense against cyber adversaries. As our world becomes increasingly interconnected, the digital realm has become a playground for both malicious actors and those who seek to protect it. In this intricate and high-stakes game, ethical hackers are the unsung heroes, working diligently to safeguard the digital infrastructure upon which our daily lives depend.

At its core, ethical hacking is a proactive approach to cybersecurity. It involves authorized individuals, known as ethical hackers or penetration testers, simulating cyberattacks on an organization's systems, networks, and applications. This simulation, performed within a controlled and safe environment, is designed to identify vulnerabilities before malicious actors can exploit them. It's akin to a digital stress test, evaluating an organization's security posture and resilience.

The motivation behind ethical hacking is not driven by ill intentions; rather, it is rooted in a commitment to protecting digital assets and sensitive information. Ethical hackers, often referred to as "white hat" hackers, employ their skills and expertise to strengthen the defenses of organizations, thereby reducing the risk of successful cyberattacks. In essence, they act as digital bodyguards, tirelessly patrolling the virtual realms in which critical data resides.

In today's threat landscape, the importance of ethical hacking cannot be overstated. Cyber threats have grown in sophistication, scale, and frequency, posing unprecedented challenges to organizations across various sectors. The methods and tools used by malicious actors are constantly evolving, and the consequences of successful cyberattacks can be severe, ranging from financial losses to reputational damage.

One of the fundamental reasons ethical hacking is crucial in today's landscape is the prevalence of zero-day vulnerabilities. These are software flaws that are unknown to the vendor and, therefore, lack patches or updates to address them. Malicious actors are always on the lookout for such vulnerabilities, as they can exploit them without fear of immediate detection or remediation. Ethical hackers, armed with their knowledge of hacking techniques, actively seek out and report zero-day vulnerabilities to vendors, allowing for timely fixes and mitigating the risk of exploitation.

The rise of nation-state-sponsored cyberattacks further underscores the significance of ethical hacking. Governments and state-sponsored groups engage in cyber espionage, cyber warfare, and cybercrime, targeting critical infrastructure, corporations, and even individuals. Ethical hackers play a critical role in detecting and thwarting these advanced and persistent threats, acting as digital guardians against nation-state adversaries.

In addition to external threats, insider threats pose a significant risk to organizations. Employees, contractors, or business partners with access to an organization's systems can inadvertently or intentionally compromise security. Ethical hackers conduct internal assessments to identify vulnerabilities and potential insider threats, helping organizations fortify their defenses from both external and internal angles.

The explosion of Internet of Things (IoT) devices has also reshaped the threat landscape. These devices, ranging from smart appliances to industrial sensors, often lack robust security measures. Ethical hackers assess the security of IoT devices and the ecosystems in which they operate, exposing vulnerabilities that could be exploited to compromise not only personal privacy but also critical infrastructure.

Ethical hacking is not merely a reactive measure but an essential component of proactive cybersecurity strategies. Organizations recognize that investing in cybersecurity is an investment in resilience. Ethical hackers partner with organizations to conduct comprehensive security assessments, including vulnerability scanning, penetration testing, and security audits, to uncover weaknesses and provide actionable recommendations for improvement.

Moreover, ethical hacking aligns with regulatory compliance requirements. Many industries and jurisdictions have established stringent cybersecurity standards and mandates. Ethical hackers assist organizations in meeting these compliance obligations, reducing legal and financial risks associated with non-compliance.

In the age of cloud computing and remote work, ethical hacking extends its reach to cloud security and remote access assessments. The migration of data and services to cloud environments has created new attack surfaces and challenges. Ethical hackers evaluate the security of cloud configurations and remote access solutions, ensuring that data remains secure, even in the absence of traditional network perimeters.

The role of ethical hacking also extends to the realm of security awareness training. Cyber threats often exploit the human element, targeting unsuspecting employees through social engineering tactics like phishing. Ethical hackers educate employees about the latest threat trends, providing them with the knowledge and tools to recognize and report suspicious activity, thus bolstering the organization's human firewall.

Ethical hacking is not a one-size-fits-all endeavor. It is a collaborative and iterative process that adapts to the evolving threat landscape. Ethical hackers continually update their skills, staying ahead of emerging threats and vulnerabilities. They employ a wide array of tools and methodologies, ranging from automated vulnerability scanners to custom-developed exploits, to comprehensively assess security.

In summary, ethical hacking is an indispensable discipline in today's threat landscape. It operates at the intersection of technology, security, and human behavior, offering a proactive and dynamic defense against cyber threats. Ethical hackers are the vanguards of cybersecurity, dedicated to fortifying digital defenses, safeguarding sensitive information, and ensuring the resilience of organizations in an increasingly interconnected world. As the battle between defenders and adversaries rages on, ethical hacking remains a beacon of hope, working tirelessly to ensure that the digital realm remains secure and trustworthy.

Chapter 2: Advanced Penetration Testing Methodologies

Advanced scoping and planning represent the foundational steps of any successful penetration testing engagement, serving as the compass that guides ethical hackers through the labyrinth of potential vulnerabilities and security weaknesses within an organization's digital infrastructure. While these concepts might seem rudimentary, they are the cornerstones upon which the entire penetration testing process rests, and mastering them is essential for achieving the desired outcomes.

When embarking on a penetration testing journey, the first and foremost task is to define the scope of the engagement. This involves clearly delineating the boundaries and limitations of the assessment, which ensures that both the ethical hacker and the client are on the same page regarding the goals and objectives of the test. A well-defined scope prevents misunderstandings and potential disruptions during the assessment, ensuring that the ethical hacker can focus their efforts on the areas of greatest concern.

Understanding the organization's objectives and specific requirements is paramount when scoping a penetration testing engagement. It's not a one-size-fits-all endeavor. Each organization is unique, with distinct goals, assets, and risk tolerances. Ethical hackers must collaborate closely with the client to gain a comprehensive understanding of the business processes, critical assets, and regulatory constraints that shape the engagement's scope.

Furthermore, scoping involves defining the rules of engagement, which outline the permitted actions and constraints during the assessment. These rules help maintain a controlled and ethical testing environment. For example, they specify whether or not the ethical hacker can attempt to exfiltrate data, disrupt services, or engage in social engineering tactics. A clear set of rules ensures that the ethical hacker operates within legal and ethical boundaries.

Advanced scoping also involves identifying the target systems, applications, and networks that will be subject to testing. Prioritizing these targets based on their criticality and potential impact on the organization's operations is crucial. Ethical hackers must weigh the potential risks against the potential benefits to determine the order in which targets should be assessed. This approach ensures that the most critical vulnerabilities are identified early in the engagement.

Once the scope is defined, the planning phase kicks into high gear. Ethical hackers must meticulously plan their approach to the engagement, taking into consideration the organization's unique challenges and requirements. This involves selecting appropriate tools and methodologies, assembling a toolkit that aligns with the scope and objectives.

In the planning phase, ethical hackers must also take into account the potential risks associated with the engagement. This includes assessing the legal and compliance implications of the test, especially in industries subject to strict regulatory requirements. Understanding the legal landscape is crucial to avoid inadvertently running afoul of the law while conducting penetration testing.

Moreover, advanced planning encompasses the creation of a detailed project plan, complete with timelines, milestones, and deliverables. This plan serves as a roadmap for the engagement, helping the ethical hacker stay on track and ensuring that the client's expectations are met. Effective project management is essential to delivering a successful penetration testing engagement.

Another key aspect of advanced planning is reconnaissance. Ethical hackers gather information about the target organization before launching the assessment. This preliminary research helps in understanding the organization's infrastructure, technologies, and potential vulnerabilities. Reconnaissance provides valuable insights that inform the testing approach and enable ethical hackers to tailor their strategies accordingly.

In addition to planning the technical aspects of the engagement, ethical hackers must consider the human element. Social engineering tactics, such as phishing attacks, can be highly effective in breaching an organization's defenses. Therefore, ethical hackers often plan and conduct social engineering exercises to assess the organization's susceptibility to these types of attacks. Advanced planning includes crafting convincing scenarios and payloads to test the vigilance of employees.

Another critical aspect of advanced scoping and planning is risk assessment. Ethical hackers must work closely with the client to identify and prioritize potential risks associated with the engagement. This includes assessing the potential impact of a successful breach, the likelihood of a security incident, and the organization's ability to mitigate and recover from such incidents. A risk assessment informs decisions about where to focus testing efforts and resources. Furthermore, ethical hackers must plan for contingencies and unexpected developments during the engagement. Cybersecurity is an ever-evolving field, and threats can emerge or change rapidly. Advanced planning includes establishing incident response procedures and communication channels with the client in case an unforeseen incident occurs during testing. Being prepared for the unexpected is a hallmark of a well-executed engagement.

In summary, advanced scoping and planning are foundational to the success of any penetration testing engagement. They serve as the compass and roadmap, guiding ethical hackers through the complex terrain of an organization's digital infrastructure. By defining the scope, setting clear rules of engagement, and meticulously planning every aspect of the assessment, ethical hackers can effectively identify vulnerabilities, assess risks, and provide actionable recommendations to strengthen an organization's cybersecurity posture. As the cybersecurity landscape continues to evolve, mastering advanced scoping and planning remains a crucial skill for ethical hackers, ensuring that they can navigate the challenges and complexities of today's digital world.

In-depth penetration testing techniques represent the heart and soul of ethical hacking, delving deep into the intricacies of an organization's digital infrastructure to unearth vulnerabilities and potential weaknesses that could be exploited by malicious actors. These techniques go beyond surface-level assessments, providing a comprehensive view of an organization's security posture and helping to fortify its defenses.

One of the fundamental techniques employed in in-depth penetration testing is network reconnaissance. This phase involves actively gathering information about the target organization's network, systems, and applications. Ethical hackers use various tools and methodologies to map out the network's topology, identify open ports, and discover potential entry points. Network reconnaissance lays the groundwork for the subsequent phases of testing by providing a clear understanding of the organization's digital landscape.

Once the network is thoroughly mapped, ethical hackers move on to vulnerability scanning and assessment. This involves the systematic identification and evaluation of vulnerabilities within the target environment. Vulnerability scanners, such as Nessus or OpenVAS, are used to automate the process of discovering known vulnerabilities in systems and applications. Ethical hackers then assess the severity of these vulnerabilities, considering factors like their potential impact and exploitability.

In-depth penetration testing techniques also encompass manual vulnerability assessment, where ethical hackers go beyond automated scanning tools to uncover subtle or unique vulnerabilities that may not be detectable by automated means. This hands-on approach requires a deep understanding of the underlying technologies and meticulous examination of configurations, code, and system behavior.

Web application penetration testing is another critical aspect of in-depth testing. Websites and web applications are common targets for attackers, making them a prime focus of ethical hackers. In this phase, ethical hackers assess the security of web applications by identifying vulnerabilities like SQL injection, Cross-Site Scripting (XSS), and Cross-Site Request Forgery (CSRF). Advanced techniques, such as fuzzing and manual code review, are employed to scrutinize web application security thoroughly.

Advanced exploitation techniques are a hallmark of in-depth penetration testing. Ethical hackers leverage their expertise to exploit identified vulnerabilities in a controlled manner, simulating real-world attack scenarios. This step helps organizations understand the potential impact of a successful breach and the pathways that attackers might exploit. By exploiting vulnerabilities, ethical hackers demonstrate the urgency of remediation and provide actionable recommendations for mitigating risks.

Privilege escalation is a crucial aspect of in-depth penetration testing, especially in environments with multi-tiered access controls. Ethical hackers aim to escalate their privileges from standard user accounts to gain higher-level access. This mirrors the tactics used by malicious actors seeking to compromise critical systems or data. By demonstrating privilege escalation techniques, ethical hackers highlight areas where organizations may need to enhance their access controls.

Post-exploitation activities are an integral part of in-depth penetration testing. Ethical hackers maintain persistence within the compromised environment, simulating the actions of real attackers who aim to maintain control for extended periods. This phase involves activities like backdooring systems, creating hidden accounts, and evading detection mechanisms. By emulating post-exploitation tactics, ethical hackers help organizations understand the importance of continuous monitoring and incident response.

In-depth penetration testing often includes lateral movement exercises, where ethical hackers explore the target environment to identify additional entry points and potential vulnerabilities. This mimics the actions of attackers who move laterally through a network to escalate their privileges or access sensitive data. Detecting and mitigating lateral movement techniques is essential for maintaining a robust security posture.

Furthermore, ethical hackers engage in data exfiltration exercises to demonstrate the risks associated with data breaches. By extracting sensitive data from the target environment, they illustrate the potential consequences of a successful attack, such as the exposure of confidential information or customer data. This drives home the importance of data protection and encryption measures.

In-depth penetration testing techniques also encompass anti-forensics and evasion strategies. Ethical hackers explore methods to hide their tracks and make it difficult for incident responders to trace their activities. By demonstrating these tactics, they emphasize the need for organizations to invest in robust forensic capabilities and incident response planning.

In summary, in-depth penetration testing techniques represent a comprehensive and multifaceted approach to ethical hacking. By combining network reconnaissance, vulnerability assessment, web application testing, advanced exploitation, privilege escalation, post-exploitation activities, lateral movement exercises, data exfiltration, and anti-forensics strategies, ethical hackers provide organizations with a holistic view of their security vulnerabilities and potential risks. These techniques help organizations identify and address weaknesses in their defenses, ultimately strengthening their cybersecurity posture in an ever-evolving threat landscape.

Chapter 3: Red Team Operations and Adversarial Simulation

Building a red team for effective operations is a multifaceted process that requires careful planning, a deep understanding of cybersecurity, and a strategic approach to adversarial simulation. Red teams play a pivotal role in helping organizations identify and remediate security vulnerabilities, strengthen their defenses, and enhance their overall cybersecurity posture.

To begin, it's essential to understand the purpose of a red team. A red team is an independent group within an organization responsible for simulating adversarial activities with the goal of uncovering weaknesses in security controls, policies, and procedures. Unlike traditional penetration testing, which often follows a predefined scope, red teams operate with a broader and more flexible mandate, emulating real-world threat actors who may target an organization without warning.

The first step in building an effective red team is assembling a team of skilled professionals with diverse backgrounds and expertise. Red team members should possess a wide range of technical skills, including penetration testing, vulnerability assessment, reverse engineering, and incident response. Additionally, individuals with expertise in social engineering and physical security may be valuable assets, as red team engagements can encompass a variety of attack vectors.

Creating a clear and well-defined charter for the red team is crucial. The charter outlines the team's objectives, scope, and boundaries, ensuring that all stakeholders understand the goals of the red team operations. It's essential to establish rules of engagement, ethical guidelines, and the scope of activities the red team is authorized to perform. These guidelines help maintain transparency, align expectations, and prevent misunderstandings.

Red team operations should be conducted with meticulous planning. The team should begin by conducting a thorough reconnaissance of the organization, gaining insights into its infrastructure, personnel, and potential vulnerabilities. This information is critical for crafting realistic attack scenarios and tailoring engagements to the specific organization's needs.

One of the primary objectives of a red team is to challenge an organization's defenses and detection capabilities. To achieve this, red teams often employ advanced and creative tactics, techniques, and procedures (TTPs) that mimic the evolving tactics of real-world threat actors. By emulating sophisticated adversaries, red teams help organizations identify gaps in their security controls and improve their ability to detect and respond to attacks effectively.

Communication and collaboration are vital aspects of red team operations. The red team should work closely with the organization's blue team, which is responsible for defense and incident response. This collaboration ensures that the organization's defenders gain valuable experience in identifying and mitigating threats posed by the red team. It also fosters a culture of continuous improvement, where lessons learned from red team engagements inform defensive strategies.

Red team engagements should be conducted with the utmost professionalism and ethical considerations. It is essential to obtain proper authorization and informed consent from relevant stakeholders before initiating any activities. Engagements should adhere to legal and ethical boundaries, and red team members should act responsibly and transparently throughout the process.

As part of red team operations, the team may engage in adversarial simulation exercises that encompass various attack vectors. This can include social engineering campaigns, physical security assessments, and digital intrusion attempts. These exercises aim to test an organization's preparedness, from its personnel's ability to recognize phishing attempts to the effectiveness of its physical security measures.

Red team assessments should provide organizations with actionable recommendations for improving their security posture. These recommendations should be prioritized based on risk and potential impact, allowing the organization to focus on addressing the most critical vulnerabilities and weaknesses first. Red teams often present their findings and recommendations to the organization's leadership and stakeholders, emphasizing the importance of remediation efforts.

In addition to periodic red team engagements, organizations may consider establishing a persistent red team program. This involves maintaining an ongoing red team capability that continually assesses and challenges the organization's defenses. A persistent red team can provide continuous insights into evolving threats and help organizations adapt their security strategies accordingly.

In summary, building a red team for effective operations is a strategic initiative that requires careful planning, a diverse skill set, clear guidelines, and a commitment to ethical and responsible engagement. Red teams play a crucial role in helping organizations identify and address security vulnerabilities, ultimately enhancing their cybersecurity resilience in an ever-evolving threat landscape. By emulating real-world adversaries and conducting adversarial simulations, red teams contribute to a proactive and proactive security posture that is well-prepared to defend against emerging threats.

Simulating real-world adversaries is a core aspect of red team operations, aiming to replicate the tactics, techniques, and procedures (TTPs) that threat actors may employ against an organization. By doing so, red teams help organizations assess their readiness and effectiveness in defending against evolving and sophisticated threats.

The goal of simulating real-world adversaries is not to cause harm or disruption to the organization but rather to identify vulnerabilities and weaknesses in the existing security measures and response capabilities. To achieve this, red teams adopt a mindset that mirrors that of genuine threat actors, thinking critically and creatively to bypass security controls and gain unauthorized access.

When simulating real-world adversaries, red teams conduct reconnaissance activities to gather information about the organization, its assets, and its employees. This information serves as the foundation for crafting realistic attack scenarios tailored to the organization's specific circumstances. Understanding an organization's infrastructure, technology stack, and personnel allows red teams to create targeted and credible threat simulations.

Red teams also employ social engineering techniques to test an organization's human-centric security controls. Social engineering involves manipulating individuals within the organization to divulge sensitive information, click on malicious links, or take actions that could compromise security. These techniques may include phishing emails, pretexting, baiting, and tailgating, among others.

In addition to social engineering, red teams assess physical security measures by attempting unauthorized physical access to restricted areas or assets. This can include bypassing access control systems, lock-picking, or gaining entry through deceptive means. Physical security assessments help organizations evaluate their ability to protect critical assets physically.

Digital intrusion attempts are a central element of simulating real-world adversaries. Red teams use various attack vectors, such as exploiting software vulnerabilities, launching brute-force attacks, and utilizing malware to gain a foothold within the organization's network. These activities aim to assess the robustness of an organization's security controls, including firewalls, intrusion detection systems, and endpoint security solutions.

Once inside the organization's network, red teams focus on lateral movement and privilege escalation, mimicking the tactics of advanced threat actors. They seek to escalate their privileges and move laterally through the network to access critical systems and data. This phase of the assessment helps organizations understand their exposure to internal threats and the effectiveness of their internal segmentation and access controls.

Red teams also evaluate an organization's ability to detect and respond to security incidents. They carefully monitor their activities and evade detection as much as possible, challenging the organization's incident response and threat hunting capabilities. This stage helps identify gaps in monitoring, alerting, and incident response processes.

Throughout the engagement, red teams maintain communication and coordination with the organization's blue team, which is responsible for defense and incident response. This collaboration ensures that red team activities are conducted ethically and transparently, avoiding any disruptions to critical business operations. It also provides an opportunity for blue team members to learn from the red team's tactics and improve their defensive strategies.

One of the critical benefits of simulating real-world adversaries is the ability to identify weaknesses in the organization's defenses before malicious actors can exploit them. By uncovering vulnerabilities and security gaps, organizations can take proactive measures to remediate issues and strengthen their security posture. This proactive approach reduces the risk of security incidents and data breaches.

Upon completion of the red team engagement, a comprehensive report is typically generated, detailing the findings, techniques used, and recommendations for remediation. This report serves as a valuable resource for organizations to prioritize and implement security improvements effectively. It also helps leadership and stakeholders understand the potential impact of security vulnerabilities and the importance of investing in cybersecurity measures.

In summary, simulating real-world adversaries through red team operations is a critical component of an organization's cybersecurity strategy. By replicating the tactics and techniques of threat actors, red teams provide invaluable insights into an organization's vulnerabilities and security posture. This proactive approach enables organizations to address weaknesses, enhance their defenses, and prepare for the ever-evolving threat landscape. Through collaboration between red teams and blue teams, organizations can build a robust and resilient security ecosystem that effectively detects, responds to, and mitigates security threats.

Chapter 4: Exploiting Zero-Day Vulnerabilities

Identifying and exploiting unpatched vulnerabilities is a crucial aspect of modern cybersecurity, as it involves uncovering weaknesses in software, systems, or devices that have not been addressed by security patches or updates. In today's threat landscape, cybercriminals actively seek out and exploit these vulnerabilities to gain unauthorized access, steal sensitive data, or execute malicious code within an organization's network.

Unpatched vulnerabilities, often referred to as "zero-day vulnerabilities," pose a significant risk to organizations because they have not been publicly disclosed or patched by the software vendor. This means that there are no available fixes or updates to address these vulnerabilities, leaving systems exposed to potential attacks. Identifying and mitigating these vulnerabilities is a critical part of proactive cybersecurity efforts.

The process of identifying unpatched vulnerabilities typically begins with vulnerability research, where security professionals, researchers, or ethical hackers actively search for weaknesses in software, operating systems, or network configurations. They may use a combination of methods, including manual code analysis, automated scanning tools, and reverse engineering techniques to uncover potential vulnerabilities.

In some cases, security researchers may analyze software or hardware products for vulnerabilities, focusing on popular and widely-used applications or systems that are more likely to be targeted by attackers. This research often involves scrutinizing code for coding errors, logical flaws, or design weaknesses that could be exploited.

Once a potential vulnerability is identified, the next step is to verify its existence and impact. This involves conducting proof-of-concept (PoC) tests or creating exploit code that demonstrates how the vulnerability can be leveraged to compromise a system. The goal is to determine whether the vulnerability can be weaponized and used in a real-world attack scenario.

During the verification process, researchers follow responsible disclosure practices, which involve notifying the software vendor or relevant authority about the vulnerability's existence. This allows the vendor to initiate the patching process and develop a security update to address the issue. Responsible disclosure is essential to ensure that the vulnerability is addressed promptly and does not fall into the wrong hands.

However, not all vulnerabilities are promptly patched by vendors, and some may remain unaddressed for an extended period. In such cases, security researchers and ethical hackers may choose to follow ethical disclosure practices by informing the affected organization or industry about the vulnerability's existence, potential impact, and mitigation steps.

In addition to responsible and ethical disclosure, some vulnerabilities may be actively exploited in the wild before patches are available. These are often referred to as "zero-day exploits." Cybercriminals and advanced threat actors may use zero-day exploits to target organizations, governments, or individuals with the intention of stealing data, conducting espionage, or causing disruption.

To protect against the exploitation of unpatched vulnerabilities, organizations must implement proactive security measures. This includes robust intrusion detection and prevention systems, network segmentation, and continuous monitoring to detect and respond to suspicious activities. Organizations should also have an incident response plan in place to address security incidents promptly.

In some cases, organizations may choose to deploy virtual patching solutions or security software that can detect and block exploits targeting unpatched vulnerabilities. These measures can serve as temporary mitigation while awaiting official patches from vendors.

It's important to note that unpatched vulnerabilities are not limited to software or operating systems; they can also exist in network configurations, hardware devices, and firmware. Security professionals must conduct thorough assessments and audits to identify and address vulnerabilities across all aspects of an organization's technology stack.

In summary, identifying and exploiting unpatched vulnerabilities is a critical aspect of modern cybersecurity, requiring diligent research, responsible disclosure practices, and proactive security measures. The constant evolution of the threat landscape underscores the importance of staying vigilant, continuously monitoring for new vulnerabilities, and taking swift action to mitigate risks. By addressing unpatched vulnerabilities promptly and effectively, organizations can significantly reduce their exposure to cyber threats and enhance their overall security posture.

Zero-day vulnerability research and mitigation are critical components of modern cybersecurity, as they involve proactively identifying and addressing previously unknown security weaknesses in software, systems, or devices. These vulnerabilities are called "zero-day" because they are exploited by attackers before the affected organization or software vendor is aware of their existence. In this chapter, we will delve into the world of zero-day vulnerability research, exploring the processes, challenges, and strategies employed by security professionals to discover and mitigate these hidden threats.

Zero-day vulnerabilities pose a significant risk to organizations and individuals alike. Unlike known vulnerabilities for which patches or updates are available, zero-day vulnerabilities are concealed and can be exploited by malicious actors without any preventive measures in place. As a result, it is imperative to have a proactive approach to identifying and mitigating these vulnerabilities before they are weaponized.

The process of zero-day vulnerability research often begins with reconnaissance, where security researchers or ethical hackers search for clues or indications of potential vulnerabilities. This phase can involve monitoring underground forums, analyzing malware samples, or examining public information about software or hardware products.

Once researchers have identified a potential zero-day vulnerability, the next step is to investigate it further. This typically involves a combination of techniques, including reverse engineering, code analysis, and dynamic testing. Researchers may analyze the affected software's binary code, source code, or even network traffic patterns to gain a deep understanding of the vulnerability's nature and possible exploitation vectors.

One of the key challenges in zero-day vulnerability research is balancing the need for thorough investigation with responsible disclosure practices. Researchers must ensure that their actions do not inadvertently expose organizations to security risks while also avoiding premature public disclosure that could aid malicious actors. Responsible disclosure involves notifying the affected software vendor or organization about the vulnerability and giving them a reasonable amount of time to develop and release a patch or mitigation strategy.

The responsible disclosure process can be complex, as it requires effective communication between researchers and vendors. Researchers often struggle with ensuring that vendors take the issue seriously, respond promptly, and prioritize the development of patches. In some cases, disagreements may arise between researchers and vendors regarding the severity of the vulnerability or the urgency of the patching process.

While responsible disclosure is the preferred approach, some researchers may choose to follow ethical disclosure practices in cases where vendors are unresponsive or do not take appropriate action. Ethical disclosure involves informing the affected organization, industry, or community about the vulnerability without revealing explicit details that could be exploited by attackers. This approach can sometimes put additional pressure on vendors to address the issue.

In addition to responsible and ethical disclosure, security researchers and organizations must consider the potential for zero-day vulnerabilities to be exploited in the wild. Cybercriminals and advanced threat actors actively seek out and exploit these hidden vulnerabilities to conduct attacks such as data breaches, espionage, or targeted malware campaigns. To defend against such threats, organizations should implement robust security measures, including intrusion detection systems, network segmentation, and endpoint security solutions.

Another challenge in zero-day vulnerability research is the sheer volume of software and devices in use today. Researchers must prioritize their efforts, focusing on widely-used and critical applications or systems that are more likely to be targeted by attackers. This requires a combination of expertise, threat intelligence, and risk assessment to determine which vulnerabilities should be investigated first.

Furthermore, the discovery of a zero-day vulnerability does not guarantee immediate mitigation. Vendors may require time to develop and release patches, leaving organizations exposed to potential attacks. To address this gap, some security researchers and organizations deploy virtual patching solutions or security software that can detect and block exploits targeting zero-day vulnerabilities.

In summary, zero-day vulnerability research and mitigation are essential aspects of modern cybersecurity, requiring a delicate balance between proactive investigation and responsible disclosure. Security researchers play a crucial role in identifying these hidden threats, and their efforts contribute to a safer digital landscape. However, the challenges and complexities involved in this process highlight the need for collaboration between researchers, vendors, and organizations to effectively address zero-day vulnerabilities and protect against potential exploitation.

Chapter 5: Advanced Network and Infrastructure Attacks

Advanced network reconnaissance and enumeration are critical components of cybersecurity that enable security professionals to gather in-depth information about target networks and systems. These processes are essential for identifying potential vulnerabilities, understanding network topologies, and preparing for penetration testing or defensive measures. In this chapter, we will explore the advanced techniques and tools used in network reconnaissance and enumeration, emphasizing their importance in modern cybersecurity practices.

Network reconnaissance, also known as network discovery or information gathering, is the initial phase of a cybersecurity assessment. Its primary goal is to gather as much information as possible about the target network without actively interacting with it. The information collected during this phase serves as a foundation for subsequent activities, such as vulnerability scanning, penetration testing, or threat analysis.

To conduct effective network reconnaissance, security professionals employ various methods and tools. One common technique is passive reconnaissance, which involves gathering publicly available information about the target network. This information can include domain names, IP addresses, organization details, and even employee names obtained from public sources like search engines, social media, and DNS records.

Active reconnaissance, on the other hand, involves actively probing the target network to discover live hosts, open ports, and services. Techniques like port scanning and banner grabbing provide valuable insights into the network's architecture and the software and services running on it. Advanced port scanning tools, such as Nmap, allow security professionals to customize scans and gather extensive information while minimizing detection.

Enumeration is the subsequent step in the reconnaissance process, focusing on extracting detailed information from the target network's live hosts and services. During enumeration, security professionals use various techniques to uncover usernames, shares, system configurations, and more. This phase aims to provide a comprehensive view of the network's assets and potential vulnerabilities.

One of the most critical aspects of network enumeration is discovering active directory (AD) information in Windows-based networks. Active directory enumeration can reveal valuable data like user accounts, groups, permissions, and trust relationships. Tools like enum4linux and ldapsearch are commonly used to extract this information. In Linux environments, the Network Information Service (NIS) or Lightweight Directory Access Protocol (LDAP) enumeration techniques are employed to uncover user and system data.

For Unix-based systems, enumeration efforts often focus on network file shares and file system information. Tools like SMBclient and NFSstat are used to identify shared resources, list files, and gather configuration details. This information can be instrumental in identifying potential points of entry for attackers.

DNS enumeration plays a crucial role in mapping network resources and uncovering valuable data like subdomains and hostnames. Tools like DNSenum and DNSRecon are employed to perform DNS zone transfers, brute force subdomain enumeration, and DNS record lookups. DNS reconnaissance helps security professionals build a comprehensive picture of the network's infrastructure and identify potential weak points.

In addition to traditional enumeration techniques, modern networks pose new challenges for security professionals. With the proliferation of cloud-based services, containerization, and microservices architecture, enumerating network assets has become more complex. Security professionals must adapt and employ specialized tools and methodologies to discover and assess these dynamic components effectively.

Advanced network reconnaissance also incorporates the use of threat intelligence feeds and open-source intelligence (OSINT) to enrich collected data with known threats and vulnerabilities. By cross-referencing network information with threat intelligence data, security professionals can prioritize their efforts and focus on areas with the highest potential risks.

Moreover, automation and scripting play a significant role in advanced network reconnaissance and enumeration. Security professionals often develop custom scripts or utilize existing automation frameworks to streamline data collection and analysis. This automation enables them to gather and process large volumes of information efficiently, reducing the time required for reconnaissance activities.

In summary, advanced network reconnaissance and enumeration are fundamental processes in cybersecurity, providing critical insights into target networks and systems. These activities help security professionals identify potential vulnerabilities, prioritize their efforts, and take proactive measures to protect organizations from cyber threats. As networks continue to evolve, security practitioners must stay updated on the latest tools and techniques to adapt to the changing landscape of network security.

Infrastructure-based attack strategies are a fundamental aspect of modern cybersecurity, encompassing a range of techniques and methodologies employed by threat actors to compromise an organization's network and systems. In this chapter, we will delve into the complexities of infrastructure-based attacks, exploring how attackers leverage various elements of a network's infrastructure to achieve their malicious objectives.

At the heart of infrastructure-based attack strategies lies the understanding that an organization's network is a vast ecosystem of interconnected devices, servers, and services. Attackers recognize that targeting specific components of this ecosystem can yield valuable results. To effectively defend against such threats, security professionals must comprehend the tactics, techniques, and procedures used by adversaries.

One common infrastructure-based attack strategy is the exploitation of vulnerabilities in network devices, such as routers, switches, and firewalls. These devices play a pivotal role in directing network traffic and ensuring its security. When compromised, they can provide attackers with unauthorized access, control, and visibility into network traffic, opening the door to further exploitation.

Attackers often search for known vulnerabilities in network devices and exploit them to gain a foothold within an organization's network. Vulnerabilities like unpatched firmware or misconfigured access controls can provide attackers with entry points for launching more extensive attacks. To mitigate this threat, organizations must maintain a rigorous patch management process and regularly audit and secure their network device configurations.

Another infrastructure-based attack vector is the compromise of Domain Name System (DNS) infrastructure. DNS is a critical component of the internet, responsible for translating human-readable domain names into IP addresses. Attacking DNS infrastructure can enable attackers to redirect traffic to malicious destinations, intercept communications, or launch phishing campaigns.

In DNS-based attacks, threat actors often target vulnerabilities in DNS servers, domain registrars, or the domain resolution process itself. Cache poisoning, DNS hijacking, and DNS tunneling are techniques used to manipulate DNS responses or abuse DNS infrastructure for malicious purposes. Organizations can defend against these attacks by implementing DNS security measures like DNSSEC, monitoring DNS traffic, and employing threat intelligence feeds.

Infrastructure-based attacks can also involve leveraging legitimate network services for malicious purposes. Attackers may compromise email servers, web servers, or file-sharing services to distribute malware, steal sensitive data, or launch phishing attacks. These services are attractive targets because they are trusted by users and often have direct access to valuable information.

To defend against such attacks, organizations must adopt a defense-in-depth approach, implementing strong access controls, network segmentation, and robust email and web filtering solutions. Regular monitoring and auditing of network services are essential to detect and respond to suspicious activities promptly.

One of the most challenging infrastructure-based attacks to defend against is Distributed Denial of Service (DDoS) attacks. These attacks aim to overwhelm a network, service, or website with a flood of traffic, rendering it inaccessible to legitimate users. Attackers often employ botnets, a network of compromised devices, to orchestrate DDoS attacks.

Mitigating DDoS attacks requires a combination of network and application-layer defenses, such as rate limiting, traffic filtering, and the use of Content Delivery Networks (CDNs). Organizations must also have an incident response plan in place to react quickly when under attack, minimizing downtime and service disruption.

Infrastructure-based attack strategies can extend beyond the network layer to target cloud services and virtualized environments. Cloud infrastructure is attractive to attackers because of its scalability and the potential to compromise multiple organizations through a single breach. Organizations must implement robust access controls, encryption, and monitoring in their cloud environments to defend against these threats effectively.

Infiltration of an organization's supply chain is another infrastructure-based attack vector that has gained prominence. Attackers may compromise suppliers, subcontractors, or partners to gain access to the target organization's network. This approach can be particularly challenging to defend against, as it often involves trusted entities with legitimate access.

To mitigate supply chain attacks, organizations should conduct thorough due diligence when selecting partners, assess their security practices, and establish strong contractual obligations regarding security. Additionally, implementing network segmentation and least privilege access can limit the damage potential of a compromised supplier.

As infrastructure-based attacks continue to evolve, organizations must adopt a proactive and adaptive cybersecurity posture. Threat intelligence, continuous monitoring, and incident response readiness are vital components of an effective defense against these attacks. Organizations should also engage in regular penetration testing and red team exercises to identify vulnerabilities in their infrastructure and improve their security posture.

In summary, infrastructure-based attack strategies encompass a wide range of techniques and tactics used by threat actors to compromise network components, services, and devices. Defending against these attacks requires a comprehensive and multi-layered approach, including vulnerability management, access controls, network segmentation, and threat intelligence. By understanding the methods employed by adversaries, organizations can better protect their infrastructure and data from cyber threats.

Chapter 6: Advanced Web Application Security Assessments

In-depth web application reconnaissance is a critical phase of the penetration testing process, where security professionals gather information about a target web application to assess its vulnerabilities effectively. This reconnaissance phase is akin to gathering intelligence before embarking on a mission, and it plays a pivotal role in ensuring the success of the subsequent testing efforts.

During this phase, the penetration tester focuses on uncovering as much information as possible about the target web application, its architecture, and its potential vulnerabilities. This process often involves several key steps, each contributing to a comprehensive understanding of the web application's attack surface.

The first step in in-depth web application reconnaissance is to identify the target application's footprint on the internet. This includes discovering the application's domain names, subdomains, and IP addresses. Techniques like DNS enumeration, zone transfers, and search engine queries can help uncover these details.

Once the application's footprint is determined, the tester seeks to map its structure and functionality. This involves identifying the web pages, directories, and resources hosted on the application. Tools like web crawlers and directory brute-forcing can aid in this discovery process.

After understanding the web application's structure, the penetration tester performs fingerprinting to determine the technologies and frameworks it employs. This information is invaluable in identifying potential vulnerabilities specific to those technologies. Tools such as web application scanners and fingerprinting scripts can assist in this task.

In-depth reconnaissance also entails scrutinizing the web application's attack surface. Testers look for publicly accessible entry points like login forms, contact forms, and user registration pages. These entry points are prime candidates for testing common web vulnerabilities like SQL injection, Cross-Site Scripting (XSS), and Cross-Site Request Forgery (CSRF).

Furthermore, testers analyze the web application's content management system (CMS) and its associated plugins or extensions. Vulnerabilities in these components are often exploited by attackers to compromise web applications. Understanding the CMS and its versions helps testers identify potential weaknesses.

As part of web application reconnaissance, security professionals seek to identify third-party assets and integrations. These can include external JavaScript libraries, APIs, and content delivery networks (CDNs) used by the application. Vulnerabilities in third-party assets can indirectly impact the security of the web application.

One critical aspect of in-depth reconnaissance is understanding the web application's user authentication and authorization mechanisms. Testers analyze how user accounts are managed, including password policies, session management, and access controls. Misconfigurations in these areas can lead to serious security vulnerabilities.

Testers also look for information disclosure vulnerabilities, such as verbose error messages or exposed source code, which can provide valuable insights to attackers. Additionally, they identify sensitive information like API keys, credentials, or database connection strings that should be protected.

Throughout the reconnaissance phase, it's essential to maintain a meticulous record of all discovered information. This documentation not only aids in the testing process but also serves as a valuable reference for the penetration tester and the organization.

As part of an effective reconnaissance strategy, security professionals perform passive and active information gathering. Passive reconnaissance involves collecting publicly available data without directly interacting with the target application. This can include searching for information on forums, social media, or open-source intelligence (OSINT) databases.

Active reconnaissance, on the other hand, involves interacting with the target application to extract information. This can include performing web scraping, conducting banner grabbing to identify server versions, or analyzing HTTP response headers for clues about the underlying technology stack.

Throughout the reconnaissance phase, ethical considerations and compliance with legal and ethical guidelines are paramount. Testers must ensure that their activities do not violate any laws or ethical standards. Permission and authorization from the organization being tested are crucial before engaging in any testing activities.

In summary, in-depth web application reconnaissance is a vital phase of the penetration testing process. It involves thorough research and data gathering to understand the target application's structure, technologies, and potential vulnerabilities. A well-executed reconnaissance phase sets the stage for a successful penetration test, enabling testers to identify and remediate security weaknesses effectively. By adopting a comprehensive approach to reconnaissance, organizations can proactively protect their web applications from evolving cyber threats.

Advanced web application vulnerability exploitation is a critical phase in the world of ethical hacking and penetration testing, where skilled professionals leverage their expertise to uncover and exploit complex vulnerabilities in web applications. This phase goes beyond the basics of identifying common security flaws and delves into the intricate and sophisticated techniques that can be employed to compromise web applications.

During advanced web application vulnerability exploitation, the focus is on identifying and exploiting vulnerabilities that may not be immediately apparent or easily detected by automated scanning tools. These vulnerabilities often require a deep understanding of web application technologies, protocols, and the ability to think creatively like an attacker.

One of the fundamental concepts in advanced web application exploitation is the identification of vulnerabilities such as SQL injection, Cross-Site Scripting (XSS), and Cross-Site Request Forgery (CSRF). While these vulnerabilities are well-known, their exploitation can become highly intricate when the application incorporates advanced security mechanisms. Exploiting them effectively requires not only identifying the vulnerability but also understanding how to manipulate it within the context of the application.

SQL injection, for example, can take on various forms, including blind SQL injection and time-based blind SQL injection. In advanced exploitation scenarios, testers may need to craft payloads that evade detection mechanisms and gather sensitive data from the database. Techniques like second-order SQL injection, which involves injecting malicious payloads that execute at a later stage, are also explored.

Cross-Site Scripting (XSS) is another common vulnerability that can become sophisticated to exploit. In advanced scenarios, testers may need to bypass Content Security Policy (CSP) restrictions, exploit reflective and stored XSS vulnerabilities, and inject payloads that circumvent client-side security controls. Techniques like DOM-based XSS attacks and leveraging obscure HTML and JavaScript functionalities are part of the arsenal.

Cross-Site Request Forgery (CSRF) vulnerabilities can be similarly challenging to exploit, especially when web applications employ anti-CSRF tokens and implement security mechanisms to prevent such attacks. Advanced testers must understand the underlying mechanisms of anti-CSRF defenses and devise strategies to bypass them, potentially requiring creative social engineering techniques.

Beyond the well-known vulnerabilities, advanced exploitation often involves discovering and exploiting business logic flaws. These flaws arise from flaws in the design and logic of the application, rather than coding errors. Testers may manipulate workflows, abuse functionality, and chain multiple vulnerabilities together to achieve their objectives. Authentication and authorization mechanisms within web applications are also prime targets for advanced exploitation. Testers may seek to bypass authentication controls, exploit privilege escalation vulnerabilities, or impersonate other users to gain unauthorized access to sensitive areas of the application. In some cases, advanced exploitation involves combining various vulnerabilities and attack vectors to achieve a sophisticated attack chain. For instance, testers may start with an SQL injection to retrieve encrypted credentials, then employ cryptographic attacks to decrypt the credentials, and finally use the obtained credentials to gain unauthorized access to the application.

Moreover, advanced exploitation often requires a deep understanding of web application frameworks, programming languages, and the underlying server technologies. Testers may analyze source code, reverse engineer applications, and scrutinize custom-built functionalities to identify vulnerabilities that automated scanners may miss.

In the context of advanced exploitation, ethical hackers must exercise extreme caution and adhere to strict rules of engagement. Unauthorized or reckless exploitation of vulnerabilities can have severe consequences, both legally and ethically. Therefore, obtaining explicit permission and guidance from the organization undergoing testing is crucial.

In summary, advanced web application vulnerability exploitation is a complex and challenging phase in the field of ethical hacking and penetration testing. It requires testers to go beyond the basics and employ sophisticated techniques to uncover and exploit vulnerabilities effectively. Testers must possess deep technical knowledge, creativity, and ethical integrity to carry out these activities safely and responsibly. By conducting advanced exploitation, organizations can gain insights into their web application security postures and take proactive measures to protect against real-world threats.

Chapter 7: Advanced Wireless and IoT Security

Wireless network penetration testing at an advanced level represents a specialized and crucial aspect of ethical hacking and cybersecurity. As wireless technologies continue to evolve and become an integral part of modern business operations, the need to assess and secure wireless networks against potential threats has grown exponentially. In this chapter, we will delve into the intricacies of advanced wireless network penetration testing, exploring the methodologies, tools, and techniques employed by experts in the field. Advanced wireless network penetration testing goes beyond the basics of scanning for open Wi-Fi networks or identifying weak encryption. It requires a comprehensive understanding of wireless protocols, security mechanisms, and the ability to simulate real-world attacks to uncover vulnerabilities. One of the fundamental aspects of advanced wireless penetration testing is understanding the different types of wireless networks and their security implications. These networks include Wi-Fi, Bluetooth, Zigbee, and others. Each has its own set of vulnerabilities and attack vectors, making it essential for testers to be well-versed in the specifics of each technology.

In the realm of Wi-Fi networks, testers must explore not only the traditional 2.4GHz and 5GHz frequency bands but also newer ones like 6GHz, which are becoming increasingly common. Advanced testers often deal with complex network infrastructures, including enterprise-grade access points, controllers, and security mechanisms such as WPA3 and EAP-TLS. Advanced wireless penetration testing also involves assessing the security of Wi-Fi networks with multiple SSIDs, VLANs, and intricate network segmentation. Testers may need to bypass network isolation measures, pivot between different network segments, and identify misconfigurations that could lead to lateral movement within the network.

Additionally, advanced testers must be skilled in the art of reconnaissance. This entails not only identifying available wireless networks but also profiling them to determine potential targets. Understanding the environment, the types of devices in use, and the wireless technologies employed is essential to crafting effective attack strategies.

Wardriving, a technique where testers roam the physical environment searching for wireless networks, is often employed in advanced wireless penetration testing. This allows testers to gather valuable information about the target network landscape, discover hidden SSIDs, and determine the locations of access points.

Once testers have gathered sufficient intelligence, they move on to the attack phase. This involves exploiting vulnerabilities in Wi-Fi encryption, authentication mechanisms, and client devices. Techniques like deauthentication attacks, brute forcing WPA/WPA2/WPA3 pre-shared keys, and bypassing MAC address filtering are common in advanced wireless penetration testing.

In recent years, the rise of software-defined radios (SDRs) has greatly enhanced the capabilities of advanced testers. SDRs enable the capture and analysis of wireless signals, making it possible to intercept and decode transmissions, including those using protocols like Bluetooth Low Energy (BLE) or custom wireless communication protocols.

Bluetooth is another area of focus in advanced wireless penetration testing. With the proliferation of Bluetooth-enabled devices, including smartphones, IoT devices, and medical equipment, the attack surface has expanded significantly. Testers must be adept at exploiting Bluetooth vulnerabilities, such as BlueBorne, and conducting attacks like "Man-in-the-Middle" (MitM) or eavesdropping on Bluetooth communications.

Zigbee, a wireless communication protocol commonly used in IoT devices, presents unique challenges for testers due to its low power consumption and mesh network topology. Advanced testers may target Zigbee networks to identify weaknesses and gain unauthorized access to connected devices.

In advanced wireless penetration testing, testers also explore advanced attacks against mobile devices and their wireless connections. This includes attacks on cellular networks, Wi-Fi calling, and mobile application vulnerabilities. Testers may attempt to intercept SMS messages, hijack phone calls, or exploit mobile apps to compromise sensitive data.

Throughout the testing process, documentation and reporting play a vital role. Testers must provide detailed reports that include findings, vulnerabilities, exploitation techniques, and recommendations for remediation. These reports are essential for organizations to understand their wireless security posture and take proactive steps to mitigate risks.

In summary, advanced wireless network penetration testing is a dynamic and evolving field that requires a deep understanding of various wireless technologies, protocols, and security mechanisms. Testers in this domain must possess a diverse skill set, from signal analysis to exploiting encryption vulnerabilities, to effectively assess the security of wireless networks. As wireless technologies continue to advance, staying up-to-date with the latest developments and attack vectors is crucial for testers to provide valuable insights and help organizations secure their wireless infrastructure.

Securing and attacking IoT (Internet of Things) devices represents a complex and rapidly evolving landscape within the realm of cybersecurity. As the IoT ecosystem continues to expand, with devices ranging from smart thermostats and refrigerators to industrial sensors and autonomous vehicles, the need to understand and address the security challenges posed by these devices has become paramount.

To embark on this journey, let's first delve into the world of securing IoT devices. When it comes to securing IoT devices, one of the primary considerations is the diversity of the devices themselves. IoT encompasses a vast array of hardware and software, from resource-constrained sensors with limited processing power to powerful smart appliances equipped with sophisticated operating systems.

To tackle the security of these diverse devices, a comprehensive approach is essential. One of the foundational principles of IoT security is device authentication and authorization. Ensuring that only authorized devices can communicate with the network is critical. This can be achieved through the use of device certificates, secure boot processes, and strong authentication mechanisms. The next layer of IoT security involves secure communication channels. Encrypting data in transit and at rest is essential to prevent eavesdropping and data breaches. Protocols like TLS (Transport Layer Security) and DTLS (Datagram Transport Layer Security) are commonly used to secure communication between IoT devices and cloud servers. Another critical aspect of IoT security is regular software updates and patch management. IoT devices are often vulnerable to security flaws that can be exploited by attackers. Manufacturers must provide mechanisms for over-the-air (OTA) updates to ensure that devices receive security patches in a timely manner. Users should also be encouraged to keep their devices up to date.

Device identity management is crucial in securing IoT ecosystems. Each device should have a unique identity that is cryptographically tied to its hardware. This identity can be used to establish trust between devices and the network, enabling secure interactions and preventing unauthorized access.

Furthermore, IoT devices should follow the principle of the least privilege. They should only have access to the resources and data necessary for their intended functions. Implementing proper access controls, such as role-based access control (RBAC), helps restrict unauthorized actions by devices.

Intrusion detection and prevention systems (IDPS) specifically designed for IoT can also play a vital role in enhancing security. These systems can monitor network traffic, detect anomalies, and respond to potential threats in real-time. In addition, they can help identify compromised devices and quarantine them to prevent further damage.

Now, let's shift our focus to the other side of the coin: attacking IoT devices. Ethical hackers and security professionals often take on the role of adversaries to identify vulnerabilities in IoT ecosystems before malicious actors can exploit them.

One common approach to attacking IoT devices is passive reconnaissance. This involves scanning for publicly available information about IoT devices, such as default passwords or exposed interfaces. Attackers may also search for firmware vulnerabilities or known exploits applicable to specific devices.

Another avenue of attack is exploiting weak or default credentials. IoT devices often ship with default usernames and passwords, which users may not change. Attackers can use these default credentials to gain unauthorized access to devices, manipulate their settings, or launch attacks.

Brute force attacks are another technique employed by attackers to gain access to IoT devices. By systematically trying different username and password combinations, attackers aim to guess the correct credentials. Strong password policies and account lockout mechanisms can help mitigate this risk.

IoT devices are not immune to traditional network-based attacks. For instance, attackers may launch distributed denial of service (DDoS) attacks using compromised IoT devices as part of a botnet. Such attacks can disrupt services, overload networks, and impact device performance.

Physical attacks on IoT devices are also a concern. If an attacker gains physical access to a device, they may be able to extract sensitive data or tamper with its hardware or firmware. Protecting physical access points and using tamper-evident seals can help mitigate this risk.

Moreover, attacks on the supply chain can introduce vulnerabilities into IoT devices before they even reach the end user. Malicious actors may compromise the manufacturing or distribution process to implant backdoors or malicious firmware.

In summary, securing and attacking IoT devices are two sides of the same coin in the ever-evolving world of cybersecurity. Securing these devices requires a multifaceted approach encompassing authentication, encryption, access control, and vigilant patch management. Meanwhile, ethical hackers and security professionals play a critical role in identifying and addressing vulnerabilities before they can be exploited by malicious actors. As IoT continues to shape our interconnected world, the need for robust security measures and proactive threat mitigation strategies remains paramount.

Chapter 8: Advanced Post-Exploitation and Persistence

In the realm of cybersecurity and ethical hacking, maintaining post-exploitation access is a crucial and advanced skill that involves a variety of techniques and strategies. Once a hacker or penetration tester has successfully gained access to a target system or network, whether through exploiting vulnerabilities or using social engineering tactics, the next challenge is to ensure continued access and control over the compromised environment.

One of the fundamental techniques for maintaining post-exploitation access is the use of backdoors. Backdoors are hidden or covert entry points into a system that allow an attacker to bypass normal authentication and gain access without detection. These backdoors can be created by modifying system files, adding rogue user accounts, or installing malicious software that opens a secret communication channel between the attacker and the compromised system.

However, maintaining a backdoor is not as simple as just creating one. To avoid detection and removal by system administrators or security tools, advanced hackers use techniques to conceal the presence of backdoors. This might involve disguising them as legitimate system processes, using encryption to obfuscate communications, or making them persistent by configuring them to start automatically every time the system boots.

Rootkits are another advanced tool in the arsenal of post-exploitation access. A rootkit is a set of malicious software components that are designed to hide the presence of an attacker on a compromised system. Rootkits often replace or modify system utilities and kernel functions, allowing them to intercept system calls and manipulate the behavior of the operating system. By doing so, they can conceal files, processes, and network connections associated with the attacker.

Rootkits can be categorized into user-mode and kernel-mode rootkits, with the latter being more challenging to detect and remove. Detecting rootkits often requires specialized tools and techniques, such as memory forensics, to analyze system memory and identify anomalous behavior.

Another advanced method for maintaining post-exploitation access involves the use of covert channels for communication. These channels allow attackers to exchange data with compromised systems in a way that evades detection by security controls. Covert channels can operate over seemingly innocuous communication channels, such as DNS (Domain Name System) or HTTP (Hypertext Transfer Protocol), making them difficult to identify.

Advanced attackers may also employ techniques like process injection to maintain access. Process injection involves injecting malicious code or shellcode into a legitimate process running on the compromised system. By doing so, attackers can execute their code within the context of the legitimate process, making it harder to detect. Common process injection techniques include

DLL (Dynamic Link Library) injection, reflective DLL injection, and process hollowing.

Privilege escalation is another critical aspect of maintaining post-exploitation access. Once initial access is achieved, attackers often seek to escalate their privileges to gain higher levels of access within the compromised environment. Privilege escalation techniques vary depending on the operating system and application vulnerabilities present on the system. They may involve exploiting vulnerabilities in the system or leveraging misconfigurations to gain elevated privileges.

Persistence is key to maintaining post-exploitation access over an extended period. Attackers need to ensure that their presence is not eradicated during routine system maintenance or security audits. Achieving persistence often involves modifying system settings or configurations to ensure that the attacker's access remains intact. This can be done through the creation of scheduled tasks, registry modifications, or the use of startup scripts.

Furthermore, attackers may employ anti-forensic techniques to cover their tracks and evade detection by digital forensics investigators. These techniques can include wiping log files, clearing event logs, and overwriting deleted data to prevent recovery.

One of the most critical aspects of maintaining post-exploitation access is continuous monitoring and adaptation. Attackers must remain vigilant for signs of detection or remediation efforts by defenders. They may need to change tactics, update backdoors, or even re-exploit vulnerabilities if necessary to maintain access.

In summary, advanced techniques for maintaining post-exploitation access are a critical component of ethical hacking and cybersecurity. These techniques encompass the use of backdoors, rootkits, covert channels, process injection, privilege escalation, persistence, and anti-forensic methods. Ethical hackers and security professionals must understand these techniques to defend against them effectively, while also using them to assess the security of systems and networks. Continuous monitoring and adaptation are essential in the ongoing cat-and-mouse game between attackers and defenders in the ever-evolving landscape of cybersecurity.

In the world of ethical hacking and cybersecurity, post-exploitation data exfiltration strategies play a critical role in the overall assessment of a system's security. Once an attacker has successfully penetrated a target system, the next step often involves the extraction or exfiltration of valuable data from the compromised environment. Data exfiltration is a complex and multifaceted process that requires careful planning and execution, and it encompasses a range of advanced techniques and methods.

Data exfiltration can take various forms, and attackers employ a variety of strategies to transfer sensitive information from the compromised system to an external location under their control. These strategies often exploit covert channels, evade detection, and disguise the stolen data.

One common technique for data exfiltration is the use of command and control (C2) servers. Attackers establish a connection between the compromised system and a remote C2 server, allowing them to send and receive data without raising suspicion. These servers act as intermediaries, making it difficult for security controls to detect the illicit data transfer. Communication with C2 servers can occur over encrypted channels to further obfuscate the exfiltration process.

Steganography is another advanced method used for data exfiltration. Steganography involves embedding data within seemingly innocuous files or images, making it appear as if nothing out of the ordinary is happening. For example, an attacker might hide sensitive information within the least significant bits of an image file or within the white spaces of a document. This covert technique can bypass traditional security measures, as the files themselves do not appear suspicious.

DNS tunneling is a sophisticated technique that exploits DNS traffic to exfiltrate data. DNS queries and responses are typically allowed to traverse firewalls and security perimeters, making them an attractive vector for data exfiltration. Attackers encode their stolen data into DNS queries, and these queries are sent to a malicious DNS server controlled by the attacker. The attacker can then decode the data from the DNS responses, effectively bypassing network security controls.

Covert channels in network protocols are often exploited for data exfiltration as well. These channels allow attackers to hide their data within legitimate network traffic. For instance, covert timing channels leverage variations in packet timing to transmit data between the compromised system and an external server. By manipulating the timing of packets, attackers can encode and decode data without raising suspicion.

Advanced attackers may also employ the use of custom malware specifically designed for data exfiltration. This malware can be tailored to the target environment, making it difficult to detect with signature-based antivirus solutions. Malware can establish encrypted communication channels, compress data, and use obfuscation techniques to evade detection while exfiltrating sensitive information.

Exfiltration through third-party services is another strategy employed by attackers. They may use cloud storage services, email accounts, or file transfer protocols to move data outside the compromised network. By leveraging legitimate services, attackers can bypass network-based security controls that may be designed to detect suspicious outbound traffic.

Even techniques such as data exfiltration over physical media are utilized in some scenarios. An attacker might copy sensitive data onto removable media, such as USB drives or external hard disks, and physically remove the media from the compromised environment. While this method may seem rudimentary, it can be highly effective and difficult to detect, particularly in environments where strict access controls are not in place.

To counter these advanced data exfiltration strategies, organizations must implement robust security measures and monitoring solutions. Intrusion detection systems

(IDS) and data loss prevention (DLP) tools can help detect unusual patterns of network traffic or data transfer that may indicate an ongoing exfiltration attempt. Behavioral analysis and anomaly detection can also play a critical role in identifying suspicious activities.

Regular security awareness training for employees is crucial in preventing data exfiltration attempts that involve social engineering or insider threats. Employees should be educated about the importance of not disclosing sensitive information and recognizing phishing attempts or other malicious activities.

In summary, post-exploitation data exfiltration strategies represent a sophisticated and critical phase in the world of ethical hacking and cybersecurity. These strategies encompass a wide range of advanced techniques, from command and control servers and steganography to DNS tunneling and custom malware. To defend against these tactics, organizations must implement a multi-layered security approach, including robust network monitoring, behavioral analysis, and user awareness training. As technology evolves, so do the methods used by attackers, making it essential for security professionals to stay vigilant and adapt their defenses accordingly.

Chapter 9: Threat Hunting and Incident Response

Proactive threat hunting is a fundamental practice in modern cybersecurity, especially in complex and dynamic environments. In the ever-evolving landscape of cyber threats, organizations cannot rely solely on reactive security measures to protect their assets. Threat hunting is an active and strategic approach to identifying and mitigating threats before they can cause significant damage. It's akin to a digital detective work, where cybersecurity professionals actively seek out signs of malicious activity within their networks and systems.

To understand proactive threat hunting fully, it's essential to grasp the nature of modern cybersecurity challenges. Attackers are continually developing new techniques, tactics, and procedures (TTPs) to evade detection and infiltrate target environments. In response, security professionals need to adopt a proactive stance, actively searching for traces of malicious activity that may have already penetrated the perimeter defenses.

One of the key concepts in proactive threat hunting is the assumption of breach. This means that organizations should operate under the assumption that their networks have already been compromised. By accepting this assumption, cybersecurity teams are motivated to actively hunt for intruders rather than relying solely on defensive measures.

Proactive threat hunting can take various forms, but it often involves skilled cybersecurity analysts leveraging their expertise and intuition to search for anomalies, indicators of compromise (IOCs), and other signs of malicious activity. These professionals use a combination of manual and automated techniques to explore the vast amount of data generated by network traffic, logs, and system events.

Machine learning and artificial intelligence (AI) have become increasingly valuable tools in proactive threat hunting. These technologies can help security teams process large volumes of data quickly, identify patterns, and detect anomalies that may be indicative of a security incident. By leveraging AI and machine learning, analysts can focus their efforts on investigating the most promising leads, optimizing the use of their time and resources.

Proactive threat hunting often starts with the collection and aggregation of relevant data. This includes logs from various sources such as firewalls, intrusion detection systems, antivirus solutions, and endpoint security tools. The data is then normalized and correlated to create a comprehensive view of network activity. By examining this data, analysts can identify patterns that deviate from the norm and may indicate an ongoing security threat.

One common technique in proactive threat hunting is the use of threat intelligence feeds. These feeds provide information about known threats, including known malware, malicious IP addresses, and attack patterns. By cross-referencing network activity with threat intelligence data, analysts can quickly identify indicators of compromise and potential security incidents.

Another proactive approach to threat hunting involves the creation of behavioral baselines for network and system activity. By establishing what constitutes "normal" behavior within an organization's environment, analysts can more easily spot deviations that may indicate malicious activity. For example, a sudden increase in failed login attempts or an unusual spike in outbound network traffic could be signs of a security breach.

Advanced threat hunting often delves into the dark corners of the network, searching for hidden threats that may have evaded detection. This may involve looking at historical data to identify signs of past intrusions, analyzing the behavior of privileged accounts, or examining the activities of third-party vendors who have access to the network.

A critical aspect of proactive threat hunting is the ability to respond swiftly and effectively when a threat is identified. Once a potential security incident is detected, analysts need to validate the findings, assess the scope and impact of the threat, and develop a strategy for containment and remediation. This process often requires close collaboration between cybersecurity teams and other stakeholders within the organization.

In complex environments, threat hunting is an ongoing and iterative process. Cybersecurity professionals must continuously refine their techniques, adapt to evolving threats, and stay current with the latest tools and technologies. Threat intelligence sharing within the cybersecurity community can also play a crucial role in proactive threat hunting, as it enables organizations to benefit from the collective knowledge of the security community.

In summary, proactive threat hunting is a vital practice in complex cybersecurity environments. It involves actively searching for signs of malicious activity within network and system data, assuming that breaches have already occurred. With the aid of advanced technologies like machine learning and threat intelligence feeds, cybersecurity professionals can identify and mitigate threats before they cause significant harm. Proactive threat hunting is a dynamic and ongoing process that requires expertise, collaboration, and adaptability in the face of ever-evolving cyber threats.

In the ever-evolving landscape of cybersecurity, advanced incident response and recovery strategies are critical for organizations to effectively mitigate the impact of security incidents. As cyber threats become increasingly sophisticated and damaging, a well-defined and adaptable incident response plan is essential to minimize downtime, protect sensitive data, and maintain business continuity.

Advanced incident response goes beyond the traditional incident management approach of merely reacting to security breaches. It involves proactive measures, careful planning, and continuous improvement to enhance an organization's overall security posture. In this chapter, we'll explore the key principles and strategies that underpin advanced incident response and recovery.

At the core of advanced incident response is the concept of resilience. Resilience in cybersecurity means not only having the ability to prevent and detect security incidents but also the capability to withstand and recover from them swiftly. This involves a shift in mindset from a purely defensive approach to a more proactive and adaptive one.

One of the key components of advanced incident response is threat intelligence. Organizations need to be well-informed about the latest threats, vulnerabilities, and attack techniques. Threat intelligence feeds and services provide valuable information about emerging threats and indicators of compromise. This knowledge enables security teams to proactively adjust their defenses and incident response plans to address evolving threats effectively.

Advanced incident response strategies emphasize the importance of automation and orchestration. Manual incident response processes can be slow and error-prone. By automating routine tasks and orchestrating the response to security incidents, organizations can significantly reduce the time it takes to contain and remediate threats. Automation can also help ensure that response actions are executed consistently and in compliance with established policies.

Incorporating threat hunting into incident response is another hallmark of advanced strategies. Threat hunting involves proactively searching for signs of malicious activity within an organization's network and systems, even when no specific threat has been detected. It's a proactive approach that aims to uncover hidden threats and vulnerabilities before they can be exploited by attackers.

An integral part of advanced incident response is the establishment of a Computer Security Incident Response Team (CSIRT) or a Security Operations Center (SOC). These dedicated teams are responsible for monitoring the organization's security posture, responding to incidents, and coordinating the recovery efforts. They play a crucial role in ensuring a swift and effective response to security incidents.

A critical aspect of advanced incident response is the development and testing of incident response playbooks. Playbooks are predefined sets of procedures and actions that guide security teams in responding to specific types of incidents. They outline the steps to take, the tools to use, and the stakeholders to involve during an incident. Regularly testing these playbooks through simulated exercises helps ensure that the response process is well-practiced and can be executed smoothly in a real-world scenario.

Advanced incident response also emphasizes the importance of data protection and privacy compliance. Organizations must comply with various data protection regulations, such as the General Data Protection Regulation (GDPR) or the California Consumer Privacy

Act (CCPA). When responding to security incidents, it's crucial to handle sensitive data in a way that complies with these regulations to avoid legal and financial repercussions.

In addition to incident response, advanced strategies also focus on recovery and resilience. Organizations should have robust backup and disaster recovery plans in place to ensure the availability of critical systems and data in the event of an incident. Regularly testing these plans is essential to identify and address any weaknesses.

Continuous improvement is a fundamental principle of advanced incident response. Security teams should conduct post-incident reviews to analyze what went well and what could be improved in their response efforts. These reviews provide valuable insights for refining incident response processes and enhancing overall security.

Collaboration and information sharing within the cybersecurity community are also critical aspects of advanced incident response. Cyber threats often transcend individual organizations, and sharing threat intelligence and best practices can help the community as a whole better defend against common adversaries.

To summarize, advanced incident response and recovery strategies are essential for organizations to effectively defend against and recover from security incidents in today's complex threat landscape. These strategies prioritize resilience, threat intelligence, automation, threat hunting, playbooks, compliance, recovery planning, continuous improvement, and collaboration. By adopting these principles, organizations can better protect their assets and maintain business continuity in the face of evolving cyber threats.

Chapter 10: Advanced Ethical Hacking Challenges and Future Trends

Ethical hacking, a practice also known as penetration testing or white-hat hacking, plays a crucial role in ensuring the security and integrity of modern technologies. As our technological landscape continues to evolve at an unprecedented pace, ethical hackers face a multitude of challenges in their mission to identify vulnerabilities and protect digital assets. In this chapter, we will delve into some of the most pressing challenges that ethical hackers encounter in the ever-changing world of technology.

One of the foremost challenges in ethical hacking is keeping pace with rapid technological advancements. New hardware, software, and platforms are continually emerging, each introducing unique security risks and attack vectors. Ethical hackers must stay updated on these developments to effectively assess the security of the latest technologies and safeguard against potential threats.

Cloud computing has transformed the way businesses operate, providing scalability, flexibility, and cost-efficiency. However, it has also introduced a host of security challenges. Ethical hackers are confronted with the task of evaluating the security of cloud-based systems and ensuring that sensitive data stored in the cloud remains protected. This necessitates a deep understanding of cloud architecture, authentication mechanisms, and data encryption.

The proliferation of Internet of Things (IoT) devices presents another formidable challenge for ethical hackers. IoT devices, ranging from smart thermostats to industrial sensors, are often designed with minimal security considerations. These devices can become vulnerable entry points for malicious actors. Ethical hackers must possess the expertise to assess and fortify the security of IoT ecosystems.

Mobile devices have become integral to our daily lives, and they have also become prime targets for cyberattacks. With the widespread use of mobile apps, ethical hackers must be well-versed in mobile application security testing. This includes identifying vulnerabilities in apps, assessing the security of mobile operating systems, and understanding the intricacies of mobile device management.

The blurring of boundaries between personal and professional technology usage, often referred to as bring your own device (BYOD) policies, presents a challenge in corporate cybersecurity. Ethical hackers must develop strategies for securing corporate networks and data while accommodating the use of personal devices within the workplace. Balancing security and usability is a constant juggling act.

Cryptocurrency and blockchain technologies have gained significant traction in recent years. While they offer exciting opportunities, they also introduce novel security concerns. Ethical hackers must navigate the complexities of blockchain security, smart contract vulnerabilities, and crypto wallet protection to ensure the safety of digital assets in this decentralized landscape.

Social engineering remains a perennial challenge in the world of cybersecurity. Attackers often employ sophisticated psychological tactics to manipulate individuals into divulging sensitive information or performing actions that compromise security. Ethical hackers need to be well-versed in social engineering techniques to effectively combat this human element of cyberattacks.

The globalization of technology and the interconnectedness of systems have led to a surge in cross-border cyber threats. Ethical hackers may need to collaborate with international counterparts and adhere to diverse legal and regulatory frameworks. This necessitates a keen understanding of international cybersecurity laws and norms.

Data privacy and compliance requirements are evolving globally, with regulations like the General Data Protection Regulation (GDPR) and the California Consumer Privacy Act (CCPA) setting stringent standards for data protection. Ethical hackers must navigate the intricacies of these regulations to help organizations maintain compliance and avoid costly penalties.

Artificial intelligence (AI) and machine learning (ML) technologies are being leveraged by both attackers and defenders. Ethical hackers must explore AI-driven security solutions to identify and counteract emerging AI-based threats effectively. Understanding the nuances of AI and ML in cybersecurity is crucial for staying one step ahead of adversaries.

In summary, ethical hacking faces a myriad of challenges in adapting to evolving technologies. To succeed in this dynamic landscape, ethical hackers must remain vigilant, continually update their skills, and possess a deep understanding of emerging technologies and the associated security risks. By tackling these challenges head-on, ethical hackers play a pivotal role in enhancing the security and resilience of digital ecosystems in our rapidly changing world.

As we navigate the ever-evolving landscape of cybersecurity and hacking, it's essential to look ahead and anticipate future trends and developments in this dynamic field. This chapter explores some of the key areas where we can expect significant changes and innovations in the coming years.

One of the most prominent trends in cybersecurity is the increasing reliance on artificial intelligence (AI) and machine learning (ML) for both defensive and offensive purposes. AI-powered security tools are becoming more sophisticated, enabling organizations to detect and respond to threats in real-time. On the flip side, malicious actors are also leveraging AI to enhance their attacks, making them more targeted and harder to detect. The ongoing arms race between AI-driven security solutions and AI-powered cyber threats will undoubtedly shape the future of cybersecurity.

The Internet of Things (IoT) continues to expand, with an ever-growing number of connected devices entering our homes, workplaces, and critical infrastructure.

While IoT offers numerous benefits, such as automation and efficiency, it also presents significant security challenges. Many IoT devices lack robust security features, making them vulnerable to exploitation. Future cybersecurity efforts will need to focus on securing this sprawling network of interconnected devices, potentially through the development of IoT security standards and regulations.

Quantum computing, with its immense computational power, poses both opportunities and threats to cybersecurity. While quantum computing holds the promise of breaking widely-used encryption algorithms, it also offers the potential for creating more secure cryptographic techniques. As quantum computing matures, organizations must prepare for the post-quantum era by adopting quantum-resistant encryption methods.

The rise of 5G technology is poised to transform the digital landscape. With faster and more reliable connections, 5G networks will enable the proliferation of IoT devices, autonomous vehicles, and augmented reality applications. However, the increased connectivity also expands the attack surface for cybercriminals. Ethical hackers and security experts will need to adapt to the unique challenges posed by 5G networks, such as the potential for more extensive distributed denial-of-service (DDoS) attacks and the need for improved network segmentation.

Blockchain technology, beyond cryptocurrencies, holds great potential for enhancing cybersecurity. Blockchain's decentralized and tamper-resistant nature can be leveraged to secure various aspects of digital transactions and identity management. In the future, we can expect to see more widespread adoption of blockchain-based security solutions for safeguarding sensitive data and ensuring the integrity of digital assets.

Cybersecurity regulations and compliance requirements are continuously evolving to address emerging threats and protect individuals' data privacy. Organizations must remain agile and adaptable to comply with these changing regulations, such as the European Union's General Data Protection Regulation (GDPR) and the California Consumer Privacy Act (CCPA). Failure to do so can result in severe financial penalties and reputational damage.

The shortage of skilled cybersecurity professionals is an ongoing challenge. As cyber threats continue to evolve and multiply, there is a growing need for qualified experts to defend against these threats. Organizations and governments are investing in cybersecurity training and education programs to bridge this skills gap. The cybersecurity community can also expect to see increased collaboration between industry, academia, and government in nurturing the next generation of cybersecurity talent.

The convergence of cybersecurity and physical security is becoming increasingly important. As critical infrastructure and essential services become more digitally connected, the potential for cyberattacks to have physical consequences grows. Ethical hackers and security experts will need to broaden their skill sets to address this convergence effectively, ensuring the security of not only digital systems but also physical assets.

Threat intelligence sharing and collaboration among organizations and nations will become more crucial than ever. Cyber threats are often transnational in nature, requiring a coordinated global response. Initiatives like the Cybersecurity and Infrastructure Security Agency (CISA) in the United States highlight the importance of cross-sector and cross-border collaboration in defending against cyber threats.

Finally, ethical hacking and penetration testing will continue to be essential components of proactive cybersecurity strategies. As the threat landscape evolves, organizations will rely on skilled professionals to identify vulnerabilities and weaknesses in their systems before malicious actors can exploit them. Ethical hackers will play a pivotal role in securing digital assets and safeguarding the privacy and security of individuals and organizations.

In summary, the future of cybersecurity and hacking promises to be both challenging and exciting. With the rapid advancement of technology, the cybersecurity community must remain vigilant, adaptable, and innovative. By anticipating and addressing emerging trends and threats, ethical hackers and security experts can continue to protect our digital world effectively.

Conclusion

In summary, the "Gray Hat Vulnerability Scanning & Penetration Testing" book bundle is a comprehensive and invaluable resource for anyone looking to embark on a journey into the world of ethical hacking and cybersecurity. Across four carefully crafted volumes, this bundle offers a progressive and structured approach to mastering the art of penetration testing, from the fundamentals to advanced techniques.

"Gray Hat Essentials: A Beginner's Guide to Vulnerability Scanning" serves as an ideal starting point, equipping beginners with the foundational knowledge and skills needed to understand vulnerabilities, identify weaknesses, and initiate the scanning process. It lays the groundwork for the exciting journey ahead.

"Intermediate Gray Hat Tactics: Penetration Testing Demystified" takes the reader deeper into the realm of penetration testing. Building upon the fundamentals, it demystifies the complexities of ethical hacking, covering a wide range of techniques and strategies used by seasoned professionals.

"Advanced Gray Hat Exploits: Beyond the Basics" is where the true mastery begins. This book dives into the intricacies of advanced exploitation, delving into complex vulnerabilities and providing in-depth insights into the techniques used by real-world hackers. It challenges readers to think creatively and critically, preparing them for the ever-evolving threat landscape.

"Mastering Gray Hat Ethical Hacking: Expert-Level Penetration Testing" crowns this bundle with its expert-level insights and hands-on guidance. It takes ethical hacking to the highest level, helping readers develop the skills and mindset required to outsmart even the most sophisticated adversaries.

Throughout these four books, readers are not only provided with technical knowledge but also with the ethical framework that underpins the field of cybersecurity. The importance of responsible and lawful hacking is consistently emphasized, ensuring that readers become not just skilled practitioners but also ethical ones.

In an age where cyber threats continue to evolve and multiply, the "Gray Hat Vulnerability Scanning & Penetration Testing" book bundle equips individuals and organizations with the tools they need to defend against these threats effectively. Whether you're a novice looking to start your cybersecurity journey or an experienced professional seeking to hone your skills, this bundle offers a comprehensive roadmap to success. So, as you embark on your exploration of these books, remember that with great knowledge comes great responsibility. The world of ethical hacking is one that demands both technical prowess and a commitment to ethics and legality. May these books empower you to navigate this challenging landscape with skill, integrity, and a commitment to making the digital world a safer place for all.

www.ingramcontent.com/pod-product-compliance
Lightning Source LLC
Chambersburg PA
CBHW071235050326
40690CB00011B/2119